The Political Theory of a Compound Republic

VINCENT OSTROM

The Political Theory
of a
Compound Republic

Designing
the American Experiment

SECOND EDITION
REVISED AND ENLARGED

FOREWORD
BY DANIEL J. ELAZAR

UNIVERSITY OF NEBRASKA PRESS
LINCOLN AND LONDON

The paper in this book meets the minimum requirements of American National
Standard for Information Sciences—Per-
manence of Paper for Printed Library
Materials, ANSI Z39.48-1984.

Library of Congress
Cataloging in Publication Data

Ostrom, Vincent, 1919–
The political theory of a compound
republic.
1. The Federalist.   2. Representative
government and
representation
–United States.   3. Federal government–
United States.   4. Democracy.
I. Federalist.   II. Title.
JK155.O88   1986
342.73'029   86-7063
ISBN 0-8032-3554-2 (alk. paper)
347.30229

to

Mildred and *Al*

for their patience

and *Jim* for his

challenge

Contents

Daniel J. Elazar

Foreword

The rediscovery of the theory underlying the American federal constitution has profound implications for American democracy in our time. Since the beginnings of this rediscovery in the 1950s, no work has contributed more than Vincent Ostrom's *The Political Theory of a Compound Republic,* first published in a limited edition by the Virginia Polytechnic Institute in 1971. Until the appearance of that book, the field had essentially remained in the hands of the students of Leo Strauss, foremost among them the late Martin Diamond, who did yeoman work recovering the contribution of the American founding fathers, particularly James Madison and the other authors of *The Federalist,* to political philosophy. *The Political Theory of a Compound Republic* added a new dimension to the study of *The Federalist* by applying the political theories of its authors to questions of constitutional choice and design, questions which were derived from the concerns of public administration and political economy.

Diamond emphasized the importance of the federal dimension of the Constitution, and much of his writing focuses on it. Taking his definition of "federal" from late medieval sources and his interpretation of the United States Constitution from *The Federalist,* Diamond concluded that the federalism of the Constitution was constitutionalized decentralization rather than true federalism; the latter had been tried under the Articles of Confederation and found wanting. For Diamond, federalism—read constitutional decentralization—was an absolutely essential element of the American democratic republic. In that sense, he was a true friend of federalism.

While Diamond was formulating his argument, the late W. W. Crosskey was challenging the federal character of the U.S. Constitution in a different way. He made a lawyer's argument, namely, that the Constitution had to be read as a contract, and when so read, with full understanding of the eighteenth-century linguistic usage, it could only be understood as having established a modestly decentralized unitary state. Whereas Diamond's argument was political in the classic sense—his dispute with contemporary political science, for example, was over the political importance of institutions (including constitutions) and foundings—Crosskey's argument was utterly apolitical. In his view, because many of the delegates to the Philadelphia convention were trained as lawyers, it was as if they sat in the Pennsylvania State House and, as lawyers, negotiated among several parties a binding contract which was to be unambiguous in language and inflexible in interpretation. Crosskey's work is valuable to help us understand eighteenth-century usages and hence what was clear to the framers and what was left ambiguous, but he is simply wrong on the contract issue.

A different kind of intellectual assault on the fundamentally federal character of the Constitution came from more conventional quarters: political scientists of various kinds who accepted the position, until recently unchallenged, that the Constitution was unmistakably federal—indeed unambiguously so—but who concluded that federalism was obsolete or unjust or both. This is not the place to go into the intellectual history of their views. Suffice it to say that these views derived from two sources: (1) Jacobin-Marxist ideas which, in political science jargon, were embodied in the conception of the reified state organized according to the center-periphery model and (2) managerial theories that emerged in the twentieth century as part of the "scientific management" approach to the organization and direction of large organizations. For some, these two sources were combined to generate an un-mitigated endorsement of centralization on all fronts—the presidency, constitutional law, government administration and finance, and the party system—on the grounds of both justice and efficiency. Others sought only greater efficiency and, in its name, organizational changes whose consequences were centralizing.

In the latter case, proposals for change endorsed federal-ism in principle even when undercutting it in practice. Per-haps the most extreme expression of the former position was William Riker's conclusion to his book *Federalism*, namely, that to believe in federalism was to believe in racism. In any case, the answer of those people to the question of the importance of federalism in the American system, would be—too impor-tant for our times.

Since the presentation of those theories, the federal char-acter of the Constitution has been reexamined by Vincent Os-trom in the original edition of this work, where he suggested that it is not only quite federal indeed but properly so in terms of political and administrative theory. He not only sees the federalism of the Constitution as a given, he understands it as a precursor of what today is known as cybernetic theory.

Contrary to the fashion—or wishful thinking—among certain schools of constitutional interpretation, there is no "founder" in the American constitutional founding. The doc-ument was truly the product of a committee, perhaps the best committee ever assembled—that is another matter—but still a committee. Moreover, it was a broadly based committee, rep-resentative of a wide range of views regarding the appropri-ate regime for the fledgling United States of America (a strong name applied to a relatively weak confederation of states—so much for the uncritical acceptance of terminological evi-dence). The convention/committee included people like Alex-ander Hamilton (whose role as constitutional interpreter was more important than his role in the convention itself), who wanted as strong a unitary state as he could get, and others like George Mason who did not really want to change the Ar-

ticles of Confederation in other than marginal ways. All the
evidence points to a wide spectrum of views with regard to
federalism. These views tended to converge, both by necessity
and inclination, toward the honestly federal Connecticut compromise (of which more below).

While the legal profession was nominally overrepresented
in Philadelphia, it is common knowledge that legal training
has been a major gateway into politics in American civil society at least since the beginning of the eighteenth century.
The men at Philadelphia were political leaders—politicians, if
you will—above all else. They were engaged in the greatest of
political exercises, the design and construction of a regime,
and, as we all agree, they were political artisans of the highest
order. The business of the members of the convention, then,
was the business of politics, the judicious mixture of fidelity to
principle and felicitous compromise. Artful use of language is
a major means of combining the two. Thus the language of
the Constitution is crystal clear where possible and ambiguous
where necessary, and the document must be read in that
spirit. Nevertheless, until our own generation, one of the
things of which there was no doubt was that the Constitution
articulated a truly federal system of government. Even the
opponents of its ratification, who hold (as did Diamond 180
years later) that the term "federal" when applied to regimes
properly applies to what we today term confederations, never
challenged the federal character of the new regime after the
adoption of the Bill of Rights.

The federalism of the Constitution was made crystal clear,
just as the division and sharing of powers was left ambiguous.
For men like Hamilton, the opportunities for centralization
offered by the latter ambiguity may have been the difference
in their willingness to accept the former, and the same was true
for those on the opposite side of the matter. Thus Americans
were bequeathed what Woodrow Wilson later described as the
"cardinal question of American politics."

Twentieth-century students of the Constitution, usually relying on *The Federalist* and selected anti-Federalist publications

exclusively, concluded that the framers of the Constitution were more or less exclusively products of classical education, Hobbesian-Lockean political science, and Enlightenment philosophy. No one would deny the existence of this "chain of tradition" as a major factor in the founding of the United States of America, but there was another line of tradition actively represented in the founding as well; the Biblical-Reformed-Puritan tradition. Both traditions address the idea and practice of federalism. The first did indeed understand federalism as confederation—a strictly political affair that involved a permanent league of states in which sovereignty, indivisible by its nature, remained with the constituent units. The second tradition, however, came to federalism through theology—indeed, it was known as the federal theology, from *foedus*, or covenant, referring to the grounding of all human relationships in the original covenant between God and man described in the Bible and subsequent subsidiary pacts. By the mid-eighteenth century, this tradition viewed federalism in theopolitical terms. From this point of view, federalism was not bound by classical notions of the polis, the perfectly complete polity which could at best be leagued with others; rather, it functioned within the biblical framework of constituent polities held together by a shared common law and institutions— a concept much more like the federalism that emerged from the constitutional convention.

The Biblical-Reformed-Puritan tradition of federalism spread throughout British North America, but it took particular root and became the dominant tradition in New England. Connecticut was the first North American polity to be founded on fully federal principles, religious and political. It was literally a federation of four original towns, subsequently expanded. The constitution of that federation, the Fundamental Orders of Connecticut (1639), is a full statement of the tradition from its biblical base onward. One hundred and fifty years after the founding of Connecticut, its sons, heirs to a long federalist tradition, proposed the Connecticut compromise and saved the Philadelphia convention.

In a paper prepared for the Workshop on Covenant and Politics of the Center for the Study of Federalism, Donald Lutz has demonstrated the power and ubiquity of this Biblical-Reformed-Puritan tradition in the process of the writing and adoption of the Constitution. With Charles Hyneman he has explored all the known political writings of Americans in the era and he has categorized the sources they cite to buttress their support of the Constitution. While *The Federalist* itself relies exclusively on classical sources (a point of great significance in prior analyses), Lutz found that overall, in other public writings on the Constitution, the Bible was the most cited source by far. Indeed, the Book of Deuteronomy, with its discussion of the Mosaic constitution for Israel, alone is cited more than any other source.

Lutz's work (and that of students of eighteenth-century political history) throws an entirely new light on the subject. No longer can we assume that the Constitution is solely a product of Locke and the Enlightenment. Perhaps if *The Federalist* had not been written to persuade already secularized New Yorkers, with their individualistic political culture, but New Englanders or the Scotch-Irish Presbyterians of the back country from Pennsylvania to South Carolina instead, its authors might also have turned to biblical sources as part of their polemic.

Diamond, relying exclusively on *The Federalist*, could conclude that *Publius* pulled a sleight-of-hand in appropriating the term "federal" for the new Constitution, but for the people of Connecticut and the rest of the "Calvinists" in America, *Publius* was hardly changing definitions in midstream. Hence Ostrom's analysis, which goes beyond and beneath *The Federalist*'s polemic, can be supported by an understanding of this American Biblical-Reformed-Puritan tradition. That should not be surprising, since federalism is the *form* of American government, in the eighteenth-century meaning of the principle that informs the American polity in its every aspect.

Ostrom's personal breakthrough in understanding the larger message of *The Federalist* represented a breakthrough for political science, just as Diamond's discovery of the flaws in the Beard thesis regarding the origins of the federal constitution was a breakthrough for political philosophy some years earlier. Unfortunately, the limited, almost private, publication of the first edition prevented it from gaining the circulation it deserved. Indeed, even this writer came upon it almost by accident, to my great benefit. Reading the book helped me place my own work on federalism in a larger theoretical framework and gave me new analytical tools with which to broaden my own inquiries. With its conceptual base, it was possible to begin constructing a true theory of federalism and a truly federal theory of the political system. As a result of that almost fortuitous event, Vincent Ostrom and I began an intellectual and personal exchange which has continued to this day and which has become one of the most gratifying relationships that I have experienced in my professional life.

Over the years, as our work together increased, I would urge him to republish his book so it would become more visible and reach the audience it deserves. He was prepared to do so only after a thorough revision of its contents to reflect his own intellectual progress in the interim. Finally, over a decade after the appearance of the original, Vincent Ostrom has done what he has promised to do, namely, prepare a second edition for publication and wider distribution. Needless to say, it is all that the first edition was and more: a contribution to political philosophy, an elucidation of the American founding and the political thought that it produced, an intellectual mode that can form the basis for a proper science of public administration, a theory of constitutional choice and design, and a bridge between all of these.

Ostrom's own political theory follows in the classically American model with individualistic assumptions about political experience. Indeed, Thomas Hobbes and Harold Lasswell are his mentors, and he follows in their traditions. He sees the former as the tradition of *Publius* and *The Federalist,* albeit without the Hobbesian conclusions with regard to the best regime. By systematizing *The Federalist*'s teaching on these subjects through the application of Lasswellian linguistic rigor, Ostrom adds a dimension of his own, carrying on the great tradition established in that classic work.

The fulcrum of Ostrom's argument rests upon the concept of constitutional choice, which one day may be recognized as his greatest contribution to political thought. His development of the idea of constitutional choice, with its corollary theories of the importance of rules in political life, the constitution as artifact, and the implications of choice for constitutional design, are outstanding features that make this work essential reading for all students of political thought. It is especially vital for students of modern polities, all of which are intimately involved with constitutional design by choice.

Ostrom's chapters on a republican remedy for the republican disease, federal structures and their implications, and the distribution of authority in the organization of the national government offer us an invaluable introduction to American political theory. While there are those who will quibble with his conclusions on the basis of what the intentions of the authors of *The Federalist* were, Ostrom makes the case that the work itself says more than the intentions of the individuals who collaborated in writing the essays that constitute it. In other words, *Publius* is the founder of American federalist theory, whatever the particular opinions of Alexander Hamilton, John Jay, and James Madison. Ostrom teaches us what *Publius* has to say on the subject, and we are all indebted to him for doing so.

Chapter Eight, Ostrom's retrospective on two centuries of American federal democracy, provides us with a bridge from the revolutionary era to our times, just as Chapter Two bridges the four generations from the English to the American revolutions, from Hobbes to *The Federalist*. In Chapter Eight, Ostrom elegantly examines the ways in which federalist theory has confronted its subsequent challenges and challengers. He examines Jacksonian democracy as seen by Tocqueville, the slavery question and the Civil War, machine politics and boss rule, and the twentieth-century break with the federalist tradition, elucidating each as an exercise in constitutional choice. Ostrom argues that while the first three challenges were confronted and resolved within the spirit of federalism, the last—and perhaps most threatening—is still very much before us.

The implications of the federal principle are brought home forcefully when it is contrasted with the other conceptions of popular government developed in the modern era. Other revolutionaries in the "Age of Revolutions" that has existed since the late eighteenth century—most prominent among them the Jacobins—also sought solutions to some of the same problems of despotism that perturbed the Americans. But in their efforts to hurry the achievement of the millennium, they considered only the problem of autocratic despotism and rejected what they believed to be the highly pessimistic assumptions of the American constitution-makers that unlimited political power could even corrupt "the people." They looked upon federalism and its principles of checks and balances as subversive of the "general will," their way of expressing a commitment to the organic unity of society, which, like their premodern predecessors, they saw as superior to the mere interests of individuals. They argued that since their "new society" was to be based on "the general will" as a more democratic principle, any element subversive of its organic unity would be, *ipso facto,* antidemocratic.

By retaining notions of the organic society, the Jacobins and their revolutionary heirs were forced to rely upon transient majorities to establish consensus or to concentrate power in the hands of an elite that claimed to do the same thing. The first course invariably led to anarchy and the second to the kind of totalitarian democracy that has become the essence of modern dictatorship. While the "general will" was undoubtedly a more democratic concept than the "will of the monarch," in the last analysis it has proved to be no less despotic and usually even more subversive of liberty.

The history of the extension of democratic government since the eighteenth century has been a history of the rivalry between these two conceptions of democracy. Because of the challenge of Jacobinism, the meaning of the American idea of federal democracy takes on increased importance.

The framers of the Constitution capitalized on the American instinct for federalism which had already revealed itself in the nationwide organization for the revolutionary struggle and in the first constitution of the United States. In one sense, they simply tried to improve the American political system within the framework of the covenant idea by creating—as they put it—a "more perfect union."

The results of their work were not accepted uncritically at the time, nor did the results remain unmodified after the ratification of the Constitution. Their emphasis on the "national" as distinct from "federal" aspects of the new Union (the terms are those of *The Federalist*) did not sit well with the majority of the American people, who felt keenly that emphasis on the federal aspects was necessary to keep government limited, taxes low, and liberties secure.

The anti-federalists lost their fight to prevent ratification of the Constitution, but by immediately accepting the verdict and entering into the spirit of the new consensus, they soon won over a majority of the American people. After the Jeffersonian victory in 1800, the dominant theoretical emphasis around the nation was to be on the primacy of the states as custodians of the nation's political power, an emphasis that was to be moderated from time to time—substantially between 1861 and 1876—but not altered until the twentieth century. This emphasis provided a very hospitable environment for the development of the "states rights" heresy that colored the actions of southerners during the Civil War generation. That, in turn, has colored our assessments of federalism to this day. It is time to decouple that heresy from federalism as the form of the American compound polity, much as it is time to decouple the newer heresies of Wilsonianism and managerialism from American progressive thought. This book helps us do both.

In reality, the debate over the meaning of the American covenant and its federal principles began anew under the

Constitution, has continued ever since, and will no doubt continue so long as the American people remain concerned with constitutional government as an essential element of the American mystique. The very existence of this debate adds to the health of the body politic. Yet, from first to last, it has remained a debate over interpretation of the meaning of the federal principle and not over the validity of the principle as such.

Though the debate has involved vital questions of the first magnitude, it has been carried on within the context of a political consensus that is all the more remarkable for having changed so little in some two hundred years. Rarely, if ever, given verbal expression, this consensus is attested to by scores of commentators on the American scene from Crevecoeur to Max Lerner and from de Tocqueville to D. W. Brogan. More impressive testimony is found in the behavior of the American people when that consensus has been threatened. Abandoning their more transient allegiances, they have invariably responded to the call, changing their "normal" patterns of behavior—often to the amazement of observers lacking historical perspective—for others more appropriate to the situation. It is this deeply rooted understanding of the basics of the American political system that sustains popular government despite the mistakes of transient majorities. The consensus itself, imbued with the spirit of federalism through and through, goes much beyond a concern with the strict institutional aspects of the federal system to embrace the ideas of partnership and balance which, put together, give birth to the federal principle.

The federalist principle is not a single way of doing things, but rather two orientations. Federalism has been interpreted as limiting government action and as providing the basis for government intervention to require private individuals to behave in a morally correct way. Thus federalism as a political way provided a basis for the secession of the southern states on one hand and, on the other, for their reintegration into the Union on an equal footing with their northern sisters once the Union forces won the Civil War. It is unfashionable for contemporary

Americans to endorse John Winthrop's conception of federal
liberty, which he defined as the freedom to do what is right.
But the recent history of government enforcement of civil
rights on the basis of U.S. Supreme Court decisions is precisely
an example of federal liberty, of the abridgement of the rights
of individuals to do wrongs to other individuals.

For three and a half centuries, two under the same constitution, Americans have managed to follow the federalist way
without being conscious that they were doing so except in the
narrowest institutional sense. Now, however, the federalist
way has come under assault by the pressures of a heretical individualism, corporatism, and collectivism. This volume is devoted to elucidating the proper individualism inherent in
American political thought, in no small measure in response to
this individualistic heresy, which is no less problematic than the
collectivist and corporatist heresies now confronting Americans. An understanding of organization based upon corporatist models of efficiency coupled with a set of expectations
from government based upon collectivist models, both coming at the same time as a reorientation of individualism in the
direction of license, have all combined to weaken the federalist mainstream of the American experiment. Hence, it becomes vital for those who understand that mainstream to articulate it and to bring it to the attention of those who have
taken it for granted and are now puzzled by the transformations taking place in American society.

In a sense, the necessity for a full articulation of federalist
theory today is a reflection of the challenges that the federalist
tradition has faced in twentieth-century America. As long as
that tradition was dominant in the United States, that is to say,
was able to confront and overcome the challenges to it, there
was little need for articulation of a federalist theory. Now it
becomes a necessity. Vincent Ostrom is at the forefront of
those who are involved in developing and articulating such
theory. This book is a major contribution to that end.

The fact that both the French and Russian Revolutions
have eclipsed the American Revolution is one of the tragedies

of our time. It is up to those who seek a true understanding of politics as politics, not as messianism, to restore the American Revolution and its ideas to their rightful place. Martin Diamond once called the American Revolution the "revolution of sober expectations." Ostrom's work follows in the tradition of sober expectations. His balancing of Hobbes and *The Federalist* links sober expectations with democratic ones. Indeed, as he suggests in this book, while democracy is the only proper form of government for a free people, the maintenance and sustenance of democratic government requires a proper constitutional design based upon appropriately sober expectations. By giving us a fully articulated federalist teaching with regard to both the design and the expectations, he has enhanced our chances of succeeding in that direction.

The year 1976 marked the end of the eleventh generation of American history and the sixth generation of American independence. It also marked the end of the first generation of the postmodern epoch. The United States, aptly called by Seymour Martin Lipset the first new nation, was born at the beginning of the modern epoch, achieved its independence as that epoch reached its apex five generations later, and reached maturity during the course of the next five generations until the modern epoch came to an end.

The bulk of the adult generation today was raised when it was still possible to talk about the United States as being on the threshold of maturity—when as much time separated the founding of the American colonies from the Revolution as separated the Revolution from the modern threshold of great world responsibility, tragic foreign involvement, and constitutional crisis at home derived from the attempt to substitute imperial for republican styles of behavior in the highest offices of the land. Our children no longer have the luxury of standing on that threshold. We have crossed a divide perhaps even more formidable than the one Frederick Jackson Turner suggested was crossed when the era of the land frontier came to an end.

The Bible reminds us that every tenth generation, a new

epoch begins. During the first epoch of American history, the American people forged a unique synthesis of constitutionalism, republicanism, and democracy. As we reflect back from the vantage point of the twelfth generation, two generations into the second epoch of American history, we are well advised to consider the character and meaning of the first.

Federalism is the glue that has tied constitutionalism, republicanism, and democracy together during the first eleven generations of American history. Like all glue, it has the properties of flexibility and hardness in turn and, once set, tends to be invisible or at least unnoticed in the midst of the materials that it has joined together. It is necessary to recall that without the glue the materials fall apart. Contemporary Americans have shown that they have no less concern for constitutionalism, republicanism, and democracy than their forefathers, but it often seems as if they are neglecting the glue. If the second epoch of American history is to reflect the fulfillment of the American promise, then we will have to be as concerned with the glue as we are with the materials themselves.

Acknowledgments

A s a scholar I owe a substantial personal debt to succeeding generations of students who have always challenged
me to rethink the intellectual grounds for constituting order
in human societies. I am especially appreciative of the stimu-
lation and assistance provided by colleagues and staff at the
Workshop in Political Theory and Policy Analysis at Indiana
University. Our work there has placed a strong emphasis
upon the tie between theory and practice and challenges anyone preoccupied with political theory to address issues in ways
that are relevant to empirical inquiry.

At this juncture I cannot, with justice, identify particular
persons who have made important contributions toward this
effort to expound the political theory of a compound republic. There are too many to name. The only exceptions are
Elinor Ostrom, Daniel Elazar, Gordon Tullock, and Patty
Zielinski. A fellowship at the Center for Interdisciplinary Research at Bielefeld University in the Federal Republic of Germany provided a stimulating and productive occasion for pre-
paring a revised manuscript while pursuing other work at the
constitutional level of analysis with a multinational and multi-
disciplinary research group investigating problems of guidance, control, and evaluation in the public sector (Kaufmann,
Majone, and V. Ostrom, 1986).

The first edition of this study was published as *The Political
Theory of a Compound Republic* by the Center for Study of Pub-

lic Choice at the Virginia Polytechnic Institute and State University in 1971. That edition has been out of print for some time. The most substantial changes in this edition are in the form of a new introduction and two new concluding chapters. Otherwise, the general presentation of the argument adheres closely to the earlier publication. A Serbo-Croatian translation is being prepared by Dr. Branko Smerdel of the faculty of law at Zagreb University for publication by *Informator* in Yugoslavia.

Two Different Approaches to the Design of Public Order

Hobbes:

The only way to erect such a common power, as may be able to defend them from the invasion of foreigners, and the injuries of one another, and thereby to secure them in such sort, as that by their industry, and by the fruits of the earth, they may nourish themselves and live contentedly; is, to confer all their powers and strength upon one man or upon one assembly of men, that may reduce all their wills, by a plurality of voices, into one will: which is as much to say, to appoint one man, or assembly of men, to bear their person; and everyone to own, and acknowledge himself as author of whatsoever he that so beareth their person, shall act, or cause to be acted, in those things which concern the common peace and safety; and therein to submit their wills, everyone to his will, and their judgment, to his judgment. . . .

. . . .

And he that carrieth this person, is called SOVEREIGN, and said to have *sovereign powers*; and everyone besides, his SUBJECT. (Hobbes, 1960: 112)

Madison:

In framing a government which is to be administered by men over men, the great difficulty lies in this: you must first enable the government to control the governed; and in the next place oblige it to control itself. A dependence on the people is, no doubt, the primary control on the government; but experience has taught mankind the necessity of auxiliary precautions. This policy of supplying, by opposite and rival interests, the defect of better motives, might be traced through the whole system of human affairs, private as well as public. We see it particularly displayed in all the subordinate distributions of power, where the constant aim is to divide and arrange the several offices in such a manner as that each may be a check on the other—that the private interest of every individual may be a sentinel over the public rights. These inventions of prudence cannot be less requisite in the distribution of the supreme powers of the State. (Federalist 51: ML, 337–338; C, 349; R, 322)

CHAPTER ONE

Introduction

Many years ago, I undertook my first serious examination of *The Federalist*. Then, I was a graduate student participating in a seminar on American political theory offered by Professor Thomas P. Jenkin at the University of California, Los Angeles. The volume intrigued me. It was interspersed with axiomatic assertions and hypothetical propositions that had more general meaning than the passing exigencies of a political debate. I noted these propositions, then, more as "gems of wisdom" than as ingredients in a general theory of politics.

The "gems of wisdom" contained in *The Federalist* have also intrigued others. Woodrow Wilson, for example, refers to them as "those incomparable papers of the 'Federalist.'" He was puzzled that a campaign document written "to influence only the voters of 1788" should have had such "a strange, persistent longevity of power" to shape "constitutional criticism" one century later. As far as Wilson was concerned, "[T]he Constitution in operation is manifestly a very different thing from the Constitution of the books." The literary allusions of the campaign document were, Wilson was convinced, "obscuring much of that development of constitutional practice which has since taken place." Wilson expounded what he considered to be the new "living reality" of American politics in his doctoral dissertation on *Congressional Government*. He derived the intellectual orientation for his approach from Wal-

ter Bagehot's *The English Constitution,* and rejected the "literary theory" of *The Federalist* with its familiar "paper pictures"
of the Constitution based upon a system of checks and balances (Wilson, 1956: 30–31).[1]

In the mid-1950s, Robert Dahl, in *A Preface to Democratic
Theory,* returned to *The Federalist* to grapple with the political
theory of "Madisonian Democracy." Dahl recognized that *The
Federalist* was written as a campaign document; but he went
beyond that and attempted to reconstruct a political theory
from Madison's argument. Dahl summarized Madisonian theory in four basic definitions, one axiom, and an inferential
structure of ten hypotheses. Dahl concluded that the Madisonian formulation was clearly inadequate as a "political science" in contrast to its function as political "ideology" (Dahl,
1963: 31). However, Dahl did not give serious attention to
concepts of federalism and constitutional rule. These concepts might be viewed as the most fundamental elements in
Madisonian Democracy. Even more important is the whole
structure of theory that is used to advance the argument in
The Federalist.

A decade later in a book on *Federalism,* William Riker
offered a military interpretation of the Constitution of the
United States, and advised his readers to avoid the ideological
fallacy that federalism is related to freedom. Riker considered
such an association to be based upon political rhetoric formulated in *The Federalist* as "the main propaganda document"
issued in support of the Constitution (Riker, 1964: 17–19).
The primacy of a military motive could be established, Riker
was persuaded, by the fact that the first few papers are devoted to problems of military security.

In a recent book, *Liberalism Against Populism,* Riker modifies
his earlier position. Riker draws upon Social Choice theory to
demonstrate that populist conceptions of democracy which
rely entirely upon simple majority votes are vulnerable to ma-
nipulation by agenda setters. By contrast, Madison's analysis
of the conditions pertaining to a liberal system of government
is less vulnerable to these same findings. Constitutional limita-

tions, Riker now argues, have had an important place in keeping "rulers from subverting regular, popular elections for 200 years" (Riker, 1982: 250).

It is time, I believe, to reconsider the basic logic that both Alexander Hamilton and James Madison used in presenting their arguments in *The Federalist* and how concepts that are an integral part of that argument were used to design the structures of American government.[2] John Jay wrote 5 of the 85 essays in *The Federalist,* which are primarily related to the standing of the United States in the international community. While these essays raise important issues, they are sufficiently tangential for my purposes that I shall focus only upon those essays written by Alexander Hamilton and James Madison. I have no grounds for judging the primacy of Madison's contributions so I shall follow the practice of referring to their joint effort as though they were coauthors who chose to place their names in alphabetical order. In fact, they used the pen name, "Publius." I have too much respect for the burdens of authorship to use the anonymous designation of a pen name in referring to their efforts.

We should also remember that Hamilton and Madison were drawing upon ideas that were the subject of current and intensive discussion by an extended community of people. What they wrote drew upon ideas current in that community, but the way they articulated the general system of ideas represented important contributions. A person like John Adams or Thomas Jefferson might well have functioned as an equally capable contributor to *The Federalist.* But, that comment should not detract from the importance of *The Federalist.* In my judgment, it is the single most important American contribution to the universe of discourse in political theory.

THE PROBLEMATICAL CONTEXT OF THIS INQUIRY

The Declaration of Independence, as a preamble to the subsequent American experiments in constitutional choice, establishes the problematical context for our inquiry when the

Declaration asserts that it is "the Right of the People to alter or abolish" a government that is destructive of certain fundamental values including those of "Life, Liberty and the Pursuit of Happiness"; and to "institute new Government, laying its foundations on such Principles, and organizing its Powers in such Form, as to them seems most likely to effect their Safety and Happiness." I say "experiments in constitutional choice" because the Declaration assumes that human beings can exercise choice in creating systems of government. Such choices draw upon certain conceptions articulated as principles that are, in turn, used to specify structures or forms. When acted upon, these conceptions and structures have effects that bear significantly upon the safety and happiness of a people and other fundamental values that are important in their lives.

If people are to institute governments on the basis of their own conceptions and designs, monitor and evaluate the performance of those governments, and modify and revise their structures through time, they need to know what they are doing. One way of coming to an initial understanding of this task is to study the efforts of others as they have confronted the basic challenge of constitutional choice. I know of no better way of beginning this task than to draw upon the works of Alexander Hamilton and James Madison as they sought to explain the efforts of the Philadelphia Convention of 1787 in formulating the U.S. Constitution. When knowledgeable artisans explain what they have done in conceptualizing a design, they are having recourse to the theoretical computations that were used in formulating that design.

Theoretical computations serve as a basis for specifying relationships between conditions and consequences. If such theoretical arguments prove to be reliable in estimating the consequences that are expected to follow, they form a body of knowledge that enables artisans to explain what they are doing. When the form of artisanship applies to the institutions of government, such theoretical arguments become the ingredients for a political science that serves as a design science. The political science used in constitutional choice is not confined to academic pursuits but includes that body of knowledge used by people to monitor and evaluate the performance of those who are elected to office and to modify and revise structures of government through time.

The Political Theory of a Compound Republic is my effort to formulate the theory that is used by Hamilton and Madison to explain the design of the U.S. Constitution. I do so not as a historian explaining what happened in 1787, but as a political scientist who is attempting to understand and reconstruct the theory that was used to design the U.S. Constitution and its broader implications for the American system of constitutional government more generally. My primary interest is in reconstructing a theory that was not only useful in 1787, but might also provide us with basic conceptual tools for addressing a variety of contemporary problems.

Constitutional choice need not be limited to constitutional conventions or constitutional amendments pertaining to national governments, but can apply to all institutions of human governance. State constitutions, municipal charters, charters of corporations, voluntary associations and clubs can all be viewed as constitutional in nature. A constitution can be defined as the set of rules that specify the terms and conditions of government. Thus, it is the constitutional level of analysis that is of critical significance for a political science whether issues of constitutional choice are being addressed in the small or in the large.

In the early twentieth century, Lenin persuasively advanced the widely accepted argument that it takes a workable theory for a people to organize a revolution. It also takes a workable theory for a people to organize a system of government that is of their own design and subject to their control. Processes of constitutional choice have a fundamental place in any democratic society. Furthermore, constitutional choice is not something that is done once and exists for all time. Constitutional rules like any rules of law depend upon the intelligent exercise of judgment in their enforcement. The integrity of a constitutional system depends as much upon the use of an appropriate theory in its maintenance as in its original formulation.

There is a sense in which the American "experiments in constitutional choice" can be thought of as going back to the Mayflower Compact and the first establishment of the Plymouth Colony. Many other experiments followed in which relevant concepts and structures were articulated in a wide variety of different compacts and charters. The first effort to organize what subsequently became the state of Rhode Island, for example, was formulated as a compact among the principal communities of that area. The American Revolution can be viewed as an effort to repudiate those principles and structures where one government exercises control over communities of people who had no voice in its formulation or direction and to affirm the right of peoples to institute governments of their own choice.

Preparation for and consummation of the American Revolution, in turn, involved a whole series of experiments in organizing institutions of government for the several states on the North American continent. Continental Congresses were organized to tend to the joint interests of the American colonists. New independent constitutions were formulated among the American states, and a new effort to create a joint government was conceptualized and formed under the Articles of Confederation.

But, basic dilemmas remained. By 1785, increasing doubt existed whether the principles and forms used in formulating the Articles of Confederation were based upon workable concepts. Many argued that the government under the Articles of Confederation was a failure—that it could not do what was minimally expected of a government in much the same way that the United Nations might be considered as a failure today. There was a problem of how to account for that failure, and what to do about it, which required a theoretical explanation.

If confederation failed, Americans faced the prospect that the numerous states would be driven by potential conflict and the escalation of threats and counterthreats to a state of war with one another. The numerous American states might then simply replicate the experiences of Europe with states warring upon one another. If those conditions should prevail, the requirements of warfare could be expected to fashion the institutions of government that were best suited to struggles for dominance and survival.

A theoretical possibility also existed that Americans might simply follow the model of the English constitution and develop a national government in conformity to that model. Adhering to the English model applied to North America would have had the advantage of taking account of American interests in the governance of American affairs. But, the autonomous existence of the several American states and strong reservations about the dangers of tyranny associated with an unlimited exercise of authority placed such a resolution beyond the bounds of what was politically feasible.

Compelling necessities sometimes become the source of inventions rather than allowing social forces, in the presence of institutional failure, to work their way through to tragedy. Federalism might be viewed as one such invention. It presented an alternative both to confederation and a national government following the English model. This new concept allowed for a *limited* national government to be formed and to exist concurrently with *independent* and *limited* state governments. But the coexistence of multiple units of government depends upon the maintenance of basic limits within a rule of law. This requires constitutions to be formulated not as statements of unenforceable moral principles but as basic rules of law which apply to the conduct of government and can be enforced in relation to those who exercise the prerogatives of government.

If these conditions could be met, the contention of the Declaration of Independence might be viewed as valid: people might institute governments basing them upon conceptions and organizing their powers in such forms that would yield effects consistent with such fundamental values as safety, liberty, justice, and happiness. But, to do this requires a theory that draws upon conceptions which, in turn, can be articulated in forms that can be expected to yield consequences consistent with certain basic values.

What applied in the 1780s, it can be argued, need not be relevant to the circumstances of life in the 1980s. New knowledge, new technologies, new modes of production, transportation and communication have radically transformed American society. Patterns of governance in a highly industrialized and urbanized American society of the 1980s are vastly different than those that existed in the 1780s.

There may, however, still be basic design principles that are sufficiently fundamental to apply to quite different times and places in human societies. These principles can best be expressed by the distinctions made by a Swiss historian Adolph Gasser in his *Geschichte der Volksfreiheit und der Demokratie* (History of Freedom and Democracy). Gasser distinguishes between concepts of governance by *Herrschaft* as against *Genossenschaft*. *Herrschaft* is often translated as authority, but the intuitive meaning is lordship. The emphasis is upon dominance in a structure of superior-subordinate relationships. By contrast, *Genossenschaft* refers to comradeship and is often translated as "association." The covenanting inherent in the American tradition of constitutional choice is an expression of *Genossenschaft* as a principle of governance. Power is distributed so that all authority is subject to limits; and no one is devoid of essential prerogatives to command the services of judges to interpose proper limits on other officials. Powers of governance are organized with reference to "opposite and rival interests" as Madison expresses the principle. Power can then be used to check power as Montesquieu expressed much the same concept. Such design concepts are as relevant today as they were two hundred years ago. These and other concepts provide a basis for human beings to develop a political science that can be used to design experiments in constitutional choice.

We might anticipate many different peoples engaging in different types of experiments in constitutional choice. If we are careful to elucidate the theory that was used to design such experiments, and we assume the burden of translating from one set of conceptualizations to another, we have the opportunity to extend our understanding of the nature and constitution of order in human societies. Unfortunately, in our preoccupation with what governments should do in addressing contemporary problems, we give little critical attention to the intellectual tools that are appropriate to the constitutional level of analysis.[3] This is why it is so important to go back to the theoretical foundations used in designing the American constitutional system for grounding ourselves in a level of discourse where we can begin to understand the terms on which alternatives are available for the governance of human societies.

When I put the initial draft of these words on paper, I did so in my study at the Center for Interdisciplinary Research at Bielefeld University in Germany. I was there as a Fellow participating in a research group concerned with "guidance, control, and performance evaluation in the public sector." Our inquiries there required us to press back to the constitutional level of analysis and to recognize that different concepts were relevant to different design possibilities. I was struck by the continued relevance that the theory of *The Federalist* has for important political problems in the contemporary world, such as fashioning the institutions of government for a European Community and for European society more generally. To find a theory useful for thinking about problems does *not* mean that Europe should copy the American model. That would show intellectual poverty—of doing no more than imitating the American example. The task, rather, is to use conceptions and the associated theoretical apparatus as intellectual tools to think through problems and make an independent assessment of appropriate ways for addressing the problems of contemporary Europe.

Many peoples in the contemporary world face the problems of instituting new governments laying their foundations on such principles and organizing their powers in such forms as to them seem more likely to effect their safety and happiness, to paraphrase the American Declaration of Independence. This is a basic task that confronts all peoples who aspire to self-governance; and the discharge of that task requires an understanding of that body of knowledge that can be used to design experiments in constitutional choice. Such a body of knowledge would be concerned with the terms on which alternatives are available for constituting order in human societies. Political theory becomes meaningful as we address ourselves to the constitutional level of analysis, to the design of experiments in constitutional choice, and to the consequences that follow from such experiments.

PITFALLS

My effort to reconstruct the political theory used by Hamilton and Madison to advance their argument in *The Federalist* is subject to a number of pitfalls. I shall try to indicate some of these, both to show what I shall not attempt to do and to specify the particular perspectives (biases) that I bring to this task. Any interpretive effort can be challenged on a variety of different grounds, especially when the work being interpreted may have entailed, as I believe it did, a considerable level of originality.

Common understanding among human beings is greatly facilitated if one can be explicit about the perspective or point of view that is being taken and the problematical situation that is being addressed. Human beings draw upon their capabilities for thinking to conceptualize ways of relating to problematical situations. Working out, in a reasoned discourse, the elements and relationships involved in conceptualizing a solution to a problem is what I mean by theory. Theory can be used both to think through a problem and to offer an explanation to others. To reduce potential for misunderstanding, it is essential that I indicate some of the pitfalls in construing arguments in political theory that arise from ambiguities in language and from efforts to construe the motives and ideas of others.

Ambiguities in Language

Susanne Langer, a modern philosopher with a strong interest in language, has made the following observation which I believe to be correct:

Really new concepts, having no name in a current language, always make their earliest appearance in metaphorical statements; therefore the beginning of any theoretical structure is inevitably marked by fantastic inventions. (Langer, 1948: vi)

We should not be surprised then if the development of a new conception associated with a distinctly new formula for creating a federal system of government should be associated with basic terminological confusion. The terms "federal" (foederal) and "confederation" had both been used to refer to a government that was devised to serve as a joint instrumentality for several independent governments agreeing to enter into such a joint arrangement. The term federal derives from the Latin term *foedus* which means to covenant. Covenanting, then, is the root concept in both terms, federal and confederation. The problem is one of distinguishing between a treaty to form an alliance or league, a confederation, and something that still has some of the characteristics of an alliance or confederation by preserving the integrity of the existing units of government, but takes on the characteristics of a *limited* national government.

In *The Federalist,* we find the terms federal (foederal), confederation, and limited national government all used for the same referent. Yet, Hamilton is quite explicit in Federalist 15 and 16 in stating why he considered the concept of confederation, when applied to *the government of governments,* to be an absurdity. In short, he did not think that the defining charac-

teristics of a confederation met the minimal defining characteristics of a government. By analogy, he would consider it
an absurdity today to refer to the United Nations as a government. It is an organization or association of governments. He
clearly specifies what he considers to be the minimum defining characteristics of a limited national government in a
federal system. Its relationships to individuals is the critical
factor. I present his formulation in my discussion of an individualistic assumption about political experience in Chapter 2.

Yet, the language in *The Federalist* ambiguously uses the
terms federal (foederal) and confederation for the same referent; and the reader must supply the appropriate meaning
from the context in which these terms are variously used. It is
as though the authors of *The Federalist* had conceptualized
basic distinctions, but had not yet disciplined their use of language to conform to those distinctions. In a sense we still face
the problem when we use the term "federal" to refer to the
national government or the national administration. A federal system of government has reference to many concurrently existing governments having autonomous existence in
relation to one another in a general system of government. It
is not just the national government. To make this distinction
clear, I capitalize the term "Federal" when referring to the national government on an assumption that such terminology
has the characteristics of a proper name rather than a properly defined term. While this is the criterion I use in my own
writing, I cannot always be sure that I do not upon occasion
err. There was greater reason for ambiguity in 1787 and 1788
when basic distinctions were first being made.

Furthermore, it takes a long time to work out the implications of novel conceptions in the realm of ideas. Theories
are never complete. Rather, theories are intellectual tools for
thinking through problems. New conceptions can be introduced and be used to think through a whole new range of
problems. New conceptions can revolutionize ways of thinking about old problems. I would argue that the concepts of
federalism and constitutional rule are among the more fun-

damental conceptions to be introduced into the realm of political theory; and we still have not thought through their fuller implications any more than we have thought through the fuller implications of theories of evolution.

Construing Motives and Ideas

Beyond the ambiguities of language we confront difficulties in construing motives and ideas. We should not be surprised to find errors, ambiguities, and reservations in the arguments being advanced by Hamilton and Madison in *The Federalist*. We all err; and our expression of ideas is often subject to ambiguities and reservations that are not always expressed even when we are aware of them. Other problems arise when we know that Hamilton and Madison both expressed points of view and advanced arguments in the debates at the Philadelphia Convention and later in their lives that are at variance with arguments advanced in *The Federalist*.

Issues bearing upon the authority and standing of individual in the U.S. Constitution, for example, were not satisfactorily addressed in the original formulation. The arguments advanced in *The Federalist* to explain away the failure of the original draft of the U.S. Constitution to contain a bill of rights are clearly unsatisfactory. Yet, the discussion in Federalist 78 about a constitution as fundamental law, and what Hamilton refers to as the general theory of a limited constitution, enables one to understand why the constitutional standing of individuals cannot reasonably be ignored. It was this issue that gave rise to the formulation and adoption of the first ten amendments to the U.S. Constitution during the process of ratifying the Constitution itself.

The more disconcerting problems are posed by essential contradictions between positions taken by either Hamilton or Madison in arguments advanced during the closed debates at the Philadelphia Convention and the arguments that were advanced in *The Federalist* during a campaign to win the approval of the people of New York for ratification of the U.S.

Constitution. There is reason to be sceptical of political rhetoric; and it seems reasonable to construe remarks made in such circumstances with a substantial measure of scepticism. But, there are disturbing methodological problems that arise from adopting such a perspective that need consideration.

Scholars in American constitutional criticism who adopt this perspective often view *The Federalist* primarily as a campaign document written to propagandize the voters of New York. This attitude on the part of a scholar runs the risk of biasing an inquiry before it is initiated. One looks for evidence of distorted or biased arguments of one sort or another. One is required, implicitly, if not explicitly, to arrive at a judgment of what are the true opinions or beliefs of a protagonist. On this basis, points of disingenuousness, or essential dishonesty, are identified often couched in words of admiration for the rhetorical skill with which issues were obscured and distorted to win the support of public opinion. Arguments are then advanced about how authors "secretly" oppose or "secretly" approve certain positions. Conclusions are then reached that authors, in truth, meant the opposite of what they said. We find assertions, for example, about "*The Federalist*'s profound disapproval of the federal principle" (Yarbrough, 1985: 52), of "democracy" (Beard, 1965), or anything else for that matter.

I find the method that follows from taking this perspective to be objectionable upon several grounds. First, it is necessary to arrive at conclusions about the "true" motives and beliefs of those who are authors of ideas. Ideas are then judged on the basis of motives attributed to authors rather than on the merit of the ideas themselves. Motives or intentions are assumed to drive human action without regard to beliefs about the way that conditions affect consequences. This runs the risk of being an *ad hominem* argument that diverts inquiry from fundamental issues in political theory to what can be fruitless speculations about human motives. I know of no way to resolve issues that turn upon determining the true motivation and secret views of other human beings.

I cannot deny that human action is purposive. Actions are motivated by thoughts and preferences that reflect both meaning and intentionality. My response is to advise caution in judging motives as grounds for construing the meaning of terms. A central issue in this volume, for example, is how to construe the passage in the opening paragraph of Federalist 1 where Hamilton poses the issue of "whether societies of men are really capable or not of establishing good government from reflection and choice, or whether they are forever destined to depend for their political constitutions on accident and force" (Federalist 1: ML, 3; C, 3; R, 33). I consider this issue to be of fundamental importance to political theory. This same passage can be lightly dismissed as meaningless rhetoric intended to deceive people by "pulling wool over our eyes." I know of no way to resolve such an issue other than to give other human beings the benefit of the doubt so that we can consider the merit of ideas for the implications that they yield. The issue posed by Hamilton has implications that are of epochal proportions for human civilization. I prefer to give credence to such a possibility; but to do so in an effort to understand the conditions that are logically necessary to realize such a possibility.

Second, the search for truth is much too difficult to presume that I can know the truth either in relation to other people's motives or opinions or in relation to the beliefs that I hold as a scholar. The most I can do in relation to the beliefs that I hold about federalism and constitutional rule, for example, is to attempt to clarify those ideas, press them as far as I can in the form of conjectures, and assume that if they have merit, the reasonableness of that merit will become apparent to others. To obscure and distort can leave others exposed to live in ignorance of what I believe to be false. I can learn only as others challenge; and I bear the burden of advancing conjectures that can be challenged. I do not believe that it is necessary to establish the "true" motives of thinkers to consider the merit of their ideas.

How, then, do I deal with the contradictions between positions taken by Hamilton and Madison apart from the arguments advanced in *The Federalist*? It seems reasonable to me for fallible human beings to expound a set of ideas that they individually view as appropriate for resolving a particular problem. In the course of deliberations, it is entirely possible for individuals to modify their opinions in light of calculations that had not been taken into account and were clarified in the discussion. This is why discussion and dialogue are so important to a clarification of issues.

Where a new and unfamiliar conception is articulated as a way of addressing some problem, reasonable individuals might both judge such a conception as having merit and still have doubts about the consequences that will follow from acting upon it. I might reasonably prefer a method for dealing with a problem that had a demonstrable record of experience behind it over a new idea that had no established record and where the record of a closely related concept was a demonstrable failure. Both the concepts of federalism and constitutional rule were seriously deficient in a well-established record of experiences; and the concept of confederation was, so far as both Hamilton and Madison were concerned, demonstrable of consistent failures. Reasonable persons might both accept the plausibility of an argument and entertain doubts about its viability in practice.

I, thus, acknowledge that both Hamilton and Madison, in varying degrees, might be characterized as "nationalists" who would have preferred a national government adhering to a republicanized version of the English model to a confederation and what they viewed as the danger of replicating the European experience of states warring upon one another. There is every reason to believe that they continued to have doubts about the viability of federal arrangements and the effectiveness of words on parchment in adequately constraining the exercise of governmental authority so as to maintain the enforceability of constitutional law. But, such doubts do not foreclose the possibility that they understood the essential logic of how a federal system might work and the conditions that are necessary for making words on parchment into effective rules of law that could be enforced in relation to those who exercise governmental prerogatives. The realization of such possibilities had revolutionary implications for all of mankind. One might appreciate the revolutionary significance of these ideas, have profound doubts about their practical feasibility, and still be willing to make the experiment.

Madison, in the closing paragraph of Federalist 14, explicitly recognizes the experimental and innovative character of what was being advanced in the U.S. Constitution. He considers it to be the "glory" of the American people not to be bound by "a blind veneration for antiquity" (Federalist 14: ML, 85; C, 88; R, 104) and willing to engage in prudent experimentation. But prudence requires caution, a willingness to explore ideas, to undertake an experiment, and to make modifications in light of experience. These methodological issues are discussed, at length, in Federalist 38 and are stated in my treatment of the assumption of human fallibility with capability for learning in Chapter 2.

These reflections then lead me to the conclusion that it is entirely possible for human beings, including Alexander Hamilton and James Madison, to comprehend the logic of an argument in a field of inquiry with which they are intimately familiar, and to advance arguments about what the likely consequences would be if certain conceptions are acted upon as these conceptions are articulated within the structural specifications of a particular constitution in a more general system of constitutional government. In much the same way, I might expect a knowledgeable architect to be able to read a set of blueprints and provide me with a reasoned exposition of the implications that are likely to follow from relying upon particular conceptualizations that were used in the formulation of those blueprints. The plausibility of one architect's explanation might be checked against the explanations offered by other architects. If an adequate assessment has been made, I should be in a position to specify both the strengths and weaknesses inherent in the design and to anticipate some points of potential vulnerability in the structure that is being planned. Points of potential vulnerability may, if known, have been glossed over. But, others who understood the basic logic could identify such points of vulnerability. Once a logic is articulated, it can be independently explored and assessed by other human beings.

I fully realize that conceptualizing and designing a unit of government to function in a more general system of government is vastly different than designing a building; but the basic use of conceptions and reason to inform the process of design is much the same. An architect may prefer some particular design concept, but this should not prevent him or her from understanding other design concepts and arguing that those other design concepts may be more appropriate to particular circumstances. Madison consistently argues that human beings confront choice either of the lesser evil or the greater good, not the perfect good.

In exploring the merit of ideas, rather than speculating about motives, the burden is upon me to take, first, a sympathetic attitude and attempt to understand the basic argument being advanced and to state that argument to the best of my ability. It does no good in judging the merit of ideas to treat them as either propaganda or ideology. I happen to have a broad area of agreement with the arguments being advanced by Hamilton and Madison as I understand those arguments. But, I bear the burden of taking a sympathetic attitude and trying faithfully to reconstruct an argument even if I personally have grounds for disagreeing either with the normative assumptions used in an argument or with the plausibility of the logical inferences being made. If I were to expound Lenin's theory of constitutional choice, I would have the same obligation sympathetically to understand and articulate that argument even though I might have great doubts about the appropriateness of the logical inference in some aspects of the argument.

One of the interesting phenomena of being human is the attachment of strong emotional feelings to ideas. This is especially the case in the realm of political discourse. Words and statements of words signal emotional responses that easily provoke feelings of threat and anxiety. If we are to make effective use of our cognitive faculties, it is important for us to become aware of these tendencies and to realize that ideas as such do not pose threats. We cannot see where an argument will take us until we have understood its logical structure and implications. Feelings of threat and anxiety can impede inquiry as a quest for understanding.

My first burden is sympathetically to understand and faithfully to reconstruct the logic of an argument. Only when this condition has been met is it possible to engage in reasoned criticism. I would hope that my effort to understand and reconstruct a theoretical argument would be such that an author would agree to its accuracy if he were alive and able to read my reconstruction. He need not agree with my critical evaluation. That needs to be independently judged in the context of a longer-term discourse about ideas. If one does not meet this standard, one is creating false targets for irrelevant commentaries and misdirected criticisms.

Construing the Language of The Federalist

It is much easier to specify the standards to which I aspire than to be confident that I can realize them. The political artisan, or the designer of political institutions, is concerned with the use of language to order relationships among human beings. Human beings have a way of not staying in place like steel, concrete, bricks, mortar, boards, and nails that an architect has reference to in conceptualizing the design of a building. Words themselves do not have meanings except as human beings share communities of experience with one another in communicating through the use of words. We give meanings to words from the experience we share in communicating with one another. This creates serious difficulties both for people who attempt to live together under a common government whose design is expressed in words, as well as for scholars who wish to understand the basic logic inherent in the design of that government.

My understanding of the words I read depends critically upon how I construe the meaning of those words; and I have no reason to believe that the languages I learned in the circle of my family, acquaintances, and colleagues are adequate languages to construe the way that two authors in the late eighteenth century expressed themselves.

Indeed, I have reason to believe that modern scholarship in the twentieth century involved a radical break with the ways of thinking about political relationships that applied to the design and modification of the American constitutional system in the late eighteenth and during much of the nineteenth century. Constitutions in the modern era are dismissed as formalities having little relevance for construing political experiences. The methods of the natural sciences are assumed to be the appropriate methods to apply to the study of political phenomena. Works like *The Federalist* are treated as propaganda, or as an ideology, without relevance for a political science.

There are some of us who are persuaded that a plausible political science should be the body of knowledge that properly informs the choices that human beings might make in formulating the design for institutions of government as embodied in constitutions. The knowledge that is appropriate to reasoning through the implications that follow from the alternative possibilities that might be explored in making decisions at a constitutional level is, from this point of view, what a political science should be all about. If that knowledge is adequately grounded to address relevant constitutional decisions *and stands the test of experience,* we can have some measure of confidence that we know what we are talking about when we engage in political analysis. It is the theoretical arguments about conditions and consequences used to inform constitutional choice that should be tested as hypotheses in empirical inquiries about political experiments.

Following this line of reasoning, I would then argue that it is important to go back at least to the seventeenth and eighteenth centuries and carefully examine the issues that were being addressed by major political thinkers in the context of problems confronting people at that time. Seventeenth-century England and Scotland were engaged in a great ferment of discussion, debate, and violent struggles bearing upon basic constitutional issues. Locke's argument about limits upon the exercise of governmental authority was reflected in the English constitutional settlement of 1689 and provided the foundation for a Whig tradition in the American colonies (see Lutz, 1980). These traditions were carried on through the eighteenth century, were reiterated in Montesquieu's treatment of the constitution of liberty, and reached their fuller development in the Scottish school of moral and political philosophy especially with the works of David Hume and Adam Smith.

Both Hamilton and Madison were thoroughly schooled in Locke, Montesquieu, and Scottish philosophy. They used the mode of analysis developed by the Scottish philosophers as their method for reasoning through political problems. Thus, they were thoroughly familiar with a long-standing discussion of constitutional issues and modes of analysis that were relevant to a consideration of such issues. They were, also, intimately involved in the practice of constitutional analysis and constitutional decision making that permeated American society during the revolutionary era. Adam Smith formulated the basic foundation for modern economic theory from that tradition of work; and I am persuaded that the work of Alexander Hamilton and James Madison, drawing upon the same intellectual traditions, serves as a proper foundation for modern political theory.

Thus, I proceed on an assumption that careful attention to the community of scholarship in seventeenth and eighteenth century England and Scotland provides the proper context for reading *The Federalist* in light of the issues being addressed in the American revolutionary effort to design systems of government that would meet the requirements specified in the Declaration of Independence and resolve the issues posed by the failure of confederation. I consider the works of Hobbes, Locke, Montesquieu, Hume, and Smith to have particular relevance. The task that the Americans faced was to formulate a solution to the governance of human society that was fundamentally at variance with the solution propounded by Hobbes. Hobbes viewed the key institution of government (i.e., the sovereign) as being the source of law, as exercising dominance over society from a single center of authority, and not itself subject to law. The task that the Americans faced was to conceptualize how a system of government with multiple centers of authority reflecting opposite and rival interests could be held accountable to enforceable rules of constitutional law. The test, then, is a viable political arrangement that forecloses the basic solution propounded by Hobbes.

The contrast between Hobbes's formulation of the institutions of government and that formulated in the American experiments in constitutional choice suggests that fundamentally different approaches exist for the organization of governance in human societies. In the one, a single center of authority, the sovereign, is designed to dominate the whole. Each unit, as a sovereign state, is fully independent of other units as sovereign states. In the other, no single center of authority dominates the rest; all assignments of authority are subject to limits. Governments can coexist with one another. New communities of interests can be constituted as limited political communities having concurrent and autonomous existence in federal systems of government.

These differences in the constitution of systems of governance in human societies have their analogue in different approaches that can be taken to the organization of economic relationships. Market organization can be contrasted to centrally administered economies where the means of production are owned and managed by the state. A sovereign state has authorities that govern over society. A federal system of government is characterized by equilibrating structures that enable people to search out resolutions in commonly defined realms of choice bounded by the limits of multiple veto points. *The Political Theory of a Compound Republic* is my effort to clarify the logic inherent in the American experiments in constitutional choice on an assumption that it offers an alternative to the traditional theory of the state.

THE SCOPE OF THIS INQUIRY

My task, in view of these pitfalls, is to take some 80 essays principally written by two knowledgeable and skilled political artisans and attempt to reconstruct the basic logic that was used to conduct an analysis so that we might understand the basic concepts and mode of reasoning used to formulate the design of the American constitutional system. I am not simply summarizing the arguments made but trying to reconstruct the theory that was used in formulating those arguments. Again, I am proceeding on an assumption that a knowledgeable architect could take 80 essays written by a team of architects to explain the implications that would follow from a particular set of blueprints and state the theory and mode of analysis used by that team of architects.

In discharging this task, I take as my point of departure the basic issue that Alexander Hamilton addresses in the opening paragraph of Federalist 1, when he raises the question of whether "societies of men, are . . . capable or not, of establishing good government from reflection and choice" (ML, 3; C, 3; R, 33). I use this statement of the problem to consider presuppositions that provide a context for analysis and to formulate the basic assumptions and postulates used in the analysis. In doing so I attempt to answer the following questions: (1) What is the basic unit of analysis? (2) What is the basic motivating factor or principle for postulating the action tendencies of that basic unit of analysis? (3) What are the postulated and limiting conditions bearing upon the availability and use of information in human affairs? (4) What are the basic postulated and limiting conditions affecting the exercise of discretion and choice in human affairs? The responses to these questions are discussed under the following topics: (1) an individualistic assumption about political experience, (2) the principle of relative advantage, (3) an assumption of human fallibility with capabilities for learning, and (4) the principle of political constraint.

I assume that one who takes these basic assumptions and first principles as applying both to oneself and to all other individuals can then reason through how individuals who are assumed to have such characteristics are likely to respond to the structure of incentives inherent in specified decision situations. Political or jurisprudential reasoning in *The Federalist* tradition is no more than thinking through the implications that follow when representative individuals choose strategies in light of the structure of incentives inherent in decision situations. The better the structure of incentives in decision situations can be understood and specified, the more reliably one might estimate how structures of incentives affect choices and how choices affect consequences.

This method is antithetical to another method which assumes that an omniscient observer can see the whole picture and that the basic problems of society can be solved by allowing such an omniscient observer to exercise omnipotent authority in governing society. Anyone who has formed the habit of thinking about problems of human societies from the perspective of an omniscient observer cannot understand the logic of a compound republic until that way of viewing problems is put aside. One needs to have a self-conscious awareness that the perspectives one takes and the presuppositions one makes affect what one observes.[4]

In Chapter 3, I turn to the basic distinction that needs to be made in thinking about constitutional choice and the constitutional level of analysis. I use the distinctions formulated in *The Federalist* between a constitution and a law to specify essential elements in the process of constitutional choice, to indicate the problem of formulating constitutions as enforceable legal instrumentalities, and to conclude by considering the distinctive character of the American theory of constitutional choice.

Chapter 4, then, goes on to consider some of the basic rudiments of a political design. The problem of design is explored first; and then a series of propositions, containing basic assumptions, definitions, and postulates relevant to the design of political institutions, are explored to the point of identifying the basic problem of majority tyranny. Chapter 5 continues this mode of analysis by exploring considerations that bear upon the capacity of mankind for self-government. It is in this context that a republican remedy for the republican disease of majority tyranny is conceptualized by the compounding of a republic.

Chapter 6 elaborates that method by treating federalism as a theory of concurrent regimes and indicating how a federal system is expected to work. Chapter 7 returns to the problem of constitutional choice as it applies to the organization of a national unit of government that is subject to enforceable rules of constitutional law. Both federalism and constitutional rule are integral principles of organization in the American system of government.

Federalism can be conceptualized as *constitutional choice reiterated* to apply to many different units of government in a system of government where each unit is bound by enforceable rules of constitutional law. When people draw upon a common theory of constitutional choice both in designing units of government and in enforcing limits with reference to those who exercise authority in such a system of government, we can conceptualize a system of government where rulers are themselves subject to a rule of law. [5]

Chapter 8 takes a retrospective view of the American experiments in constitutional choice after two centuries of experience. I there engage in a reflective inquiry about the general significance of the American experiments in constitutional choice in light of subsequent experience. My concern is to view problems of institutional failure and how Americans

have addressed those problems as basic issues of constitutional importance. The analysis is a difficult one for two reasons. First, *The Federalist* provides us with only a partial view of
the multiple experiments in American constitutional choice.
Second, a basic shift occurs midway in these two centuries
where leading thinkers reject the theory of *The Federalist* for a
theory of a unitary, as contrasted to a compound, system of
government built upon a model of parliamentary democracy
and bureaucratic administration.

Political artisans concerned with administrative reorganization and political reform in the twentieth century have become
preoccupied with eliminating "fragmentation of authority"
and "overlapping jurisdictions." Separation of powers necessarily involves fragmentation of authority. Federalism necessarily involves overlapping jurisdictions. We, thus, face some
puzzling problems in reflecting upon what intellectual tools
are appropriate to determining the future of the American
experiments in constitutional choice. We expound reform
principles in the twentieth century which are the antithesis of
the design principles used to formulate the American experiments in constitutional choice in the late eighteenth century.

To gain a more general view of the American experiments
in constitutional choice, I draw upon Tocqueville's work which
avoids the more partial view of *The Federalist* and its proper
preoccupation with the U.S. Constitution as only one particular experiment in constitutional choice. Tocqueville focuses
upon the American constitutional system as a whole including
institutions of local government. Tocqueville's analysis is properly informed by a sympathetic understanding of the basic
principles of constitutional choice that distinguish the theory
of a compound republic from that of an extended unitary republic. The political theory of a compound republic is not to
be confused with traditional theories of sovereignty.

After presenting Tocqueville's assessment, I then focus
upon two issues that were a basic challenge to that system.
One is the issue of slavery. The other is the issue of political
corruption associated with the rise of machine politics and

boss rule. In each case, I indicate the way these issues have been addressed at the constitutional level of analysis.

I then turn to the repudiation of the theory of *The Federalist* as failing to address political realities. In doing so, I rely upon Woodrow Wilson's critical assessment in *Congressional Government* and in an essay on "The Study of Administration." I construe the nationalization of American government in the twentieth century as a basic challenge to the political theory of a compound republic.

In view of this basic challenge presented by the rejection of federalist theory and the nationalization of American government, I go on in Chapter 9 to further reflect upon what it means for human beings to design and create systems of government based upon reflection and choice. It is not enough to be concerned with issues of what governments should do in deciding matters of public policy. There is a deeper constitutional level of analysis that pertains to the terms and conditions that apply to the structures and processes of government and how these processes should be conducted. There is still a further level of analysis that is concerned with the effects of governmental actions. We need to see these different levels of analysis in relation to one another and the way they affect life in human societies if we are to have an adequate basis for construing the meanings of experiments in constitutional choice.

The effort of scholars in the nineteenth and twentieth centuries to repudiate earlier traditions of inquiry by contrasting theoretical formulations with living realities has posed a fundamental challenge both to scholarship and to constitutional government. I indicate the nature of that challenge, and, in turn, challenge the challengers. I advance a contestable set of arguments. I welcome others to respond with contestable arguments which seek to clarify the nature and constitution of order in human societies. Where this leaves us and what we might do about present circumstances, my dear readers, will be for you to think through and help resolve.

NOTES

1. References are to the works and editions cited in the list of References. All references to *The Federalist* will be to the Modern Library edition, to the Cooke edition published by Meridian Books, and to the Rossiter edition published by New American Library of World Literature. In those cases only the appropriate page number will be given with the initials ML for Modern Library, C for Cooke, and R for Rossiter. I have quoted from the text of the Modern Library edition.

2. I make a distinction between conceptions and theoretical apparatus. A concept like constitutional rule implies a system of rule that applies to an exercise of the prerogatives of government. But, to work out logically the conditions that must be satisfied to make that concept meaningful requires one to specify the terms and conditions of government plus the conditions for attaining the effectiveness of rules. This requires that rules be made enforceable. Explaining the logically necessary conditions for attaining an enforceable system of constitutional law requires the elaboration of a complex argument which is implied by the concept of constitutional rule. To think through that concept requires a theoretical apparatus to do so.

Noam Chomsky, in *Rules and Representations*, advances the conjecture that "knowing a language" may involve different aspects of cognition: a conceptual aspect of cognition may be distinguishable from a computational aspect of cognition (1980: 54–57). My reference to concepts or conceptions would refer to conceptual aspects; and my reference to theory would be to the computational aspects that enable us to account for the essential relationships implicated in the conceptual aspects.

3. Nevil Johnson's *In Search of the Constitution* presents an extended discussion of the lack of appropriate intellectual tools for considering the constitutional importance of many policy decisions in contemporary discussions.

4. It is possible for an analyst who takes the perspective of representative individuals to build the rudiments of analysis by indicating the action tendencies inherent in the structure of multiple institutional arrangements in human societies. Once these tendencies

have been aggregated to give a general understanding of the action tendencies in a society, it is then possible for that analyst to offer theoretically informed conjectures about the general effects of the aggregate political and social structure of a society. This is what Tocqueville does in *Democracy in America*. In Volume I, he builds the structure of institutional analysis and considers the relative effects of circumstances, institutions, and customs in the shaping of American society. In Volume II, he considers the aggregate effect of American society upon the working of the intellect of Americans, the feelings of Americans, and patterns of social relationships in American society. While Tocqueville makes an aggregate analysis that generalizes about society as a whole, he does not take the perspective of the omniscient observer. Rather, he formulates the analytical apparatus in Volume I which is used to conduct the analysis in Volume II.

The analysis in *The Federalist* is an *a priori* theoretical argument exploring the action tendencies created by the opportunities and constraints inherent in the institutional arrangements specified in the U.S. Constitution. The first 51 essays largely focus upon the marginal effect of the U.S. Constitution in a federal system. The later essays largely focus upon an analysis of the constitution of particular decision structures in the national government.

I write this note to emphasize that viewing problems from the hypothetical perspective of representative individuals does not foreclose analysis at aggregate levels of society. It does, however, require the analyst to work out the elements of analysis that contribute to the aggregate level of analysis. Tocqueville's work is illustrative of that method.

5. Much of the debate between what are today referred to as "Federalists" and "Anti-Federalists" focuses upon a common issue and concern: How can a system of government be established where officials are held accountable to a rule of law? Basic differences focus upon what were viewed as potential threats to the maintenance of a rule of law that applied to the conduct of all officials. There were those who viewed the national government as posing the most serious threat, and the states as a better repository of liberty. Fears of presidential prerogatives, judicial authority, and the absence of a bill of rights become sources of opposition to the U.S. Constitution. But,

the paramount concern was how to establish a system of government that would operate within the limits of constitutional law. Herbert J. Storing's extended essay on *What the Anti-Federalists Were For,* which appears as volume I of his *The Complete Anti-Federalist,* is deserving of careful study in relation to any study of *The Federalist.*

Given the common focus of inquiry, the term "Anti-Federalist" is a misnomer except for the fact that opposition was being stated to the U.S. Constitution. Much of the discourse is informed by similar theoretical considerations in a larger community of discourse. My own conclusion is that any system of constitutional government is always subject to multiple threats. Purely institutional constraints are never sufficient to maintain the limits of constitutional rule. An informed citizenry that knows how to maintain appropriate limits is also essential.

The overwhelming preoccupation about the maintenance of the limits of constitutional rule among both "Federalists" and "Anti-Federalists" is much in contrast with modern political discourse in the twentieth century where the paramount concern is with what authority exercises supremacy and has the last say in the conduct of government. Fragmentation of authority and overlapping jurisdictions are viewed as perversities. The real Anti-Federalists came into existence in the late nineteenth and twentieth centuries. The so-called Anti-Federalists of the late eighteenth and early nineteenth centuries were largely variants in a federalist tradition. I confine my analysis to the argument in *The Federalist* because that argument is a coherent one that can be juxtaposed to its antithesis in twentieth century political discourse.

CHAPTER TWO

Point of Departure, Basic Assumptions, and First Principles

THE POINT OF DEPARTURE

In the opening paragraph of Federalist 1, Hamilton makes an observation which poses the critical question that begins the line of inquiry in *The Federalist:*

It has been frequently remarked that it seems to have been reserved to the people of this country, by their conduct and example, to decide the important question, *whether societies of men are really capable or not of establishing good government from reflection and choice, or whether they are forever destined to depend for their political constitutions on accident and force.* (Federalist 1: ML, 3; C, 3; R, 33. My emphasis.)

He then goes on to add:

If there be any truth in the remark, the crisis at which we are arrived may with propriety be regarded as the era in which that choice is to be made; and a wrong election on the part we shall act may, in this view, deserve to be considered as the general misfortune of mankind. (Federalist 1: ML, 3; C, 3; R, 33)

Madison takes much the same view in the concluding lines of Federalist 14 where both "America" and "the whole human race" are viewed as the potential beneficiaries of an effort to create a compound republic. He viewed the American efforts to rear "the fabrics of governments" as having no parallel in human experience to that point in time. A part of that effort had been to design a "great Confederacy." Madison then goes on to conclude with the following observation:

If their works betray imperfections, we wonder at the fewness of them. If they erred most in the structure of the Union, this was the work most difficult to be executed; this is the work which has been new modelled by the act of your convention, and it is the act on which you are now to decide. (Federalist 14: ML, 85; C, 89; R, 104–105)

The contention in the Declaration of Independence that it is the "Right of the People . . . to institute a new Government, laying its foundations on such principles and organizing its powers in such form, as to them shall seem most likely to effect their Safety and Happiness" had now become more problematical. It was an open question for Hamilton whether good governments could be designed on reflection and choice. But, a question of such fundamental importance was of potential interest to all mankind. The failure of confederation had a sobering effect. The new design fashioned by the Philadelphia Convention is what gave promise of attaining a constructive resolution. Madison's discussion in particular had reference to the plurality of experiments in the "fabrics of governments" and in the "works" that betrayed so few imperfections. It was the structure of the "Union" that posed the greatest difficulties; and he viewed the work of the Philadelphia Convention as a new model to improve and perpetuate prior efforts to design a "great Confederacy." Different models were used to organize political experiments. They were to be understood on the basis of reflection; and a choice was to be made in light of the anticipated consequences. The validity of the proposition that human beings can design governments of their own choosing was to be decided by experience.

If an affirmative answer can be given to the questions posed by Hamilton—that governments *can* be established on the basis of reflection and choice—a thesis is being advanced that the government of human affairs *is* the subject of choice and that those who exercise that choice can have reference to a body of knowledge and to methods of analysis to inform choice. In other words, a science of politics is presumed. Such a political science can be used to design and organize institutions of government. Hamilton clearly acknowledges the contribution of "the science of politics" to the basic formulations in the U.S. Constitution (Federalist 9: ML, 48; C, 50–51; R, 71–72); and in the Federalist 31, he states a number of basic axioms in a theory of ethics and politics.

The presumption that governments can be established by "societies of men" on the basis of reflection and choice has a corollary presumption that the organization of governments can be *maintained* or *modified* on the basis of reflection and choice. If this presumption is accepted as a logical possibility, then, we can infer that the "ultimate authority" to devise, revise, and alter the terms of government resides with the "societies of men" who chose to constitute themselves as political communities. *Constitutional decision making*, in such a conception, is an essential political prerogative for modifying and altering the terms of government.

A correlative presumption would also exist that all instrumentalities of government, where government is derived from reflection and choice, can exercise only a limited and derived authority. Madison, in speaking of the relationship of the people to the proposed Federal and state governments, expressed the same idea when he observed, "[T]he ultimate authority, wherever the derivative may be found, resides in the people alone . . ." (Federalist 46: ML, 305; C, 315; R, 294). A further presumption exists that a system of government conceived through reflection and choice would be based upon a political formula reserving certain decision-making capabilities for people to function in a political community as *inalienable* rights. "Inalienable" need imply only that such rights involve the assignment of a political authority that is *not* subject to appropriation, possession, or alienation by others, including public officials vested with authority to tend to the collective interests of a political community. Presumably, any political constitution, which is based upon the authority of people to decide the terms and conditions of government, must necessarily contain correlative reservations about the authority of people which are not subject to alienation. Such reservations are expressed either as a limitation upon the authority of instrumentalities of government, or as an "any-one" rule assigning authority to individual persons. If an "any-one" rule can be sustained, then the authority of everyone is assured. [1]

The doctrine of popular sovereignty inherent in the assertion that "societies of men" can by reflection and choice establish, maintain, and alter the terms of government might be considered to be a logical possibility given certain assumptions, but an empirical impossibility given conditions which deviate from those assumptions. In this sense, the doctrine of popular sovereignty might be dismissed as a utopian concept with little or no relevance for the development of a political science. The authors of *The Federalist* would contend that the establishment of government by accident and force was the prevailing condition for most of mankind. The special task confronting the American people was to demonstrate that the *improbable* was *possible:* that a people could by its conduct and example establish and maintain a system of government based upon reflection and choice.

To go beyond the revolutionary assertion that it is the right of a people to institute a new system of government "laying its foundation on such principles and organizing its powers in such form" as they may choose "to effect their Safety and Happiness" required that the principles of political organization be expounded and that these principles be incorporated into the design of political institutions. Political science, as one might expect, was an intellectual preoccupation among Americans in the late eighteenth and early nineteenth centuries. New concepts were being introduced into American political science. New elements of design were being introduced into constitutions in order to realize the possibility that governments might be organized on the basis of deliberate choice among societies of men.

The political circumstance of the late 1780s provided a critical juncture for a theory holding that societies of men could establish and maintain the terms of government through reflection and choice. The conditions of government under the Articles of Confederation had led to frustration and dissatisfaction. A political stalemate existed; and there was little opportunity for resolving that stalemate within the constitutional decision rules of the Articles of Confederation. The task of revising the terms of government required recourse to a constitutional system based upon a fundamentally different conception. In establishing the source of the error and in formulating an alternative arrangement, the authors of *The Federalist* argued that it was necessary to go back to first principles or basic assumptions. These first principles or basic assumptions were never enumerated and enunciated as elements in a treatise on political theory. We can, however, through an examination of their argument, formulate several basic assumptions or first principles that are inherent in their analysis apart from the concept used as their point of departure.

One of their first assumptions is the proposition that *individuals are the basic units to be considered in the design of political institutions*. Actions of a government derive from the interests of individuals; to be effective, actions of government must relate to the conduct of individuals; the operations of governments, as such, are the coordinated conduct of individuals acting in specialized capacities. A second assumption in the political theory of *The Federalist* is that individuals are self-interested and will seek to enhance their relative advantage. A third assumption is that of human fallibility with capability for learning. As advocates of a proposal designed to correct a previous error, the authors of *The Federalist* devote considerable attention to the problem of human error. Finally, they advance a position, which I shall identify as the principle of political constraint, based upon an assumption that conditions of reason and justice, and conditions of social organization, depend upon some form of political order.

"[T]he principle of LEGISLATION for STATES or GOVERN-
MENTS, in their CORPORATE or COLLECTIVE CAPACITIES"
(Federalist 15: ML, 89; C, 93; R, 108. Hamilton's emphasis.) in
contradistinction to "the principle of legislation for the individual citizens of America" (Federalist 17: ML, 101; C, 105; R,
118) was identified as the basic misconception in the design of
the American confederation. Hamilton called it "the great
and radical vice" of the confederation (Federalist 15: ML, 89;
C, 93; R, 108). Both Hamilton and Madison consider a political system based upon the concept of governing corporate or
collective entities, as distinguished from individual persons, to
be a fundamental fallacy and to be "incompatible with the
idea of GOVERNMENT" (Federalist 15: ML, 90; C, 94; R, 108.
Hamilton's emphasis).

Prior to the American effort to organize a Federal government based upon the political formula of the Constitution of
1787, the constitutions of all existing confederacies had, according to Madison, been grounded on the assumption that
the authority of the confederation applied to the government
of principalities, city-states, or states comprising that confederation. The congresses or councils of those confederations could resolve, but the execution of any resolution was
dependent upon the actions of the constituent members. The
constitutions of these confederacies had been "vitiated by the
same erroneous principles" (Federalist 37: ML, 226; C, 233;
R, 226) as the American confederation.

The basic lesson for Hamilton and Madison in the American experiment with confederation is that people as individual persons are the fundamental units to be considered in
organizing any political association. The "true springs" (Federalist 15: ML, 92; C, 96; R, 110) by which human behavior is
actuated have reference to individuals as persons rather than
to collectivities as corporate entities. The individual person is
the doer of acts. The way each individual as a person relates

himself to others is the basis of all social organization. The *raison d'etre* of government is to constrain and order the behavior of individuals, "[b]ecause the passions of men will not conform to the dictates of reason and justice, without constraint" (Federalist 15: ML, 92; C, 96; R, 110). This principle is as applicable to an official acting in a governmental capacity as it is to any person acting in his or her capacity as an individual citizen or as a private person. Madison draws upon this individualistic conception of political relationships to derive his formula for the distribution of authority. He observes that

the constant aim is to divide and arrange the several offices in such a manner as that each may be a check on the other—that the private interest of every individual may be a sentinel over the public rights. (Federalist 51: ML, 337; C, 349; R, 322)

Since individuals exercise discretion as doers of acts, the authority of a government must extend to "the persons of the citizens" (Federalist 15: ML, 91; C, 95; R, 109). "Government," according to the authors of *The Federalist*, "implies the power of making laws" (Federalist 15: ML, 91; C, 95; R, 110). They go on to argue:

It is essential to the idea of a law, that it be attended with a sanction; or, in other words, a penalty or punishment for disobedience. If there be no penalty annexed to disobedience, the resolutions or commands which pretend to be law will, in fact, amount to nothing more than *advice or recommendation*. (Federalist 15: ML, 91; C, 95; R, 110. My emphasis.)

An association which is limited to giving *advice* and making *recommendations* without the ability to enforce its prescriptions as working or operable rules of conduct cannot meet the essential requirement of a government. Thus, an effort to govern collectivities without reference to the accountability of individuals for their action is "incompatible with the idea of GOVERNMENT" (Federalist 15: ML, 90; C, 94; R, 108). An effective government must enforce rules that apply to individuals.

Where collectivities are the exclusive object of political resolutions, and when sanctions are applied to a collectivity, there is no capacity to discriminate between the innocent persons and the wrongdoers who comprise the population of a collectivity. Guilt by association is a necessary consequence of applying sanctions against collectivities, *per se.*

Hamilton infers that justice cannot be done when sanctions are applied to collectivities. Remedies applied by courts and ministers of justice, he suggests, "can evidently apply only to men" (Federalist 15: ML, 91; C, 95; R, 110) in their individual capacities. He considers military force, or the "coercion of arms," to be the basic form of collective sanction which "must of necessity be employed against bodies politic, or communities, or States" (Federalist 15: ML, 91; C, 95; R, 110). Where remedies are limited to the use of collective sanctions, judgment regarding individual responsibility becomes an impossibility and necessarily gives way to the exigencies of government by an indiscriminating use of force.

When a corporation is fined for the violation of law, who bears the burden of the fine? Is it the individual or individuals responsible for taking the particular decision in violation of law? Or, is the burden passed on to either shareholders of the corporation, customers, or both? The application of criminal sanctions to collectivities, in this case a corporation, shields the wrongdoers from culpability and transfers the burden to others who may be innocent bystanders. This, Hamilton would argue, is not consistent with the requirements of justice.

From an extended consideration of the "great and radical vice," the fundamental fallacy, of conceiving collectivities, *per se,* as the objects of political action, Hamilton concludes that the design and construction of a *limited* national government in a federal system of government must be based upon a conception of political experience as pertaining to individuals. He then pursues the implications of his conclusion:

[I]f it be possible at any rate to construct a federal government capable of regulating the common concerns and preserving the general tranquility, it must be founded, as to the objects committed to its care, upon the reverse of the principle contended for by the opponents of the proposed Constitution (i.e., the principle of legislation for states, or communities, in their collective capacities). *It must carry its agency to the persons of the citizens.* It must stand in need of no intermediate legislations; but must itself be empowered to employ the arm of the ordinary magistrate to execute its own resolutions. The majesty of the national authority must be manifested through the medium of the courts of justice. *The government of the Union, like that of each State, must be able to address itself immediately to the hopes and fears of individuals; and to attract to its support those passions which have the strongest influence upon the human heart. It must, in short, possess all the means, and have a right to resort to all the methods, of executing the powers with which it is intrusted, that are possessed and exercised by the governments of the particular States.* (Federalist 16: ML, 98–99; C, 102–103; R, 116. My emphasis and parenthetical note.)

From this line of argument, I conclude that political associations are conceived as means for individuals to act in concert, to act jointly in relation to each other through institutional arrangements assigning special prerogative, or authority, for some individuals to act on behalf of others. Such an association can for some purposes be conceptualized as a thing unto itself—as a shorthand device for naming and characterizing the persons who choose to act in cognizance of a common set of rules which serve as a mutual referent in coordinating their actions, one with another. But, any effort to conceive collectivities as things unto themselves is apt to give rise to a fallacy of assuming that names reflect events to which one can attribute existence, discretion, action, and responsibility apart from the associations involved.

Yet we still have an interesting analytical question: What does it mean to act on a "fallacious" or "erroneous" conception? *The Federalist* argument is that persons in many political associations had acted upon erroneous conceptions in the past. Actions based upon a conception involving the government of people in their collective capacities had occurred through long periods of history. Apart from the constitution of early confederations, Madison and Hamilton might well have contended that the great empires of the Persians, the Macedonians, the Romans, the Mongols, and the British were based upon the superimposition of the rule of an imperium upon diverse people organized as collectivities in relation to their local or municipal institutions. In such cases, an imperial exercise of government over collectivities in their corporate capacities should lead to the consequences that Hamilton and Madison anticipated: the use of collective sanctions, including recourse to military force and the coercion of arms, without an ability to realize reason and justice in relationships of the individual to the imperium and of the imperium to the individual.

Action based upon an erroneous or false conception should give rise to consequences, and those consequences can be discerned and evaluated. Action based upon a different conception can be expected to produce different consequences, and those consequences can be discerned and evaluated. Thus, the significance of the two alternative conceptions must rest upon: (1) a comparative examination of the differences inherent in operationalizing actions appropriate to each and (2) a comparative assessment of the consequences, in terms of independent criteria or standards of evaluation. The conception which provides the better explanation for anticipating the successful realization of events is the preferred conception.

Hamilton derives his formulation for creating a limited national unit of government that will operate concurrently with state governments from the concept that individuals form the basic unit in the design of all political institutions. Instead of a general regime being superimposed upon a structure of subordinate regimes, as would be inherent in the government of collectivities in their corporate capacities, Hamilton conceives that a limited national government can be made operational only by establishing a concurrent structure with full redundancy of means and methods of operation, but specialized as to the tasks to be accomplished. The scale and purpose of organization would vary, but the means and methods would be the same in designing the structure for a system of concurrent governments in a compound republic. Citizens would then function concurrently in two or more governments that serve different communities of interest.

Conceiving of individuals as being the basic units exercising responsibility in political relationships does not presume that individuals as such exist apart from ordered social relationships with others in a society. Language derives from shared social relationships; and the accumulated learning derived from the use of languages to communicate with one another is what makes human civilization and political organization possible. But it is still individuals who form the basic units that comprise political communities. Conditions of freedom and justice can prevail only so long as individuals are assumed to be responsible for their own actions; and judgments can be rendered in relation to presumptions of individual responsibility. The price of freedom and justice, then, turns upon the responsibility of individuals for the decisions they make and the actions they take both in relation to their own interests and the interests of others.

THE PRINCIPLE OF RELATIVE ADVANTAGE

If an individualistic assumption about political experience is adopted as a basic assumption, what principle can be expected to govern the behavior of individuals? First, Hamilton assumes that individuals will always be confronted by circumstances involving a scarcity of goods and resources.

I believe it may be regarded as a position warranted by the history of mankind, that, *in the usual progress of things, the necessities of a nation, in every stage of its existence, will be found at least equal to its resources.* (Federalist 30: ML, 185; C, 190; R, 190. Hamilton's emphasis.)

People may vary in wealth and prosperity. Some goods may at times be in such abundant supply that they can be treated as free goods. But the aggregate supply of resources will be such that the aggregate demands of a nation cannot be met without principles of economy. Choices are necessary.

Second, both Hamilton and Madison assume that individuals will have reference to self-interest or "self-love" in the pursuit of opportunities and possibilities. It is from this base of self-interestedness that human energy, ambition, and productivity arise. The latent sources of conflict or "causes of faction are thus sown in the nature of man . . . " (Federalist 10: ML, 55; C, 58; R, 79). The very design of political institutions depends upon connecting the interests of the individual with the assignment of decision-making capabilities so that the interest of one is constrained by the interests of others. "Ambition must be made to counteract ambition" (Federalist 51: ML, 337; C, 349; R, 322).

Third, Madison is quite explicit in assuming that individuals will always be confronted by the problem of choosing from imperfect options. He formulates a principle of relative advantage when he observes that "choice must always be made, if not of the lesser evil, at least of the GREATER, not the PERFECT, good . . ." (Federalist 41: ML, 260; C, 269; R, 255. Madison's emphasis). At another point, he comments: "No man would refuse to give brass for silver or gold, because the latter had some alloy in it" (Federalist 38: ML, 239; C, 246; R, 237).

The emphasis throughout Madison's discussion is clearly one of choosing the greater good rather than the lesser good despite the imperfect qualities attributed to men and their political institutions. At times, Madison deals with the principle of relative advantage as an analytical postulate assuming that individuals will pursue their greater advantage under given conditions. At other points, he urges careful consideration of the advantages or benefits as well as the inconveniences and disadvantages in the sense that persons *should* choose the alternative offering the greater advantage. The principle of relative advantage serves both as an analytical postulate in understanding how persons will behave and as a normative criterion about how they ought to behave. Any intellectual ambiguity implied by the use of a basic assumption as an analytical postulate, on the one hand, and as a normative criterion, on the other, derives in part from other assumptions made about the human condition. The assumption of human fallibility implies that a person may be unable to distinguish the greater from the lesser good because one lacks either sufficient knowledge about the nature of events perceived as "goods," a reasoned comprehension of one's own "true" preferences, or both.

Hamilton is emphatic in distinguishing a short-run individualistic calculus, which is apt to emphasize human ambition or human passion, from a long-term calculus, which permits reasoned considerations of "policy, utility and justice." He poses the issue in one of his many rhetorical questions:

> Has it not, on the contrary, invariably been found that momentary passions, and immediate interests, have a more active and imperious control over human conduct than general or remote considerations of policy, utility, or justice? (Federalist 6: ML, 30; C, 31; R, 56)

The answer he intends is an initial "yes." However, that is only his starting point. He views the essential nature of the political process as permitting the interposition of essential constraints, and allowing reason to work its way through to a more enlightened judgment that takes account of general, long-run considerations. The political process is one that should enable human reason to be transformed from a consideration of momentary passion and immediate interest into a more general and long-term consideration of "policy, utility or justice." We shall return to this consideration in the subsequent discussion of the principle of political constraint.

Madison is also emphatic in stressing the imperfect character of political institutions: "[I]n every political institution, a power to advance the public happiness involves a discretion which may be misapplied and abused" (Federalist 41: ML, 260; C, 269; R, 255–256). Since perfect solutions cannot be expected, the practical formulator of constitutions must con-

sider the disadvantages in relation to the advantages inherent
in alternatives rather than consider the existence of disadvantages to be evidence that a solution is not perfect, and, therefore, to be rejected. Goods are rarely, if ever, unqualified goods
or unmixed blessings. The capacity to assess accurately the
greater advantage requires a knowledgeable sophistication.
Even then, such calculations may be a matter of substantial
doubt and uncertainty resulting from imperfect information.

Beyond the mixed bag of advantages and disadvantages, or
benefits and costs, inherent in the evaluation of any occurrence or possibility, Madison also implies that valued occur-
rences which may be good for some can also be detrimental to
others. His very definition of a "faction" is predicated upon
this distinction: "A number of citizens . . . who are united and
actuated by some common impulse of passion, or of interest,
adverse to the rights of other citizens, or to the permanent and
aggregate interests of the community" (Federalist 10: ML, 54;
C, 57; R, 78. My emphasis). Such circumstances require citizens to give careful attention to an extended social calculus
of one's interests *vis-à-vis* others' interests in the context of a
more general community of interests and to select those opportunities which will realize the greater good rather than the
lesser good.

AN ASSUMPTION OF HUMAN FALLIBILITY WITH CAPABILITY FOR LEARNING

The authors of *The Federalist* confronted an especially difficult
dilemma concerning human fallibility in presenting their
case. On the one hand, they contended that the Articles of
Confederation were based upon an erroneous concept. This
assertion, as we have seen, was extended to cover *all other
known confederations* (Federalist 37: ML, 226; C, 233; R, 226).
They specifically rejected as fallacious the concept that a government could govern other governments or states in their
collective capacities. Instead, they advanced a thesis that units
of government as political associations must be related to the

persons of individuals, to their hopes and fears, and to the significance of their behavior as calculable action. Rather than assert any *special* claim to enlightenment for establishing the validity of *their* conceptions, Hamilton and Madison contend that both the authors of the proposed constitution and their critics are fallible. [2] In short, men "ought not to assume an in-fallibility in rejudging the fallible opinions of others" (Federalist 37: ML, 226; C, 233; R, 226).

Madison pursues a rather extended discussion about the circumstances of human fallibility in Federalist 37 and 38 in introducing his political analysis. The faculties of the human mind—of sense, perception, judgment, desire, volition, memory, and imagination—are not well enough understood, he asserts. Neither is "the great kingdom of nature" (Federalist 37: ML, 228; C, 235; R, 227–228). The imperfection of the human senses, Madison argues, obscures the perfection of nature. When we consider

the institutions of man, in which . . . obscurity arises as well from the object itself as from the organ by which it is contemplated, we must perceive the necessity of moderating still further our expectations and hopes from the efforts of human sagacity. (Federalist 37: ML, 228–229; C, 235; R, 228)

Language as "the medium through which the conceptions of men are conveyed to each other" (Federalist 37: ML, 229; C, 236; R, 229) is another source of imperfection in human understanding. "[N]o language is so copious as to supply words and phrases for every complex idea, or so correct as not to include many equivocally denoting different ideas" (Federalist 37: ML, 230; C, 236; R, 229). Hence, language gives rise to unavoidable inaccuracies which increase with the complexity and novelty of the events being considered.

Madison continues to argue that "when the Almighty himself condescends to address mankind in their own language, his meaning, luminous as it must be, is rendered dim and doubtful by the cloudy medium through which it is communicated" (Federalist 37: ML, 230; C, 236–237; R, 229). From this, one must infer that even the word of God, when communicated through the vehicle of human language, can be only imperfectly understood. Thus, human understanding, even of the word of God, is fallible! Indistinctions of the object, imperfection in perception and conception, and the inadequacy of language as a vehicle to express and communicate ideas all contribute to imperfection in human knowledge and understanding (Federalist 37: ML, 230; C, 237; R, 229).

What, then, are fallible individuals to do when they must assume their own fallibility in considering the fallible opinions of others? Madison states his argument in the form of a parable about a patient afflicted with a strange disease. He offers three considerations for the fallible decision maker to use in facing a problematical situation (Federalist 38: ML, 236ff; C, 242ff; R, 233ff). First, a fallible decision maker should consider the degree of agreement among the more knowledgeable persons regarding the adequacy of any proposed solution. The relative unanimity of the delegates to the Philadelphia Convention in approving the draft of the new constitution, thus, was a recommendation for its adoption. Second, the fallible decision maker should make his own reasoned analysis of each alternative offered after "calculating its probable effects" in light of existing knowledge, and then make his choice in terms of the greater good (Federalist 37: ML, 224; C, 231; R, 224). Third, the fallible decision maker confronted with uncertainty and doubt must undertake the experiment and ascertain by actual trial whether the proposed remedy will alter the situation and improve his condition. Both Madison and Hamilton are emphatic in regarding experience as "the oracle of wisdom" (Federalist 15: ML, 92; C, 96; R, 110). If the plan of the convention contained errors based upon inadequate experience and understanding, these errors "will not be ascertained until an actual trial shall have pointed them out" (Federalist 38: ML, 235; C, 241–242; R, 233).[3]

Thus, fallible decision makers must anticipate the possibility of a reconsideration of their situation, a reformulation of their problems, and a change of strategies in light of experience and new information. The condition of human fallibility requires analysis, reason, deliberation, choice, experience, reconsideration, and an opportunity to alter, amend, or change as new information and new understanding give rise to new possibilities. Human life and the constitution of political institutions, as Madison indicates in his parable of the patient, can never be more than a provisional experiment subject to change in light of experience (Federalist 38: ML, 236; C, 243; R, 234).

THE PRINCIPLE OF POLITICAL CONSTRAINT

In answering his own question, "Why has government been instituted at all?," Hamilton asserts, "Because the passions of men will not conform to the dictates of reason and justice, without constraint" (Federalist 15: ML, 92; C, 96; R, 110). In other words, constraint is requisite for the application of reason and justice in the conduct of human affairs.

Madison at a different juncture poses another rhetorical question: "But what is government itself, but the greatest of all reflections on human nature?" He responds: "If men were angels, no government would be necessary. If angels were to govern men, neither external nor internal controls on government would be necessary" (Federalist 51: ML, 337; C, 349; R, 322).

Human intelligence and reason when conditioned by an assumption of human fallibility and an individualistic pursuit of relative advantage can lead to the contemplation of a myriad of possibilities. Most possibilities inherent in human endeavors affect the opportunities not only of an individual thinker and doer, but of many other individuals as well. If men were angels, presumably their actions would reflect a pure goodness—all actions would benefit both an actor and others. If the quality of pure goodness were endowed by man's genetic inheritance, then, according to Madison, governments would be unnecessary. When men pursue their individual advantage to the detriment, disadvantage, or injury of others, constraint is necessary if the greater good is to be realized.

We need then to assume that, wherever human beings exist and use language to communicate with one another, a cultural heritage exists and a principle of political constraint is operative in human relationships. In human societies there are both conditions that facilitate mutually productive relationships and those that yield mutually destructive relationships. The problem is how to facilitate the one and constrain the other by constituting order in human societies.

The Logic of Mutually Productive Relationships

Given the condition of human fallibility—the circumstance that anyone can have only an imperfect awareness of the consequences that follow from his or her actions—the possibility exists that action in the pursuit of one's advantage can lead to unintended consequences and cause injuries to others. Some measure of political constraint is essential even in assuring resolution of such innocent sources of conflict as circumstances which derive from the unintentional harm or injury that one's action may inflict upon others. Remedies, in such situations, are essential if appropriate structures of incentives are to provide reinforcement for preferred forms of learned behavior. Means must be available to right wrongs, if preferred forms of behavior are to prevail in social learning.

In the absence of constraint, opportunity exists for individuals to pursue their advantage at the cost or detriment of others. An incentive would then exist for those being deprived to attempt to minimize such costs by impeding or deterring actions that were detrimental to their interests. Reciprocal interaction based upon one seeking one's own self-interest at the expense of others may, thus, lead to consequences that are mutually detrimental as each seeks to deter others by the use of threats and coercive actions. Political constraint, which will facilitate actions of beneficial consequences and limit actions of detrimental consequences, is essential if individuals are to have mutually productive relationships with one another.

An arrangement for facilitating productive relationships and for deterring detrimental or injurious relationships can only be supplied as a matter of deliberate choice by interposing constraint into the potential variety of human behavior through commonly understood rules of conduct. The function of law is to introduce constraint, as a matter of policy or of choice, into the potential variety of human behavior. Individuals can then pursue their own advantage while at the same time taking account of the interests of others. A constraint introduced into the potential variety of all possible human behavior as a consequence of choice or as a matter of policy is, by definition, a political constraint. Legal and political arrangements, or institutions, are devices for resolving conflicts arising from a heterogeneity of interests so that human beings can take advantage of one another's capabilities in communities that are bound by common principles of political constraint.

Because of the potential disjunction between an individual's calculation of one's immediate, short-term interest and the calculation of one's general, long-term interest, an essential condition of political organization is to interpose processes for due deliberation. Methods must be devised so that reasoned consideration of social consequences will be extended in both space and time. Due process in a political sense, thus, implies that efforts will be made to encapsulate conflict, and to transform conflict into a symbolic one allowing for reasoned contention on behalf of different positions. Carrying on conflict at the symbolic level by recourse to human reason enables people to anticipate the probable consequences of their actions before taking overt actions and forcing others to bear those consequences. Justice can only be rendered through reasoned contention among self-interested and fallible human beings in a stable and orderly social environment.

Thus, reason and justice in the conduct of human affairs depends upon political constraint. However, the existence of political constraint is *not* a sufficient condition to assure reason and justice in the conduct of human affairs. The use of sanctions inherent in the principle of political constraint may also be a means of compounding wrongs rather than of righting wrongs. Instruments of coercion can be used to oppress and tyrannize others.

The principle of political constraint, and the correlative condition requiring use of coercive sanctions to order social relationships, necessarily implies that some persons will be assigned responsibility for making decisions and for taking actions where the extraordinary powers of applying coercive sanctions are a matter of legitimate, or rightful exercise of political prerogative. The constitution of any structure of governance consequently implies an *unequal* distribution of decision-making capabilities among the persons subject to the authority of government. Fundamental conditions of inequality must, therefore, necessarily exist in any system of government. Patterns of order with their rule-ruler-ruled relationship can be presumed to exist in all human societies.

The prerogatives of public authority create a unique opportunity for individuals to pursue their own advantage at the expense of others. Madison asserts the proposition, "[I]n every political institution, a power to advance the public happiness involves a discretion which may be misapplied and abused" (Federalist 41: ML, 260; C, 269; R, 255–256). The principle of political constraint conditioned by assumptions of self-interest and of human fallibility implies that any political order is necessarily an imperfect order. It is subject to usurpation, corruption, and abuse; and individuals can use the opportunities inherent in the exercise of political prerogatives to advance their own interests at the expense of others.

Madison emphasizes that the exercise of oppressive power has a price in any society. A powerful faction can oppress the weak in the same way that strong individuals can oppress the weak in the absence of political constraint. Only by limiting the power of those who exercise political prerogatives is there any likelihood that such prerogatives will be used to realize justice as the end of government and of civil society (Federalist 51: ML, 340; C, 352; R, 324). A political system based upon reflection and choice must contain methods for dealing with the essential conditions of political inequality and with the usurpation and corruption of political authority. Such a political system must also apply remedies that are appropriate to its own reform. Both "rulers" and "ruled" must find their range of opportunities constrained by rules of law. Then we might meaningfully contemplate the possibilities that people are masters; and rulers, their servants. Democracy as the rule of people might then be a meaningful concept.

A concept of political reform which implies a deliberate and conscious effort to modify and change political institutions without having to redesign and rebuild a whole new political order is inherent in the arguments being advanced throughout *The Federalist*. There are no Hobbesian speculations about the conditions of man in a state of nature in contradistinction to man in a commonwealth.[4] We can infer that the authors of *The Federalist* expect to find men only in states of society where some principle of political constraint operates in the conduct of human relations, and that men have throughout history shared in societies structured by various forms of political institutions.

If human beings have basic confidence that the conditions of life are organized to facilitate the working out of mutually agreeable relationships, they can approach one another in quite different ways than if they have to assume that they are always exposed to threats and exploitation by others. People behave quite differently when threatened or provoked than when extended respect and reciprocity. The task in constituting a political order is how to rig the games of life in a way that is fair and grounded in principles of respect and reciprocity among people who share communities of interest with one another. When conflicts escalate into threats and counterthreats, it is essential to have institutions of government that afford reserve capabilities for resolving conflict in ways that are fair and where respect is accorded to each individual as a human being.[5]

The Logic of Mutually Destructive Relationships

The state of organized warfare, in contrast to a Hobbesian state of unorganized warfare—a war of "every man, against every man" (Hobbes, 1960: 82)—receives considerable attention in *The Federalist* as a condition which reflects the limits of political organization. At the same time, organized warfare is a critical condition that must be taken into account in the constitution of any political system.

A state of warfare occurs when, in the absence of an appropriate instrument of political constraint, different peoples become involved in a dynamic interaction where each seeks to realize a relative advantage at the expense of others and has recourse to violent means to do so. Each mobilizes its destructive capability to impose a forceful constraint upon others. Warfare is the classical case where the pursuit of relative advantage leads each party to take actions that are detrimental to the other. The principle of relative advantage becomes a choice not of the greater good, but of the lesser evil. The criteria for action in such conflicts are essentially controlled by the discretion of the adversary rather than by a joint exercise of discretion to realize mutually productive possibilities. The requirements of the conflict dominate all other social calculations.

These principles are clearly stated by Madison when he observes:

One:

The means of security can only be regulated by the means and the danger of attack. (Federalist 41: ML, 262; C, 270; R, 257)

Two:

It is in vain to oppose constitutional barriers to the impulse of self-preservation. It is worse than in vain; because it plants in the Constitution itself necessary usurpations of power (i.e., a necessity to usurp power by ignoring constitutional limitations), every precedent of which is a germ of unnecessary and multiplied repetitions. (Federalist 41: ML, 262; C, 270; R, 257. My parenthesis.)

Three:

If one nation maintains constantly a disciplined army, ready for the service of ambition or revenge, it obliges the most pacific nation who may be within the reach of its enterprises to take corresponding precautions. (Federalist 41: ML, 262; C, 270; R, 257)

An illustration:

The fifteenth century was the unhappy epoch of military establishments in the time of peace. They were introduced by Charles VII of France. All Europe has followed, or been forced into, the example. Had the example not been followed by other nations, all Europe must long ago have worn the chains of a universal monarch. Were every nation except France now to disband its peace establishments, the same event might follow. The veteran legions of Rome were an overmatch for the undisciplined valor of all other nations, and rendered her the mistress of the world. (Federalist 41: ML, 262; C, 270–271; R, 257)

Four:

[T]he liberties of Rome proved the final victim to her military triumphs; . . . the liberties of Europe, as far as they ever existed, have with few exceptions, been the price of her military establishments. (Federalist 41: ML, 262; C, 271; R, 257)

Five:

A standing force, therefore, is a dangerous, at the same time that it may be a necessary, provision. On the smallest scale it has its inconveniences. On an extensive scale its consequences may be fatal. On any scale it is an object of laudable circumspection and precaution. A wise nation will combine all these considerations; and, whilst it does not rashly preclude itself from any resource which may become essential to its safety, will exert all its prudence in diminishing both the necessity and the danger of resorting to one which may be inauspicious to its liberties. (Federalist 41: ML, 262–263; C, 271; R, 257–258)

Hamilton develops an analogous form of reasoning to draw another set of inferences.

One:

Safety from external danger is the most powerful director of national conduct. Even the ardent love of liberty will after a time, give way to its dictates. The violent destruction of life and property incident to war, the continual effort and alarm attendant on a state of continual danger, will compel nations the most attached to liberty to resort for repose and security to institutions which have a tendency to destroy their civil and political rights. To be more safe, they at length become willing to run the risk of being less free. (Federalist 8: ML, 42; C, 45; R, 67)

Two:

The disciplined armies always kept on foot on the continent of Europe, though they bear a malignant aspect to liberty and economy, have, notwithstanding, been productive of the signal advantage of rendering sudden conquests impracticable, and of preventing that rapid desolation which used to mark the progress of war prior to their introduction. (Federalist 8: ML, 41; C, 44; R, 66)

Three:

But standing armies . . . must inevitably result from a dissolution of the Confederacy. (Federalist 8: ML, 43; C, 46; R, 67–68)

Four:

They [the states] would, at the same time, be necessitated to strengthen the executive arm of government, in doing which their constitutions would acquire a progressive direction towards monarchy. It is of the nature of war to increase the executive at the expense of the legislative authority. (Federalist 8: ML, 43; C, 46; R, 68)

These allusions to the logic of organized warfare were directed to the problem of constituting an effective unit of government among the peoples comprising the several states of the United States of America. Both Hamilton and Madison anticipate that an inability to attain effective political solutions to problems arising among the peoples of the different states must necessarily lead toward military solutions. The task they confronted was to institute a system of government which would be capable of solving problems by reflection and choice. Only by the constitution of a system of government which took account of the community of interests shared by the several states could the American people hope to occupy an insular position upon the land mass of a major continent. With an appropriate constitution they might enjoy the potential wealth of a continent, while attaining the relative security of an island.

Madison pursues this argument in the following terms:

The Union itself, which it cements and secures, destroys every pretext for a military establishment which could be dangerous. America united, with a handful of troops, or without a single soldier, exhibits a more forbidding posture to foreign ambition than America disunited, with a hundred thousand veterans ready for combat. . . . A dangerous establishment can never be necessary or plausible, so long as they continue a united people. But let it never, for a moment, be forgotten that they are indebted for this advantage to the Union alone. The moment of its dissolution will be the date of a new order of things. . . . [T]he face of America will be but a copy of that of the continent of Europe. It will present liberty everywhere crushed between standing armies and perpetual taxes. The fortunes of disunited America will be even more disastrous than those of Europe. The sources of evil in the latter are confined to her own limits. No superior powers of another quarter of the globe intrigue among her rival nations, inflame their mutual animosities and render them the instruments of foreign ambition, jealousy and revenge. In America the miseries springing from her internal jealousies, contentions, and wars, would form a part only of her lot. A plentiful addition of evils would have their source in that relation in which Europe stands to this quarter of the Earth, and which no other quarter of the earth bears to Europe. (Federalist 41: ML, 263–264; C, 271–272; R, 258–259)

The political constitutions of Europe, according to both Hamilton and Madison, were based upon the prevalence of organized warfare as the dominant political condition. The exigencies of warfare, the conditions of surviving in mutually destructive contests of violence, had forged the constitutions of Europe. These constitutions were derived more from accident and force than from reflection and choice. The opportunity confronting the American people in 1787 was one of extending the principle of political constraint so that people might attempt to govern their own affairs, reaching out to continental proportions, on the basis of reason and justice without being preoccupied with a threat of violence, or without being required to mobilize engines of war to impede enterprising adversaries. In short, could a political solution be devised which would associate the people of numerous simple republics together in a limited national government and provide them with the institutional facilities of a compound republic for governing both their separate and diverse interests and their common interests?

ELEMENTS IN STRUCTURES OF INFERENTIAL REASONING

Systems of government are, from the arguments advanced by Hamilton and Madison, composed of human beings who are properly to be viewed in their standing as individual persons. It is individuals who are being taken into account in creating the design for a system of government. In thinking about the structure of government, it is individuals who, in their relationships with one another, comprise the active elements that give motion to any system of government. They are both the instruments and objects of governmental action. Individual persons, as the basic units of which governments are composed, are capable of thinking for themselves and determining their own course of action by calculating the relative advantage of the alternatives that are available to them in any choice situation. The essential parts in those mechanisms which we call a system of government are, thus, always capable of thinking for themselves and acting in ways that take account of their own relative advantage. They are, also, capable of making mistakes and of making choices without knowing all of the consequences that follow from their choices.

Such individuals are likely to find themselves in situations where potential conflict will pose a threat, where a threat will provoke a counter-threat, and where an exchange of threats will generate mutually destructive consequences. An awareness of the perverseness of such circumstances can lead to the contemplation of alternative circumstances where conflict can be constrained so that individuals might pursue their mutual advantage in taking account of each other's interests and gain the advantage of mutually productive possibilities. Anticipating how individuals will choose among the opportunities that are available to them in specifiable choice situations is what drives the logic of inferential reasoning in the political theory used by the authors of *The Federalist*.

Situations that provoke threat and the potential for mutually destructive conflict are always to be contemplated in relation to possibilities where relationships could be reordered in ways that permit those involved to develop and maintain mutually productive relationships with one another. Life in human societies can be viewed as a game where individuals pursue their opportunities in relation to a system of rules. The point of any political analysis is to estimate the effect of rules upon the choices that are made and the consequences that follow from those choices. Where rules create perverse incentives, and human beings act in ways that are mutually detrimental to one another, a question arises as to whether a change of rules can yield different choices that enable human beings to relate to one another in more constructive ways.

The overwhelming preoccupation in *The Federalist* is with the circumstance that any system of rule depends upon officials who have responsibilities for the enforcement of rules. What is to prevent those officials from being arbitrary and using their authority to exploit others? Or, in the extreme case, what is to prevent rulers from using instruments of coercion to oppress and war upon those who are subject to their rule? Is it possible to create a system of rule where rulers will themselves be subject to an enforceable rule of law? This is the fundamental issue in the design of the American constitutional system.

In pursuing their analyses, Hamilton and Madison: (1) take the perspective of an individual as the basic unit of analysis (where other analyses represent aggregations of individuals as basic units of analysis), (2) contemplate the structure of incentives and disincentives inherent in hypothetical choice situations, (3) anticipate how those incentives and disincentives affect the actions individuals are likely to take, and (4) estimate the consequences that are likely to follow. These are the elements that drive the logic of inferential reasoning in their analysis. Anyone who follows this method can better understand the arguments being advanced in *The Federalist*. Anyone who uses this method can, also, become an analyst who has the possibility of reasoning through problems involving the choice of institutional arrangements for the governance of human societies.

NOTES

1. I am indebted to Ronald Oakerson for the concept of an "anyone" rule. The concept is developed more fully in Chapter 7 regarding the authority of persons.

2. The Platonic tradition of ideal forms is based upon criteria of rationality which presume a special claim to enlightenment as justifying the philosopher-king and the peculiar constitution of the Pla-

tonic Republic as an ideal type. Hamilton and Madison make no such special claim to enlightenment.

3. Milovan Djilas (1957: 37) argues in the case of the Soviet experiment in constitutional choice that the leaders of the Russian revolutionary effort had expectations, based upon theoretical conceptions advanced by Marx and Lenin, that the state would wither away and democracy would be strengthened. Instead, Djilas argues, "the reverse happened." A new ruling class was created; and state power to rule over society was increased. Djilas's critique of the "experiments" grounded in Marxist-Leninist theory presents a fundamental challenge to the empirical warrantability of that formulation.

What it would mean to anticipate that a "state" would "wither away" depends upon what one means by state. From one point of view, a federal system of government can be considered as an alternative to a circumstance where a state, as a monopoly of the legitimate use of force, rules over society. Society might then be viewed as becoming self-governing through a multitude of democratically organized instrumentalities of governance rather than being in a state of subjection dominated by the rulership of the state.

4. Hamilton does characterize men as "ambitious, vindictive, and rapacious," but here he is alluding to men in political elites cloaked with presumptions of sovereign prerogative (Federalist 6: ML, 27; C, 28; R, 54).

5. Rousseau, I believe, correctly formulated the "solution" to patterns of governance based upon struggles for dominance: "Man was born (to be) free and everywhere he is in chains. One who believes himself the master of others is nonetheless a greater slave than they" (1978: 46. My parenthesis). Mutual respect and reciprocity afford the basis for a different resolution than is realized through struggles for dominance.

CHAPTER THREE

Constitutional Choice

The political analysis advanced in *The Federalist* relies upon the concept of a constitution as an instrument for articulating the design of a government formulated on the basis of reflection and choice. The concept of a constitution implies several distinctions that are essential to the political theory of a compound republic. First, the American theory of constitutional decision making implies that some laws are more fundamental than others. Second, distinctions among laws also reflect distinctions about decision-making processes. Processes of constitutional decision making are conceptualized apart from other processes of political decision making. Finally, a constitution which is viewed as an operative legal instrument demands more exacting design and draftsmanship than if a constitution were viewed as a statement of general moral principles lacking legal force in limiting the exercise of governmental prerogatives.

The American approach to constitutional choice, thus, defines the political context in which processes of constitutional decision making occur. The work of the Philadelphia Convention, the preparation and publication of *The Federalist,* and the addition of amendments to the Constitution all occurred in this process. This approach of conceiving a constitution to be a legal instrumentality for a limited government also requires a structure of political relationships that makes it possible to enforce rules of constitutional law against governmental authorities.

A DISTINCTION BETWEEN A CONSTITUTION AND A LAW

In Federalist 53, Madison distinguishes a "constitution" from a "law": a constitution is "established by the people and *unalterable* by the government, and a law [is] established by the government and alterable by the government" (Federalist 53: ML, 348; C, 360; R, 331. My emphasis). This distinction implies that a government in a limited constitutional republic does not have the prerogative of defining its own authority. The correlative inference implied by a theory of limited constitutions is that constitutional decision making is concerned with making decisions about the general decision rules applicable to the conduct of a government, but does not include the prerogatives of making decisions about agency and other relationships within a unit of government and operational decisions in the recurrent affairs of a government. A government is concerned with making and enforcing laws, collecting taxes, appropriating funds, appointing personnel, and managing public affairs consonant with the rules in a constitution. These are governmental decisions taken within the rules laid down in a constitution "established by the people and unalterable by the government" (Federalist 53: ML, 348; C, 360; R, 331). People are also effectively precluded from taking operational decisions through constitutional decision making processes; theirs is a limited authority, too. Policy and operational decisions are established by governments and are alterable by governments under the decision rules established by a constitution for the conduct of government.

If governments were free to define their own authority, there would be no incentive for them to impose limits upon that exercise of authority. Furthermore, those who exercise governmental authority would, then, have incentives to use those prerogatives to their own advantage and to the disadvantage of those who oppose them. Constitutions are intended to interpose limits and constrain the pursuit of opportunities to those that are consistent with what Hamilton identifies as "the general theory of the limited constitution" (Federalist 81: ML, 524; C, 543; R, 482).

THE PROCESS OF CONSTITUTIONAL DECISION MAKING

Madison examines the authority of the Philadelphia Convention to propose changes in constitutional decision rules, and while doing so considers the nature of constitutional decision making as a political process. In alluding to the right of the American people to alter and to abolish their government and to institute a new government as expressed in the Declaration of Independence, Madison recognizes that "it is impossible for the people spontaneously and universally to move in concert toward their object" of altering the terms of government "most likely to effect their safety and happiness" (Federalist 40: ML, 257; C, 265; R, 253). Changes in the terms of government must then be proposed as *"informal and unauthorized propositions,* made by some patriotic and respectable citizen or number of citizens" (Federalist 40: ML, 257; C, 265; R, 253. Madison's emphasis). In referring to *"informal and unauthorized propositions,"* Madison uses the criterion of a lawyer to mean propositions not having legal force and effect. Instead, he identifies such propositions as merely *"advisory and recommendatory"* (Federalist 40: ML, 256; C, 264; R, 252. My emphasis). The authority of the Philadelphia Convention was not to establish, to create, or to enact a constitution, but to recommend a revised constitution for consideration by the confederate Congress and the legislatures of the several states. The action of the Philadelphia Convention was thus *advisory* and *recommendatory,* and the draft document prepared by the Philadelphia Convention was subject to consideration by the confederate Congress and each state legislature prior to consideration by conventions called in each state for purposes of ratifying the Constitution as recommended by the Philadelphia Convention. The call of the conventions for ratification depended upon prior actions by both the confederate Congress and the state legislatures.

The organization of constitutional decision making by the separation of the *recommendatory process* from the *ratification process* implies that a process of *deliberation* would intervene before the choice of ratification is made. *The Federalist* was written to inform people who were participating in such a process of deliberation and to contribute toward a reasoned choice in the ratification of the U.S. Constitution.

Considerable emphasis is given in *The Federalist* not only to the disjunction between the recommending and ratifying processes but also to the concept that constitutional decisions, as distinguished from operational governmental decisions, must be taken on the basis of extraordinary decision rules intended to assure a general consensus or substantial unanimity, in matters affecting the substance of a constitution. Madison insists that the basic decision rule for the ratification of the proposed constitution was not a *majority* of the people of the union or a *majority* of the states, but "was the *unanimous* assent of the several States that are parties to it . . ." (Federalist 39: ML, 247; C, 254; R, 243–244. Madison's emphasis). The Constitution could be placed in operation in those states which had approved, once conventions in nine of the thirteen states had ratified the Constitution, but no state was compelled to join without its assent.

The presumption that substantial unanimity is an appropriate standard in thinking about constitutional choice is shared by others who have thought about the problem. Thomas Hobbes, for example, has observed that "[i]t is in the laws of a commonwealth, as in the laws of gaming: whatsoever the gamesters all agree on, is injustice to none of them" (Hobbes, 1960: 227). Playing games means that in any particular play of a game, some will win and others will lose. Winning is rewarding; losing is depriving. Yet, people are able to agree generally upon a set of rules as being fair despite the fact that in each

game some will win and some will lose. The standard of unanimity, thus, becomes a measure of fairness in the constitution
of a democratic community even though any one person can
expect to be among the losing minority in many of the decisions that are taken in the conduct of government.

It is the basic unanimity about constitutional considerations
that yields a high level of consensus and shared community of
understanding in a democratic society that lay beneath the
sometimes bitter contestation that goes on in election campaigns where some can win and some must lose. Fallible creatures may both disagree and make serious errors of judgment
in the short run, but the differences pertain to what each sees
as benefitting the community of people who rely upon institutions of government to take collective decisions for their joint
benefit. It is from this point of view that Buchanan and
Tullock, in *The Calculus of Consent,* argue that conceptual
unanimity, not majority voting, is the base rule in a democratic society. Citizens in a democracy would then be primarily
concerned with what is fair for everyone rather than trying to
exploit one's fellow citizens for one's own advantage. If everyone pursued the latter strategy, democratic societies would
soon degenerate into a circumstance where various elements
of a society would be at war with one another.

In the ratification of the U.S. Constitution, there are some
grounds for speculating as to whether the "nth" state was indeed free to refuse ratification of the Constitution; and the
Civil War might be used as an illustration to suggest that such
might not have been the case. On the other hand, authoriza-
tion for Canada's admission to the United States of America is
contained in Article XI of the Articles of Confederation, but
Canada never acceded to membership in the American Union.

The strategic opportunities inherent in these constitutional
decision rules were exploited, in turn, to force a major revision in the U.S. Constitution during the ratification process.
The most serious objection to the Constitution was an alleged
insufficiency of a bill of rights limiting the authority of Congress and specifying the authority of persons in the new re-

gime. To remedy this situation, conventions in several of the larger states, following the example of Massachusetts and Virginia, ratified the Constitution, and, at the same time, adopted resolutions calling upon Congress to propose amendments to the Constitution providing for a bill of rights. Such resolutions included declarations formulating the basic provisions for a bill of rights. North Carolina and Rhode Island withheld their ratification until Congress had submitted several resolutions to the states for amendments to the Constitution having the effect of adding a bill of rights. Thus, the decision rules inherent in the ratifying process were used to press Congress, during its first session, into submitting several major amendments to the Constitution for consideration by the states. North Carolina and Rhode Island ratified only after Congress had acted. These two states functioned as hold-outs to assure appropriate action by Congress in meeting the demands of the several states regarding a bill of rights.

CONSTITUTIONS AS LEGAL INSTRUMENTALITIES

Hamilton is explicit in defining the concept of a limited constitution as one which necessarily implies limits upon the legal and political competence of governmental authorities. Under a limited constitution Hamilton concludes that "every act of a delegated authority, contrary to the tenor of the commission under which it is exercised, is void" (Federalist 78: ML, 505; C, 524; R, 467).

> To deny this, would be to affirm, that the deputy is greater than his principal; that the servant is above his master; that the representatives of the people are superior to the people themselves; that men acting by virtue of powers, may do not only what their powers do not authorize, but what they forbid. (Federalist 78: ML, 505–506; C, 524; R, 467)

Hamilton specifically rejects the contention that legislative bodies are competent constitutional judges of their own political prerogatives. The members of a legislative body would in that case be judges of their own cause and, as such, would hold a position contrary to the theory of a limited constitution. Instead, Hamilton argues:

> It is far more rational to suppose, that the courts were designed to be an intermediate body between the people and the legislature, in order, among other things, to keep the latter within the limits assigned to their authority. The interpretation of the laws is the proper and peculiar province of the courts. A constitution is, in fact, and must be regarded by the judges, as a fundamental law. (Federalist 78: ML, 506; C, 525; R, 467)

In Hamilton's view, "[T]he judiciary, from the nature of its functions, will always be the least dangerous to the political rights of the Constitution . . . " (Federalist 78: ML, 504; C, 522; R, 465). The judiciary controls neither "the sword" nor "the purse" of the community; and has "no direction either of the strength or the wealth of the society." Instead, it must rely upon "judgment" and reason as its instrumentality for action. The judiciary has no force to implement its judgments, but must rely upon the aid of the executive to carry them out. As a consequence, Hamilton argues that an independent judiciary is "peculiarly essential in a limited Constitution," if government is to be grounded on reasoned choice (Federalist 78: ML, 505; C, 524; R, 466).

Hamilton's thesis, derived from "the general theory of the limited constitution," is that the provisions of a constitution have binding force as a legal instrumentality, and that judges must construe the provisions of a constitution as the fundamental law. No act contrary to a constitution can be valid (Federalist 78: ML, 505; C, 524; R, 467). This thesis stands in marked contrast to John Austin's conclusions in *The Province of Jurisprudence Determined*. In a monarchy, or in a unitary state where supreme authority is exercised by a collegial legislative body, constitutional law is, in Austin's view, not positive law, but only positive morality. In such a political system, "whether constitutional law has thus been expressly adopted, or simply consists of principles current in the political community, it is merely guarded, against the sovereign, by sentiments and feelings of the governed" (Austin, 1955: 259). The governed in such circumstances have no redress against a supreme political authority through the courts of law. Acts which might be "unconstitutional" cannot in such circumstances be held "illegal." Constitutional law, under those circumstances, has no more force as positive law than the prescriptions of international law have when applied to sovereign nation states. Austin concludes: "Each is positive morality rather than positive law. The former (constitutional law) is guarded by sentiments current in the given community, as the latter (international law) is guarded by sentiments current among nations generally" (Austin, 1955: 262. My parentheses). Moral sentiments are much too fragile to maintain the enforceability of rules of constitutional law without instrumentalities for citizens, through due processes of law, to resist the arbitrary actions of officials.

Formulating a constitution which was intended to have legal force in limiting the legal and political competence of governmental authorities poses quite a different problem in legal draftsmanship than the formulation of a set of general moral principles which serve only as an expression of moral sentiments. A limited constitution cannot rely upon the expediency of vesting "ultimate authority" or the "last say" with any particular governmental body. The design of a limited constitution, thus, requires reference to a theory of political organization which stands in marked contrast to a theory of unlimited sovereignty.

THE SPECIAL CHARACTER OF AMERICAN CONSTITUTIONAL THEORY

American constitutional theory as expounded in *The Federalist* bears a close kinship to what is sometimes referred to as social contract theories of seventeenth- and eighteenth-century Europe. Similarities are usually emphasized; but there are also many points of basic contrast. Several distinctions require emphasis in understanding the American experiment in constitutional choice.

First, the essential prerogatives in the American theory of a limited constitution are defined by the terms of the covenant rather than a willing act of unqualified submission to a sovereign. The Hobbesian assumption that "covenants, without the sword, are but words" (Hobbes, 1960: 109) is congruent with the American theory of constitutional decision making only when one adds: "And the sword, without covenants, is but an instrument of tyranny." Use of the sword is legitimate only when used in accord with the terms of a covenant to maintain reason and justice in the conduct of human affairs. The terms of the covenant specify the basic political formula controlling the operations of any basic structure of government in the American theory of constitutional decision making.

Second, the theory of a limited constitution assumes that constitutional decision making is a continuing, albeit intermittent, process involving amendment and revision as well as the formulation of an "original" constitution. The presumption that a social contract is based upon unanimity has its counterpart in the requirement of American constitutional theory that constitutional decision making is based upon extraordinary decision rules intended to reflect consensus of the political community. Government in the American theory of constitutional decision making exercises a limited authority without the political prerogative of altering its own constitutional terms of reference. Enactments by the required majority of a legislature and endorsement by an executive can be invalidated on constitutional grounds. If alternative political remedies are not effectively available within the existing constitutional framework, the constitutional terms of reference can be changed through extraordinary processes of constitutional amendment and constitutional revision. The draft constitution of 1787 was the product of an effort at constitutional revision rather than an effort to formulate an original constitution. Its ratification by several of the states, already noted, was conditioned by a demand for further revisions which were subsequently adopted as a bill of rights contained in the first ten amendments. Subsequent amendments of major importance have also been added. The rise of machine politics and boss rule in the nineteenth century led to major constitutional changes in state constitutions as a part of the Progressive reform movement.

Third, both Madison and Hamilton recognized that "the general theory of the limited constitution" applied to other forms of political association in the context of American experience. The terms of government in each of the states was the subject of state constitutional decision making. *The Federalist* makes no reference to processes of constitutional decision making as occurring in the organization of private associations or among municipal or quasi-municipal corporations within the states. But, such a conception is not inconsistent with Hamilton and Madison's theory of constitutional decision making and governmental organization. Constitutional decision making is, thus, a continuing, recurring process in which American citizens participate in formulating the basic rules for the government of various forms of political association. Popular participation in constitutional decision making must be considered apart from popular participation in the regular cycle of elections for selecting the personnel of government who exercise the prerogatives established by constitutional decisions.

Fourth, in the American theory of the limited constitution, the binding force of law is not the "ultimate" word in the sense of being the command of *a* sovereign. Instead, the binding force of law in the American political community depends upon the legal and political competence of its authors. The constitutional law of the nation differs from the constitutional and statutory laws of the 50 states. Public and private law are not rigidly separated. Property law is not simply a field of private law; it refers to a diversity of interests and rights held in public proprietorships as well. A contract or a will can be viewed as a part of the relevant system of law for those who are bound by the provisions of such instruments. To sustain a "law" and one's lawful claim under law may require willful violation of another "law." Justice is realized not by willful submission to authority, but by a reasoned contention on behalf of the legitimacy of one's interests in relation to the interests of others.[1] Citizens can maintain limits upon the exercise of governmental authority only as they are willing to challenge the provisions of ordinary law and determine whether or not they conform to the requirements of constitutional law.

Finally, the American theory of the limited constitution implies that no "governmental" authority has the last say. The competence of all decision makers is defined by diverse decision rules. All decision makers are bound by requirements of due process of law. Various forms of action afforded by administrative remedies, judicial remedies, legislative remedies, and constitutional remedies are among the diverse strategies which can be pursued by interested persons in seeking resolution to problems arising from life within American society.

A theory of constitutional choice implies that various decision rules in a constitution are formulated as a part of a coherent structure. If people are to exercise control over the authority of government, they must give critical attention to the basic design of a constitution that will enable them to enforce limits of constitutional law upon governmental authorities. Constitutional law, without a capacity for enforcement, can only be, in John Austin's terms, positive morality not positive law. When Thomas Hobbes developed his theory of sovereignty, he was quite explicit in emphasizing that the sovereign is the source of law, above the law, and cannot be held accountable to law. The American system of constitutional law required that Hobbes's conception of sovereignty be foreclosed in the design of their political institutions. The task of devising a political system where governmental officials are bound by enforceable rules of constitutional law is no simple task. Subsequent chapters will examine the political theory developed in *The Federalist* to explain the American solution to this fundamental problem of political organization.

NOTES

1. Many of the statements in this paragraph stand at substantial variance with European concepts of code law reflected in the work of scholars like Max Weber (Rheinstein, 1967) or Wolfgang Friedmann. Friedmann's commentary of *Law in a Changing Society,* for example, contains no reference to constitutional law. The domain of "public law" is treated as "administrative law" subject to determination by processes of administrative review as in French jurisprudence.

CHAPTER FOUR

Some Rudiments of Political Design

THE PROBLEM OF DESIGN

If an effort is made to establish "good government" on the basis of "reflection and choice" (Federalist 1: ML, 3; C, 3; R, 33), such a government would be an artifact devised as a deliberate act of design. The task of devising a constitution as a deliberate act of design is one of reason, of work, and of craftsmanship. The product as an artifact will reflect the basic conceptions and propositions held by its authors about the organization of political affairs. Any artifact thus reflects the materials, the concepts used, and the choices made by its makers. These serve as working ingredients, basic assumptions, and operating principles. What an artisan fashions, how he draws upon his concepts and materials, and uses them, depends upon his objectives or purposes.

The authors of *The Federalist* were aware of the difficulties of craftsmanship in formulating a constitution and explicitly discussed the problem of design. Madison's discussion of design criteria is reminiscent of an engineer considering trade-offs among such factors as speed, load, and safety. To secure more of one may require some sacrifice of another.

The design problem confronting the Philadelphia Convention according to Madison was one of "combining the requisite stability and energy in government, with the inviolable attention due to liberty and to the republican form" (Federalist

37: ML, 227; C, 233; R, 226). He goes on to formulate the design problem and to analyze it in the following way:

One:

Energy in government is essential to that security against external and internal danger, and to that prompt and salutary execution of the laws which enter into the very definition of good government. (Federalist 37: ML, 227; C, 233; R, 226)

Two:

Stability in government is essential to national character and to the advantages annexed to it, as well as to that repose and confidence in the minds of the people, which are among the chief blessings of civil society. . . . [T]he people of this country, enlightened . . . as the great body of them are, in the effects of good government, will never be satisfied till some remedy be applied to the vicissitudes and uncertainties which characterize the State administrations.[1] (Federalist 37: ML, 227; C, 234; R, 226–227)

Three:

On comparing, however, these valuable ingredients with the vital principles of liberty, *we must perceive at once the difficulty of mingling them together in their due proportions.* (Federalist 37: ML, 227; C, 234; R, 227. My emphasis.)

Four:

The genius of republican liberty seems to demand on one side, not only that all power should be derived from the people, but that those intrusted with it should be kept in dependence on the people, by a short duration of their appointments; and that even during this short period the trust should be placed not in a few, but a number of hands. (Federalist 37: ML, 227; C, 234; R, 227)

Five:

Stability, on the contrary, requires that the hands in which power is lodged should continue for a length of time the same. (Federalist 37: ML, 227; C, 234; R, 227)

Six:

A frequent change of men will result from a frequent return of elections; and a frequent change of measures from a frequent change of men: whilst energy in government requires not only a certain duration of power, but the execution of it by a single hand. (Federalist 37: ML, 227–228; C, 234; R, 227)

Madison clearly conceives that the design of political institutions must satisfy the requirements of multiple design criteria. The design criteria are neither fully compatible nor fully contradictory. Elements functioning as components of a whole are never so fully integrated as to be mutually reinforcing nor so fully independent as to be mutually exclusive. The contradictions are such that an effort to maximize one value will tend to impair another, but not in equal proportions.

We must conclude then that the design of a constitution for an operational system of government can never derive from the maximization of any single value and that the logic of ideal types or pure forms has only limited utility in creating empirical artifacts. The issue takes on special significance when political scientists attempt to use what Robert Dahl has called the "method of maximization" to analyze the "Madisonian" and other theories of democracy. Dahl suggests that "Madisonian theory postulates a non-tyrannical republic as the goal to be maximized" (Dahl, 1963: 63).

The maximization rule is Dahl's not Madison's. Both Madison and Hamilton are quite explicit about the problems of judgment, discretion, and compromise which must be inherent in the constitution of a political system. More safety may be procured at the price of less liberty, liberty at the price of less safety. Liberty and republican form must be considered as elements among the design criteria to be evaluated in relation to other design criteria such as "safety," "energy," and "stability."

The principle of relative advantage in *The Federalist* presumes declining marginal utility for most values. The greater good thus requires a proportioning of values where values do *not* maintain constant ratios.[2] Thus, maximization of an aggregate value position will usually deviate significantly from the maximization of a *particular* value. Furthermore, maximization of an aggregate value position is impossible without recourse to a single scale of values like Benthamite utility. The task is one of "mingling them together in their due proportion" to gain the best aggregate advantage. Madison refers to this as an "arduous" task and implies that any political solution must be a compromise among the conceptual elements entering into the solution. Every choice has its price; and that price is calculated on multiple scales of value requiring different computations. Liberty and justice cannot be computed on a scale of dollars and cents.

On the other hand, ideal types or perfect forms may be useful conceptual devices for understanding the limitations inherent in empirical conditions. Madison employs a postulate of omniscience, or perfect information, in his use of the concept of God to demonstrate the imperfection of human language. He also uses a concept of "pure democracy" to conclude that an idealized form of popular government "can admit of no cure for the mischiefs of faction" (Federalist 10: ML, 58; C, 61; R, 81). A theory of perfect forms can serve as a point of departure for the development of a qualified or conditional form of analysis that may be applicable to empirical possibilities.

Much is said through *The Federalist* about energy, safety, liberty, justice, and republican form. Different elements in a constitution are designed to take account of one or another of these criteria, but the way that each is related to others is essential to the general design. The element of safety from external threat, for example, requires speed and dispatch commensurate to any potential source of danger. Presidential authority to act with dispatch in response to external dangers is based upon a concept of one-man rule. The concepts of due dependence on the people, of representation, and of majority vote are significant factors in establishing republican form. The concept of liberty, in turn, is closely tied to the authority of persons.

Thus, the task of devising a constitution requires a consideration of various exigencies and of making provision for different decision rules appropriate to those exigencies. Arrangements for one-man rules and for any-one rules must be mingled in their due proportion with majority-vote rules if the requisites of energy, safety, liberty, justice, and republican form are to be appropriately combined in constitutional arrangements.

The concept of "usurpation" as used in *The Federalist* can also be derived from the problem of design. Any artifact designed to meet certain criteria and thus to serve certain purposes or functions may also create opportunities for others to use in ways that were never contemplated by the designers. Such possibilities necessarily derive from the lack of perfect foresight and the capacity of human beings to gain an advantage from being able to manipulate elements of constraint in their environment. This possibility necessitates change over time in the structure of political institutions and in the concepts used to organize political institutions.

The concept of usurpation returns us to the assumptions and first principles which we have already examined. Fallible creatures need to make provisions for learning and for change. The principle of relative advantage depends upon a principle of political constraint if people are to derive mutual advantage from one another's capabilities. The authors of *The Federalist* explicitly denied any presumption of infallibility. They presented their analysis for contemporaries to consider in arriving at their decision on authorizing the draft of a new constitution, but they were careful to insist that the proper test for their formulations lay in an actual trial. Provision for amendment and revision could take care of needed change under no more exacting requirements than those established to authorize the new constitution. That imperfections would exist in its design, or that new strategies could be devised to use the political formulae of the new constitution to gain advantage for some at the expense of others, was clearly recognized, when Hamilton asserted:

> I never expect to see a perfect work from imperfect man. The result of the deliberations of all collective bodies must necessarily be a compound, as well of the errors and prejudices, as of the good sense and wisdom, of the individuals of whom they are composed. The compacts which are to embrace thirteen distinct States in a common bond of amity and union, must as necessarily be a compromise of as many dissimilar interests and inclinations. How can perfection spring from such materials? (Federalist 85: ML, 570–571; C, 591; R, 523–524)

SOME BASIC PROPOSITIONS ABOUT THE DESIGN OF POLITICAL INSTITUTIONS

The design of a particular constitution depends upon certain basic assumptions, terms, and propositions used by its designers in building political constraint into the structure of interpersonal relationships so that people can govern their affairs. *The Federalist* does not address itself directly to an explicit formulation of such propositions. But, it does address itself to related issues which enable us to reconstruct some of the basic assumptions and rules for the design of political institutions. Hamilton in Federalist 6 and 23, and Madison in Federalist 10 and 51, assert a variety of propositions which we can use to reconstruct the basic elements involved in the structure of political relationships. Several basic propositions used in *The Federalist* express its conception of the rudiments of political organization involved in the structuring of authority relationships. However, in Proposition 1, I am forced to supply my own formulation of the beginning point which I believe to be inherent in the logical argument of *The Federalist*.

Proposition 1. Every person is presumed to be the best judge of that person's own interest.[3]

I know of no place in *The Federalist* where Proposition 1 is explicitly formulated as a direct proposition. But, this proposition is a fundamental presupposition underlying the general argumentation at a number of points. Hamilton, for example, in a closing appeal to his fellow citizens in the state of New York observes:

Every man is bound to answer these questions to himself, according to the best of his conscience and understanding, and to act agreeably to the genuine and sober dictates of his judgment. (Federalist 85: ML, 569; C, 589; R, 522)

This assertion presumes that one is the best judge of one's own interest, including an individual's interest in the common affairs of a political association.

In Federalist 10, Madison also argues that "[a]s long as the reason of man continues fallible, and he is at liberty to exercise it, different opinions will be formed" (Federalist 10: ML, 55; C, 58; R, 78). So long as a man's "self-love" can attach itself to his opinions, a great diversity of opinions will be held with strong attachments. Issues arising from a diversity of opinions will inevitably generate conflict. Madison indicates a distinct preference for finding means to resolve conflicts rather than for avoiding conflicts by destroying the liberties which lead to a diversity of opinion. Madison extends this argument to assert that the diverse faculties, or capabilities, of men will also generate a great diversity of interests. He views the origin of property rights as arising from the diverse faculties of men and indicates that "the first object of government" is the protection of these diverse faculties among men (Federalist 10: ML, 55; C, 58; R, 78).

This line of argument is not meaningful unless one assumes that the first object of government is to maintain the creativity of individual persons and that each individual is presumed to be free to decide what is in his or her own best interest as long as that interest does not adversely affect the interests of others. From this consideration I adduce Proposition 1: *Every person is presumed to be the best judge of that person's own interest.*

Montesquieu asserts a comparable proposition in his discussion of the constitution of liberty from which Hamilton and Madison draw in the formulation of their political science. Montesquieu states: "A man who is supposed a free agent ought to be his own governor" (Montesquieu, 1966: 154). Thus, the proposition that every individual is presumed to be the best judge of that individual's own interests is a beginning point for specifying who is to assume initial responsibility for governing the affairs of each person as a participant in a political association. Each person must assume initial responsibility for the government of his or her own affairs.

Proposition 2. No man is a fit judge of his own cause in relation to the interests of others[4] (Federalist 10: ML, 56; C, 59; R, 79).

Proposition 3. With equal, nay with greater reason, a body of men are unfit to be both judges and parties at the same time (Federalist 10: ML, 56; C, 59; R, 79).

A crucial point in most political theory turns on the question: Who is fit to rule (i.e., who is fit to determine and tend to the interests which derive from the actions of others)? *The Federalist* responds that *no one, per se,* is fit to rule. Hamilton, for example, quite explicitly asserts that the private passions— the attachments, enmities, interests, hopes, and fears—of

leading individuals in the communities of which they are members . . . have in too many instances abused the confidence they possessed; and assuming the pretext of some public motive, have not scrupled to sacrifice the national tranquillity to personal advantage or personal gratification. (Federalist 6: ML, 28; C, 29; R, 54)

He declares in his conclusion that "men of this class" will in too many instances abuse the confidence they possess, whether they are the favorites of a king in a monarchy or the favorites of a people in a republic. Rank in an aristocracy or membership in an elite does not, *per se,* make one a fit judge of his or her own cause in relation to the interests of others. Nor is a body of men fit to judge its own cause in relation to the interests of others.

Resolution of the problem created by presuming that *no one, per se,* is fit to rule others is a principal issue in the political theory of *The Federalist.* Fitness to rule depends upon the qualified capacity of persons who occupy positions of special political prerogative to work out settlements under the terms of decision rules which are subject to review and reconsideration by others. Transactions and social relationships can be broadly based upon a decision rule of willing consent; but every decision maker should be subject to multiple exposures in dealing with the interests of others. The structure of authority in the American political system, thus, assumes that all transactions and social relationships implicate many others even though a particular transaction may be confined to only two parties. Whenever a dyadic relationship ceases to be an agreeable one, and individuals are unable to reach a satisfactory resolution of their interdependent relationships, the offices of third persons are established to assist in the resolution of conflict. The structure of authority in the American political system is based upon a special calculus providing recourse to alternative decision-making arrangements so that no person, nor any one group of persons, can be the ultimate judge of his, her, or their own causes that affects the interests of others. The following propositions serve as elements for building such a structure of authority relationships.

Proposition 4. Ambition must be made to counteract ambition (Federalist 51: ML, 337; C, 349, R, 322).

Human ambition, the inspiration for all actions, is the energizing force which Madison would use to constitute the interpersonal structure of authority relationships. A unit of government or a political association, more generally, cannot be founded upon ambition alone. Rather, it stands upon the proposition that "[a]mbition must be made to counteract ambition."

Considerable confusion has derived from Madison's use of this proposition as a cornerstone in the political theory of *The Federalist.* Richard Hofstadter, for example, restates this proposition to mean: "It is too much to expect that vice could be checked by virtue; the Fathers relied instead upon checking vice with vice" (Hofstadter, 1954: 7). Unfortunately, the vice or virtue of an act cannot be judged exclusively by the initiator of an act. The worth of an act can be established only by evaluating the preferences, opinions, and judgments of others who may be affected by it. If a mutuality of interest exists in the evaluation of an act as beneficial to everyone concerned, then human ambition can indeed be virtuous! Whenever an act is mutually beneficial to all who are affected, *no* political problem exists. We have already examined this circumstance in the context of Madison's assertion that "if men were angels, no government would be necessary." Men whose acts are entirely virtuous in everyone's calculations can freely pursue their advantage and simultaneously benefit others without interposing any element of political constraint.

Where mutually beneficial relationships are absent, an act perceived to be virtuous by one may be perceived by others as pernicious meddling in their affairs. The pejorative use of the term "do-gooder" indicates the potential for vice in good intentions.[5] The potential lack of conjunction in evaluating vices and virtues is the condition which gives rise to the need to counteract ambition with ambition, and thus to provide an opportunity for an expression of conflicting interests. Vice and virtue cannot be presumed. The vice or virtue of an act can only be determined by an evaluation of the consequences of action by anyone affected.

Among fallible persons, each individual is presumed to be the best judge of that individual's own interest in the initial articulation of that interest. Both an actor and anyone adversely affected by an act are appropriate judges of their individual interests, but are inappropriate judges of the interests of others in relation to their own interest. In the absence of agreement among the parties to a conflict, a unilateral determination by one of the parties will not yield orderly and productive social relationships. The principle of political constraint implies that a variety of specialized institutional arrangements need exist so that *anyone* may invoke procedures

to bring a third party into a dispute and begin processes for
mediating, resolving, or adjudicating the conflict of interests.[6]
The constitution of any political association thus depends
upon introducing a social calculus into the structure of decision rules to qualify and condition ambition by consideration
for the interests of others.

Proposition 5. The interest of the man must be connected
with the constitutional rights of the place [i.e., position][7] (Federalist 51: ML, 337; C, 349; R, 322).

The use of counteracting ambitions or conflicting interests
in the architecture of human institutions is accomplished by
tying "the interest of the man" to "the constitutional rights of
the [position]." This process of creating a union of individual
interest and of public right is, in turn, accomplished by assigning an authority to act subject to limitations or constraints
inherent in the rights and interests of others.

Propositions assigning authority or capabilities to act, together with such correlative limitations as take account of the
interests of others, comprise the law that is operative in any
society. Thus, a system of law in a society can be viewed as a
system of *decision rules* potentially applicable to all transactions
and relationships in a society.[8] In turn, the particular form of
a human institution or social organization can be viewed as a
political artifact; that is, an arrangement which is authorized,
maintained, and revised by reference to a set of decision rules
contained in a system of law. For example, a property right,
when viewed from such a conception, is not a thing which is
the object of ownership, but the authority that a person can
exercise in relation to others with regard to the objects that
are the subject of property relationships. I am the proprietor,
for example, who has the authority to use, control, and dispose of my own skills as an artisan, subject to limitations which
recognize the lawful interests of others. I have a property
right to my own labor. Others have property rights to their
own labor. I can dispose of my skills as an artisan to work for
others, but I am the one who has authority to make those
decisions.

Madison emphasizes that the process of tying the "interests of the man" to the exercise of a public right ought to occur throughout "the whole system of human affairs," in public as well as private affairs. How such relationships are constituted make for critical differences in the character of political institutions.

Proposition 6. The means ought to be proportioned to the end; the persons, from whose agency the attainment of any end is expected, ought to possess the means by which it is to be attained (Federalist 23: ML, 142; C, 147; R, 153).

In assigning authority to persons who are to act on behalf of a community of interests which are shared by those who form a political association or a unit of government, Hamilton asserts in Proposition 6 that the appropriateness of decision rules must be determined by the end or the objective sought. Where, for example, dangers are very great in relation to the aggregate values of those involved, and where the element of surprise may also be high, we would anticipate that the time and effort expended on due deliberation or due process should be held to a minimum. Under these exigencies, the choice of a decision rule enabling *one man* to commit a collectivity to take action may be an appropriate decision rule.[9]

From such calculations Hamilton concludes, "Of all the cares or concerns of government, the direction of war most peculiarly demands those qualities which distinguish the exercise of power by a single hand" (Federalist 74: ML, 482; C, 500; R, 447). This is the rationale justifying the propriety of the constitutional provision designating the President to be "commander-in-chief of the army and navy of the United States, and of the militia of the several States *when called into the actual service* of the United States" (Federalist 74: ML, 481–482; C, 500; R, 447. Hamilton's emphasis). Thus, the constitution of a republic provides for a limited one-man rule as well as for other decision rules.

Other decision rules apply to other exigencies, but the controlling concept in Proposition 6 is a fiduciary relationship about the ends to be attained and the means appropriate to attaining those ends. A trustee in a fiduciary relationship must have authority that is competent to discharge the trust. At the same time, a trustee in a fiduciary relationship can be held accountable for a proper discharge of a trust. To hold to account is to limit authority in relation to other authorities. Rather than identify a single controlling decision rule, a proper constitution would include a mix of decision rules applicable to different fiduciary relationships.

Proposition 7. In every political institution, a power to advance the public happiness involves a discretion which may be misapplied and abused (Federalist 41: ML, 260; C, 269; R, 255–256).

Proposition 6 implies that interests which members of a political community share in common will require special decision rules authorizing some person or some group of persons to act on behalf of the collectivity. Such authority implies a capability to use sanctions to enforce common rules, and thus, to exercise lawful coercion on behalf of the common good. A constitutional decision to vest the prerogatives of commander-in-chief with one man *necessarily* implies a *radical inequality* in decision-making capabilities. Such radical inequalities in the assignment of decision-making capabilities may be essential for the security and safety of a people in protecting themselves against external threats and dangers of war. At the same time the assignment of such a decision-making capability to advance "the public happiness" also involves a discretion which may be misapplied and abused.

While the case of a one-man decision rule represents an extreme case, the principle of Proposition 7 can apply to any decision rule which relaxes the requirement of willing consent on the part of each and every person involved in a political association. The rule of willing consent is not a sufficient rule for political order since each individual would then be the judge of one's own interest in relation to the interests of others. Decision rules which assign special prerogatives on the part of officials to act on behalf of others within a collectivity imply a power which can be misapplied and abused. Those who comprise a majority coalition where collective action can be taken by majority vote can use their capability to impose deprivations upon others.

The creation of fiduciary relationships inherent in the exercise of political authority necessarily involves the powers that can be misapplied and abused. The problem is how to hold those who exercise the basic prerogatives of government accountable in their discharge of a public trust.

Proposition 8. [T]he constant aim is to divide and arrange the several offices in such a manner as that each may be a check on the other—that the private interest of every individual may be a sentinel over the public rights (Federalist 51: ML, 337; C, 349; R, 322).

Proposition 9. The accumulation of all powers . . . in the same hands, whether of one, a few, or many, and whether hereditary, self-appointed, or elective, will lead to tyranny[10] (Federalist 47: ML, 313; C, 324; R, 301).

Propositions 8 and 9 are complementary propositions designed to modify the requirement in Proposition 6 that authority be commensurate with the objective in order to reduce the abuse or misapplication of public authority. Only by dividing and arranging the several offices so that each may be a check upon the other is it possible to meet the condition that no one is a fit judge of one's own cause in relation to the interests of others and to hold officials accountable for their discharge of a public trust. Thus, the action of every judge and every public officer, according to the political theory of *The Federalist*, must be subject to review and scrutiny by others. No one is fit to exercise the prerogative of a Hobbesian sovereign. Each person can assume moral responsibility for the government of his own affairs only to the extent that he or she is free to challenge those, including public authorities, who may threaten essential interests.

A naive faith that persons assigned the extraordinary prerogatives of public authority will not abuse those prerogatives is an unwarrantable assumption. Instead, each decision maker or each set of decision makers will be exposed to having the

consequences of their decisions considered by other independent decision makers. In this way, individuals occupying different positions of political authority will have an incentive to
protect their own interest in the proper exercise of public authority, and thus, to maintain the integrity of their position
and to prevent its usurpation by others.

This method of dividing and arranging the several offices
so that each may be a check upon the other is seen by Madison
as the fundamental problem in framing the structure of government. He views this method as an application of a more
general principle of using opposite and rival interests to
structure the whole system of human affairs—private as well
as public. The contribution of *The Federalist* is to extend this
principle to distributing authority for the exercise of the "supreme powers of the State" (Federalist 51: ML, 338; C, 349;
R, 322).

Proposition 10. By a faction, I understand a number of citizens who . . . are united and actuated by some common . . .
interest, adverse to the rights of other citizens, or to the permanent and aggregate interests of the community[11] (Federalist 10: ML, 54; C, 57; R, 78).

Proposition 11. Liberty is to faction what air is to fire (Federalist 10: ML, 55; C, 58; R, 78).

If we accept the analysis of the previous propositions, we
can assume that the structure of authority in a political community provides a great variety of opportunities for individuals to enter into combination with other individuals. Many
of these combinations will facilitate the interests of some, but
at the cost of others, and will, thus, evoke political conflict.
Such conflict can be expected to generate yet more combinations. Factions will form to attempt to dominate the decision-
making arrangements for exercising prerogatives of public
authority. The decision rules of a political system will inevitably permit some to form winning combinations. A winning
combination, as a faction or coalition, can exploit the opportunities inherent in public decision rules to derive an advantage detrimental to the interest of other citizens or to the

long-term, aggregate interest of the community of persons forming a unit of government.

The freedom of all citizens to enter into combinations and to participate in the political process implies that a great diversity of activity and a great variety of combinations can be expected to form. Such combination can be further expected to generate conflict and to exploit the full range of strategic opportunities inherent in the decision rules of the political system. If advantage can be gained by forming a combination to beat the game, enterprising persons can be expected to form such winning combinations. Constitutional decision makers in fashioning a political system based upon liberty and republican form, thus, must consider tendencies toward combinations and the consequences such tendencies will have for the corruption of a political system.

Proposition 12. If a faction consists of less than a majority, relief is supplied by the republican principle, which enables the majority to defeat its sinister views by regular vote (Federalist 10: ML, 57; C, 60; R, 80).

This proposition implies a definition of republican rule as a rule requiring majority vote to make a binding commitment in the conduct of government. When such a voting rule is used, Madison anticipates that the principle of majority vote will enable a republican government to defeat the designs of a minority faction by the political condition of its "regular vote." He indicates that the conflict generated by a minority faction may be a costly matter: "It may clog the administration, it may convulse the society; but it will be unable to execute and mask its violence under the forms of the Constitution" (Federalist 10: ML, 57; C, 60; R, 80).

It can be argued that Madison passes over the problem of minority factions too lightly, even though he does recognize that the task of defeating such a faction can be a costly process. The problem of a minority faction which may be generated by collusion between the leading elements of the major parties or factions in a republic is not treated as a distinct problem. The leaders of two or more parties or factions may collude to control the centers of power and exploit a people to the advantage of party leaders and to the detriment of members of the society. Such a minority faction may, however, be viewed as equivalent to a majority faction.

Proposition 13. When a majority is included in a faction, the form of popular government . . . enables it to sacrifice to its ruling passion or interest both the public good and the rights of other citizens (Federalist 10: ML, 57; C, 60–61; R, 80).

The solution afforded by the principle of majority vote in preventing a minority faction from imposing its will upon others will not suffice when a majority comprises a faction. A majority faction is one that can win by the "regular vote." Consequently, a majority faction or a majority winning coalition can preempt the political game by majority vote and exploit the advantages of winning at the expense of the losing coalition and of the long-term aggregate interests of the community.

CONCLUSION

Proposition 13 poses a central difficulty for the authors of *The Federalist*. A republican form of government is clearly insufficient to provide a remedy against a majority faction unless special advantage can be taken of the opportunities of using ambition to counteract ambition (Proposition 4) and of arranging the several offices in such a manner that each may be a check on the other (Proposition 8). If such principles can be used in the design of the political structure of a compound republic, as distinguished from a simple republic, then a solution to the problem of majority faction can be attained.

Political power can be used by a winning coalition to exploit and tyrannize others. Rule by majority faction is equivalent to tyranny of the majority. The political theory of a compound republic is an effort to resolve this problem. The *essential problem* was posed by Madison when he observed:

To secure the public good and private rights against the danger of such a (majority) faction, and at the same time to preserve the spirit and the form of popular government, is then the great object to which our inquiries are directed. (Federalist 10: ML, 57–58; C, 61; R, 80. My emphasis and parenthesis.)

We have reviewed basic propositions of political design applicable to the structure of authority relationships. Majority factions yield what Hamilton and Madison regard as a republican disease. We turn next to their formulation of a republican remedy for the republican disease.

NOTES

1. These "vicissitudes and uncertainties" were unquestionably aggravated by the dynamics of unconstrained conflict where states were beginning to act to the detriment of one another. Threats and counterthreats were in danger of escalating into war.

2. See Chapter 5, Figure II as contrasted to Figure I to note the difference.

3. I deliberately used the verb "is presumed" to reflect the status of this proposition as a *presumption*. The presumption may not be empirically valid in all cases. Thus, some people may be held to be incompetent and not responsible for their individual actions. The presumption is assumed to be generally valid unless contrary grounds can be established.

4. This is a reformulation of Madison's statement: "No man is allowed to be a judge in his own cause, because his interest would certainly bias his judgment, and, not improbably, corrupt his integrity" (Federalist 10: ML, 56; C, 59; R, 79).

5. Folk adages which assert, like Samuel Johnson, that "the way to hell is paved with good intentions" also revealed the potential for vice in virtuous intentions.

6. Thus, the capacity to "call the police" as a first step in dealing with a dispute is an initial element in a political process and is usually based upon an "any-one" rule. The Detroit City Police Department, however, once announced to the local citizenry that, for reasons of economy, police would not respond to calls involving less important problems like family squabbles and petty burglaries. If this policy continued one might expect a modification in the constitution of

family life among some families or the development of alternative methods for processing family conflicts.

7. In addition to the usual associations with "space," the term "place" also has standard dictionary definitions which include: (1) position, situation, or circumstance: *if I were in your place*; (2) a job, post, or office: *persons in high places in government*; (3) official employment or position: *several places that have not been filled*. From Random House Dictionary of the English Language.

8. Commons and Hohfeld provide fuller expositions of this point of view.

9. Buchanan and Tullock provide a modern rationale for such a conclusion in their *Calculus of Consent*.

10. This reformulates Madison's proposition. I have substituted the last four words for his "may justly be pronounced the very definition of tyranny." I assume that Madison's definition of tyranny implies an *abusive and oppressive usurpation of authority*. His proposition, then, is not a simple definition, but an assertion about the consequences of vesting all powers in a single decision structure.

11. Madison's full definition is stated: "By a faction, I understand a number of citizens whether amounting to a majority or minority of the whole, who are united and actuated by some common impulse of passion, or of interest, adverse to the rights of other citizens, or to the permanent and aggregate interests of the community."

CHAPTER FIVE

A Republican Remedy for the Republican Disease

The political theory of a compound republic grounds basic elements in the structure of authority relationships upon propositions which assert, among others, that: (1) every person is presumed to be the best judge of that person's own interest, (2) no one is a fit judge of one's own cause in relation to the interests of others, (3) no body of men are fit to be judges and parties at the same time, (4) ambition must be made to counteract ambition, (5) authority should be assigned so that the persons from whose agency the attainment of an end is expected ought to possess the means by which it is to be attained, and (6) the constant aim is to divide and arrange the several offices in such a manner that each may be a check on the other. The initial analysis concluded that the form of popular (democratic) government enables a majority to sacrifice the public good and the rights of other citizens to its ruling passion.

The first several propositions are congruent only with a concept that people will participate in the government of their own affairs. Such a conclusion is consistent with a positive answer to the question: Are societies of men really capable of establishing good government from reflection and choice? The conclusion regarding majority factions casts substantial doubt upon the possibility of deriving an affirmative answer. The distinguishing characteristics of the political theory of a compound republic come from the resolution of this problem. The tension between the conclusion about majority factions and the possibility that societies of men might estab-

lish good government from reflection and choice was a major
problem to be solved: *"the great object to which our inquiries
are directed"* (Federalist 10: ML, 58; C, 61; R, 80. My emphasis). Thus, we need to give careful attention to the analysis of
the problem of self-government as it is conceptualized in *The
Federalist.*

"THE CAPACITY OF MANKIND FOR SELF-GOVERNMENT"

In his analysis of the "plan of government" formulated by the
Philadelphia Convention, Madison turns to the question of
whether the general form and aspects of the government are
"strictly republican" (Federalist 39: ML, 242–243; C, 250; R,
240). He considered this an essential criterion among the several design criteria pertinent to the plan of government. He
observes:

It is evident that no other form would be reconcilable with the genius
of the people of America; with the fundamental principles of the
Revolution; or with that honorable determination which animates
every votary of freedom, (than) to rest all our political experiments
on the capacity of mankind for self-government. (Federalist 39: ML,
243; C, 250; R, 240. My parenthesis.)

Madison concludes that if the plan of the convention departs
from this essential principle of basing a national government
upon the capacity of mankind for self-government, then advocates of the constitution must abandon their position as no
longer defensible. Republican forms, however, are subject to
some fundamental limitations. We shall consider these limitations and the means to overcome them in the balance of this
chapter.

A Size Principle

Fragments of a surprisingly sophisticated and forceful argument regarding essential limits upon the capacity of mankind
for self-government are developed at various junctures in *The
Federalist.* The argument is an effort to formulate a size prin-

ciple in relation to group decision making concerned with the common or joint interests of persons forming a unit of government. The most explicit formulation of this size principle occurs in discussion of the size of the House of Representatives, particularly in Federalist 55 and 58. But, the argument is a general one applicable to any decision-making group.

A statement of the size principle is expressed thus:

One:

Nothing can be more fallacious than to found our political calculations on arithmetical principles. (Federalist 55: ML, 361; C, 374; R, 342)

Two:

Sixty or seventy men may be more properly trusted with a given degree of power than six or seven. (Federalist 55: ML, 361; C, 374; R, 342)

Three:

But it does not follow that six or seven hundred would be proportionably a better depositary. (Federalist 55: ML, 361; C, 374; R, 342)

Four:

And if we carry on the supposition to six or seven thousand, the whole reasoning ought to be reversed. (Federalist 55: ML, 361; C, 374; R, 342)

Five:

The truth is, that in all cases a certain number at least seems to be necessary to secure the benefits of free consultation and discussion, and to guard against too easy a combination for improper purposes; as, on the other hand, the number ought at most to be kept within a certain limit, in order to avoid the confusion and intemperance of a multitude. (Federalist 55: ML, 361; C, 374; R, 342)

From these several propositions, extracted from a single paragraph in Federalist 58, I can derive two representations.

Along the horizontal axis in each representation is measured
the number of individuals who might be included within a
decision-making group. Quality of deliberation is represented
along the vertical axis. Both measures share a common zero
point. The upward sloping straight line in Figure I represents
what *The Federalist* would call a fallacious concept that an
increase in the number of persons included in a decision-
making group involves a uniform improvement in the quality
of deliberations. Or, in other words, the bigger the group, the
better.

Figure II implies that an increase in the number of persons
included within a decision-making group does not involve a
uniform addition to the quality of deliberations. When the
number is very small, an increase in size may contribute a
larger than average increment to the quality of deliberation.
However, a size is reached where further increments will
create a decreasing marginal contribution from each participant. While the general characteristic of the curve in Figure II can be inferred from the propositions on political calculations, the precise shape of the curve is not known. Thus,
my representation assumes some arbitrary qualities. Beyond a
certain size, each person added to a decision-making group

FIGURE I

A "Fallacious" Use of "Arithmetical Principles" for
Determining the Size of a Decision Making Group

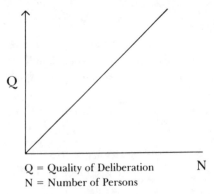

Q = Quality of Deliberation   N
N = Number of Persons

will diminish its quality of deliberations. The analysis in *The Federalist* implies that such a hypothetical possibility could occur if the constitution of a government does not take account of the limitations inherent in a size principle.

"In all very numerous assemblies," the authors of *The Federalist* argue, "passion never fails to wrest the sceptre from reason" (Federalist 55: ML, 361; C, 374; R, 342). And this proposition is asserted to be true without regard to the character of the persons participating (i.e., independent of their individual personalities) in a numerous assembly. This judgment is supported with an emphatic conclusion that "had every Athenian citizen been a Socrates, every Athenian assembly would still have been a mob" (Federalist 55: ML, 361; C, 374; R, 342).

The basic constraining condition existing in *any deliberative group* derives from the circumstance that *only one speaker can be heard and understood at a time.* Simultaneous speeches by two or more persons addressing a single audience simply constitute noise and evoke confusion. Orderly deliberation requires that speech, and thus communication, be rationed on the basis of a one-at-a-time rule.

Deliberation based on a one-at-a-time rule implies that in

FIGURE II

A Proper Use of Political Calculation for Determining
Size of a Decision-Making Group

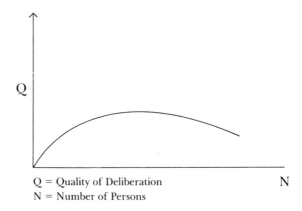

Q = Quality of Deliberation   N
N = Number of Persons

all deliberative bodies "the greater the number composing them may be, the fewer will be the men who will in fact direct their proceedings" (Federalist 58: ML, 381; C, 395; R, 360). This principle applies to any deliberative body whether an assembly of citizens, as in the case of Athens, or in a representative assembly, as in the case of a modern legislative body. With the essential constraint inherent in a one-at-a-time rule, the larger the group, the proportionately less opportunity each individual member will have to express his thoughts.

In a large legislative body like the U.S. House of Representatives, it would take in excess of 70 hours of time on a legislative calendar to allocate only 10 minutes to each of 435 members, assuming no loss of time in the conduct of proceedings. Ten minutes does not give much opportunity for a reasoned presentation of arguments on important issues. The House of Representatives is unable to have as effective deliberations as the Senate simply as a result of its larger size. The House of Commons in Great Britain with more than 600 members faces even more difficult problems. The chamber of the House of Commons is too small to accommodate all members; and debate is dominated by members of the Government and the leading members of the opposition party. An ordinary member of the House of Commons rarely has an opportunity to speak. The leadership dominates the proceedings.

The operation of any large deliberative assembly, whether in a direct democracy or in a representative assembly, will depend upon the selection of a few to exercise prerogatives in setting the agenda and controlling deliberation. The dominance of the leadership will increase and the influence of each member of a group upon its deliberations will decline as the number increases in size. Democratic arrangements give way to oligarchical control. And so it follows, as argued in *The Federalist*, that "the larger the number, the greater will be the proportion of members of limited information and of weak capacities" (Federalist 58: ML, 381; C, 396; R, 360). And thus: "In the ancient republics, where the whole body of the people assembled in person, a single orator, or an artful statesman, was generally seen to rule with as complete a sway as if a sceptre had been placed in his single hand" (Federalist 58: ML, 382; C, 396; R, 360).

In concluding discussion of this size principle, the authors of *The Federalist* warn:

The people can never err more than in supposing that by multiplying their representatives beyond a certain limit, they strengthen the barrier against the government of a few. Experience will forever admonish them that, on the contrary, *after securing a sufficient number for the purposes of safety, of local information, and of diffusive sympathy with the whole society* (Madison's emphasis), *they will counteract their own views by every addition to their representatives. The countenance of the government may become more democratic, but the soul that animates it will be more oligarchic* (my emphasis). The machine will be enlarged, but the fewer, and often the more secret, will be the springs by which its motions are directed. (Federalist 58: ML, 382; C, 396; R, 360–361)

This size principle severely constrains the organization of any deliberative body. The several thousand citizens who participated in the assembly of Athens clearly exceeded the number of persons who could effectively participate in a direct democracy. As a consequence, Madison's conclusion that "a pure democracy . . . can admit of no cure for the mischiefs of faction" (Federalist 10: ML, 58; C, 61; R, 81) is also consistent with this reasoning. Oligarchical tendencies will arise to dominate the proceedings of any numerous assembly. Safety in numbers, beyond rather confined limits, is a false presumption. The operation of this size principle yields counterintuitive results—that is, results that run counter to common-sense intuitions about what is true or evident.

The Principle of Political Representation

The problem posed by the size principle can be partly resolved by a scheme of representation in which the function of legislation is exercised by deputies which the people choose to

represent them in a legislative assembly. Madison thus distinguishes a democracy from a republic by saying that a republic
involves "the delegation of the government . . . to a small
number of citizens elected by the rest" (Federalist 10: ML, 59;
C, 62; R, 82). Through the institutional device of elected representation, the government of a republic can extend to a
larger number of people and to a larger region than a direct
democracy can.

Madison warns, however, that the size principle is also applicable to a representative assembly in a republic. On the one
hand, "[T]he representatives must be raised to a certain number, in order to guard against the cabals of a few" (Federalist
10: ML, 59; C, 62–63; R, 82), no matter how small a republic
may be. On the other hand, in a large republic, the representatives "must be limited to a certain number, in order to guard
against the confusion of a multitude" (Federalist 10: ML, 60;
C, 63; R, 82). Securing a proper proportion of representatives
for safety and at the same time avoiding the oligarchic tendencies in the deliberations of a multitude presents one problem affecting the size of a republic.

In addition, the size of a constituency is constrained by the
need to have information on local conditions which are relevant to common policies. If the constituency is too small, a
representative will be unduly attached to local interests and a
multitude of representatives would impair the deliberative
process. On the other hand, "By enlarging too much the
number of electors (i.e., constituents), you render the representative too little acquainted with all their local circumstances
and lesser interests . . . " (Federalist 10: ML, 60; C, 63; R, 83.
My parenthesis). The size principle applies both to representative bodies and to the aggregate size of units of government.
Without attention to the constraint of the size principle, "The
countenance of the government may become more democratic, but the soul that animates it will be more oligarchic"
(Federalist 58: ML, 382; C, 396; R, 360–361).

The size principle can be somewhat relaxed when certain
occupational groupings in a society assume a specialized role

in representing the interests of others. As a consequence, Hamilton contends, "actual representation of all classes of the people, by persons of each class" (Federalist 35: ML, 213; C, 219; R, 214) is not necessary. Merchants, he argues, are the natural patrons and friends of those engaged in "the mechanic and manufacturing arts." Members of the "learned professions . . . form no distinct interest in society, and according to their situation and talents, will be indiscriminately the objects of the confidence and choice of each other, and of other parts of the community." Lawyers, for example, make it their professional business to represent the interests of others. Landed interests will tend to be represented by "the middling farmer" or "moderate proprietors of land" (Federalist 35: ML, 214; C, 220; R, 215). Hamilton thus anticipates that representatives will be selected predominately from moderate landholders, merchants, and members of the learned professions.

Hamilton anticipates that in the normal course of events "these three descriptions of men" will be able to understand and attend to the interests of the "different classes of citizens." A man whose situation leads him to "extensive inquiry and information" about "the momentary humors or dispositions which may happen to prevail in particular parts of the society" may be a more competent spokesman for those interests than "one whose observation does not travel beyond the circle of his neighbors and acquaintances" (Federalist 35: ML, 215; C, 221; R, 216). If such a man, who makes it his business to serve the interests of others, is "a candidate for the favor of the people, and . . . is dependent on the suffrages of his fellow-citizens for the continuance of his public honors," he will "take care to inform himself of their dispositions and inclinations, and should be willing to allow them their proper degree of influence upon his conduct." "This dependence, and the necessity of being bound himself, and his posterity, by the laws to which he gives his assent," Hamilton concludes, "are the true, and they are the strong chords of sympathy between the representative and the constituent" (Federalist 35: ML, 215; C, 221; R, 216).

By utilizing the affinity that merchants, or members of the learned professions have toward the interests of carpenters, blacksmiths, linen manufacturers, stocking weavers, and other specialized groups in society, it becomes possible to represent all their interests without having a representative spokesman for each and every interest. Thus, the regularity and wisdom of deliberation need not be sacrificed to the size of a legislature which is sufficiently large to represent all interests by persons directly affiliated with each interest group.

Hamilton also recognizes that "the door" to political representation "ought to be equally open to all" (Federalist 36: ML, 217; C, 223; R, 217), even though the situation of moderate land proprietors, merchants, and members of the learned professions may better enable them to represent the interests of others. "There are strong minds in every walk of life that will rise superior to the disadvantages of situation, and will command the tribute due to their merit, not only from the classes to which they particularly belong, but from the society in general" (Federalist 36: ML, 217; C, 223; R, 217). Such persons are eminently qualified to represent the interests of others.

In the final analysis, political representation is best served when "every considerate citizen" can "judge for himself where the requisite qualification is most likely to be found" (Federalist 36: ML, 216; C, 222; R, 217). Voters, in short, should be free to select their own representative and to determine the qualifications of their political representatives. If political representation can be best performed by persons whose social circumstance and interests lead them to inquire about the interests of others and to seek political resolution to problems that take account of those interests in a way that wins their support as voting constituents, then the size of representative bodies can be held within bounds that permit orderly debate and deliberation by a miniscule fraction of the aggregate population. Still, such persons are limited to the condition that only one person can be heard by any one audience at any given time. The ratio of representative to constituent population being discussed in *The Federalist* for the House of Representatives was 1 : 30,000. Today, this ratio is 1 : 500,000. One might, also, infer that the House of Representatives has long since reached the size where its "democratic countenance" is animated by an "oligarchic soul." If the United States had been organized as a simple unitary republic, one can reasonably infer that the republic long ago would have fallen victim to the constraint inherent in the size principle. The Senate, as a smaller deliberative body, is still capable of meaningful debate.

THE REPUBLICAN DISEASE

Madison perceives that "[t]he latent causes of faction are . . . sown in the nature of man" (Federalist 10: ML, 55; C, 58; R, 79). Ambition guided by limited and fallible understanding leads to a great diversity of opinion. Ambition served by limited, varying capabilities leads to diverse, competing claims regarding the acquisition and possession of goods and skills as property. A division of a society into different interests, groups, and parties ensues from the competing aspirations of individuals to make decisions and to control events viewed as property. A free laborer is a proprietor at liberty to dispose of his own efforts as he sees fit (subject to constraint, of course). The general structure of property law is thus a major element in defining the power structure of a society; and, as Madison well understood, "[T]he most common and durable source of factions has been the various and unequal distribution of property" (Federalist 10: ML, 56; C, 59; R, 79).

"The regulation of these various and interfering interests," Madison reasons, "forms the principal task of modern legislation, and involves the spirit of party and faction in the *necessary* and *ordinary* operations of the government" (Federalist 10: ML, 56; C, 59; R, 79. My emphasis). If an unqualified principle of majority rule prevails in a system of government based upon legislative supremacy, then no force will exist to break the dominance of a majority faction. The parties forming a majority faction would then be judges of their own cause; "[A]nd the most numerous party, or, in other words, the most powerful faction must be expected to prevail" (Federalist 10: ML, 57; C, 60; R, 80). Majority rule permits a dominant faction to prevail; and the processes of reasoned discourse cannot be carried on where a group of men is the judge of its own cause. It can simply dominate without further opportunity for challenge and discussion. The capacity of a majority faction to prevail, to usurp political prerogatives for its advantage at the expense of others, thus, is the source of the basic malady in a government based upon democratic or republican rule.

Hamilton analyzes the republican disease in a sweeping view of political history. "It is impossible," he states,

to read the history of the petty republics of Greece and Italy without feeling sensations of horror and disgust at the distractions with which they were continually agitated, and at the rapid succession of revolutions by which they were kept in a state of perpetual vibration between the extremes of tyranny and anarchy. If they exhibit occasional calms, these only serve as short-lived contrasts to the furious storms that are to succeed. If now and then intervals of felicity open to view, we behold them with a mixture of regret, arising from the reflection that the pleasing scenes before us are soon to be overwhelmed by the tempestuous waves of sedition and party rage. If momentary rays of glory break forth from the gloom, while they dazzle us with a transient and fleeting brilliancy, they at the same time admonish us to lament that the vices of government should pervert the direction and tarnish the lustre of those bright talents and exalted endowments for which the favored soils that produced them have been so justly celebrated. (Federalist 9: ML, 47–48; C, 50–51; R, 71–72)

Hamilton does not explicitly say how "little, jealous, clashing, tumultuous commonwealths" become "the wretched nurseries of unceasing discord" (Federalist 9: ML, 49–50; C, 52–53; R, 73) in the context of his essay in Federalist 9. The logic of mutually destructive conflicts which he pursues in Federalist 7, 15, 16, 27, and 28 provides one basis for deriving conclusions about how republics become "the wretched nurseries of unceasing discord." If Madison's formulation about majority faction can be used to characterize the cause of the republican disease, then we can infer, from the logic of mutually destructive conflict, how those conditions will lead to its contagion within a family of independent republics.

If a majority faction can dominate the government of a republic and use its dominance to gain advantage for itself at the expense of others, the losers will try to minimize their disadvantage by seeking the support of allies. The more extreme the deprivation, the more willing the deprived become to use extreme measures in the absence of alternative methods for seeking more agreeable solutions. Conflict may escalate to a point where factions within a society regard each other as enemies and seek to use the coercive instrumentalities of government to war upon each other. If a neighboring republic is dominated by a faction congenial to an oppressed faction in one republic, domestic issues will soon impinge upon the relationships between two republics. The conflicts will escalate in mutual recrimination, conspiracies to interfere in each other's affairs, and efforts to impose collective sanctions. And so, the constitutions of republics must give way to the requirements for maintaining a state of organized warfare. If such consequences are to be avoided, both the cause and the epidemiology of the republican disease must be understood in devising a constitutional system which can "secure the public good and private rights against the danger of such a (majority) faction, and at the same time . . . preserve the spirit and the form of popular government . . . " (Federalist 10: ML, 57–58; C, 61; R, 80. My parenthesis).

A REPUBLICAN REMEDY

Madison's prescription that "all our political experiments" should rest upon "the capacity of mankind for self-government" (Federalist 39: ML, 243; C, 250; R, 240) contains the formula for a remedy to the republican disease. Madison's formula assumes radical proportions only if taken quite literally: *all* our political experiments should be based upon the principle of self-government. Application of the principle of self-government to *concurrent* governments in a federal system of government is the major innovation in the political theory of a compound republic.

No single center of authority need dominate all of the rest. Smaller communities of interest can be organized on principles of self-government and maintain autonomy in the governance of their own internal affairs. Other interests that are shared by several different communities can be organized as autonomous self-governing authorities. The principle can be extended from regional to national and international communities of interest. Republican institutions can be nurtured both in small communities and in larger communities. The probability of any one faction gaining dominance in all units of government in a federal system is significantly smaller than one faction gaining dominance over a single center of ultimate authority in a unitary nation-state.

Madison concludes his famous analysis in Federalist 10 with the observation, "In the *extent* and *proper structure* of the Union, therefore, we behold a republican remedy for the diseases most incident to republican government" (Federalist 10: ML, 62; C, 65; R, 84. My emphasis). The remedy lay in both the *extent* and *proper structure* of arrangements for a republican system of government. Instead of relying upon a unitary arrangement inherent in the constitution of a single republic, the major remedy of *The Federalist* lay in *compounding* a republic so that self-government can operate concurrently in the government of different communities of interest. In this way, the cause and the spread of the republican disease can be remedied by treating both the *extent* and *proper structure* of multiple units of government as allowing for the articulation of multiple and concurrent communities of interest where no one community of interest need deny or dominate the rest.

Some have read Madison's observation as applying only to the extent of a republic. Simply to extend the area of a republic would encompass a greater variety of interests. But, the oligarchical tendencies inherent in the size principle would facilitate easy dominance by one faction over the other interests if only a single center of governmental authority were created in a nation as a whole. No single monopoly of public authority exists in a compound republic. Multiple authorities are established representing diverse communities of interest. Each is governed by republican principles of self-government. *Proper structure* is as important a qualification as *extent* in working out a remedy to the republican disease.

Madison's reference is to the extent and proper structure of the *Union*. The concluding sentence leaves little doubt that federal arrangements in a compound republic are being referred to:

[A]nd according to the degree of pleasure and pride we feel in being republicans, ought to be our zeal in cherishing and supporting the character of Federalists. (Federalist 10: ML, 62; C, 65; R, 84)

It is federal principles that afford a remedy to republican diseases.

The method of compounding a republic through the concurrent operation of principles of self-government can be extended to a point where each decision maker is exposed to alternative decision-making arrangements. Thus, compounding republics can meet the criterion that no person can be a fit judge of his or her own cause in relation to the interest of others. Each person stands exposed to the actions and judgments of others; and each from an individual vantage point participates in the government of society.

A federal system of government permits each unit of government to deal with the size principle in a way that is congruent with both the spirit and form of republican government while permitting opportunity for orderly deliberations. Each elector can participate in diverse constituencies, and each unit of government will respond to the different interests of diverse constituencies. Thus, a federal constitution provides a happy circumstance for avoiding the paradox that a constituency be either too large or too small. According to Madison, "the great and aggregate interests" of a people can be reflected in large constituencies with reference to a national legislature, while "the local and particular" interests of a people can be reflected in smaller constituencies with reference to state legislatures or to local councils (Federalist 10: ML, 60; C, 63; R, 83).

By using concurrent and overlapping units of government to resolve the paradox posed by the size principle, further advantages flow from a federal constitution. A much larger territory and a much larger population can be brought within the compass of republican institutions. By extending the sphere of republican institutions, "you take in a greater variety of parties and interests; you make it less probable that a majority of the whole will have a common motive to invade the rights of other citizens" (Federalist 10: ML, 61; C, 64; R, 83). If a majority faction should usurp the public authority of one particular government to the detriment of its citizens, those citizens would have legitimate recourse to *alternative* units of government and alternative decision structures to advance their contentions and to seek resolution of their grievances.

On the basis of the reasoning inherent in a theory of federalism, Madison further concludes:

In the extended (and compound) republic of the United States, and among the great variety of interests, parties, and sects which it embraces, a coalition of a majority of the whole society could seldom take place on any other principles than those of justice and the general good. (Federalist 51: ML, 340–341; C, 352–353; R, 325. My parenthesis.)

The possibility of a majority faction dominating all decision structures in the compound republic of America is not precluded. But, the probability of that occurring is greatly reduced by organizing a democracy as a federal system of government. A coalition of the majority of the whole society exposed to challenge in diverse decision structures among concurrent governments would tend to search out decisions that are consistent with criteria of justice and the general good in the conduct of political affairs.

This reasoning led Madison to a further and more radical conclusion:

> [T]he larger the society, provided it lie within a practical sphere, the more duly capable it will be of self-government. (My emphasis.) And happily for the republican cause, the practicable sphere may be carried to a very great extent, by a judicious modification and mixture of the federal principle. (Federalist 51: ML, 341; C, 353; R, 325. Madison's emphasis.)

Madison elsewhere suggests that the "natural limit of a republic is that distance from the centre which will barely allow the representatives to meet as often as may be necessary for the administration of public affairs" (Federalist 14: ML, 81; C, 85; R, 101).

The implication of this reasoning suggests that tasks of constitutional innovation being undertaken in 1787 and 1788 might be repeated in the future to develop incremental units of government as new communities of interests arise. If people are prepared to act upon the principle that *all* political experiments be based upon the capacity of mankind for self-government, then the larger the society participating in a federal system of government, the more duly capable mankind will become of governing human affairs on the basis of reflection and choice. A theory of federalism, in short, provides an alternative to either imperialism or the reign of mutually destructive conflict in governing human affairs. Hamilton, Madison, and Jay signified their zeal for the *federal principle* by naming their work *The Federalist*.

CHAPTER SIX

Federal Structures and Their Implications

INTRODUCTION

In response to those who "have decried all free government as inconsistent with the order of society," Hamilton enumerates various devices for ameliorating the "imperfections" of republican government while retaining its "excellences." Among these arrangements he includes:

[1] the regular distribution of power into distinct departments; [2] the introduction of legislative balances and checks; [3] the institution of courts composed of judges holding their offices during good behavior; [4] the representation of the people in the legislature by deputies of their own election. (Federalist 9: ML, 48; C, 51; R, 72)

Each of these contributes to a division of labor in political decision making based upon qualified independence among decision makers rather than upon an unqualified structure of dependence in a superior-subordinate relationship.

Hamilton then proposes "ENLARGEMENT of the ORBIT," within which "popular systems of civil government" are to "revolve," as an essential remedy for the vicissitudes of petty republics (Federalist 9: ML, 49; C, 51–52; R, 73. Hamilton's emphasis). The central task is to extend the structure of political organization to a realm involving a community of interests among peoples comprising numerous republics. A formulation for this solution is derived from Montesquieu, with a significant modification being added in *The Federalist*.

In analyzing the problems of constituting a republic in relation to the requirement of defense against organized warfare, Montesquieu had concluded:

> If a republic be small, it is destroyed by a foreign force, if it be large, it is ruined by internal imperfection. (Montesquieu, 1966: 126)

This conclusion as applied to a unitary republic implies serious limits to a republican form of government. The size principle discussed in Chapter 5 implies that oligarchical tendencies in large republics will yield serious internal problems of institutional failure. Threats of external aggression mean that small republics are vulnerable to attack by large despotic neighbors. Thus, Montesquieu anticipates that both large and small republics are likely to fail for different reasons.

But, a different resolution can be derived for a compound republic. According to Montesquieu, as quoted by Hamilton, a "CONFEDERATE REPUBLIC" afforded "a kind of constitution that has all the internal advantages of a republican, together with the external force of a monarchical, government" (Federalist 9: ML, 50; C, 53; R, 74. Hamilton's emphasis). Hamilton continues to draw upon Montesquieu in the following:

> This form of government is a convention by which several smaller *states* agree to become members of a larger *one*, which they intend to form. It is a kind of assemblage of societies that constitute a new one, capable of increasing, by means of new associations, till they arrive to such a degree of power as to be able to provide for the security of the united body.
>
> A republic of this kind, able to withstand an external force, may support itself without any internal corruptions. The form of this society prevents all manner of inconveniences.
>
> If a single member should attempt to usurp the supreme authority, he could not be supposed to have an equal authority and credit in all the confederate states. Were he to have too great influ-

ence over one, this would alarm the rest. Were he to subdue a part, that which would still remain free might oppose him with forces independent of those which he had usurped, and overpower him before he could be settled in his usurpation.

Should a popular insurrection happen in one of the confederate states, the others are able to quell it. Should abuses creep into one part, they are reformed by those that remain sound. The state may be destroyed on one side, and not on the other; the confederacy may be dissolved, and the confederates preserve their sovereignty. (Federalist 9: ML, 50–51; C, 53–54; R, 74–75. Hamilton's emphasis.)

Given the basic assumptions in *The Federalist,* the superimposition of a simple, collective decision-making structure upon a number of existing states organized in their corporate capacities is insufficient to govern the affairs of a confederate republic (see Chapter 2). Thus, Montesquieu's concept of a confederation is vulnerable to the same erroneous conception that applied to the American confederation. Instead, it was necessary to constitute an additional political structure which would "carry its agency to the persons of the citizens" concurrently with previously established structures of government. A limited national government in a federal system of government could be formed to represent the American people in taking political decisions regarding matters which lay beyond the domain of individual states. As Madison observes, "The federal and State governments are in fact but different agents and trustees of the (same) people, constituted with different powers, and designed for different purposes" (Federalist 46: ML, 304–305; C, 315; R, 294. My parenthesis).

The new Federal or national government, thus, was to be a government with limited jurisdiction, but one of general competence within the scope of its limited jurisdiction. The competence of the respective units of government in the proposed federal system is summarized by Madison in the following observation:

[T]he general government is *not* to be charged with the *whole power* of making and administering laws. Its jurisdiction is limited to certain enumerated objects, which concern all the members of the republic, but which are not to be attained by the separate provision of any. The subordinate governments, which can extend their care to all those other objects which can be separately provided for, will retain their due authority and activity. (Federalist 14: ML, 82; C, 86; R, 102. My emphasis.)

Each government, state and national, was designed to have a will of its own and to have substantial independence from the other. Each could carry its agency to the person of the citizen, address itself to the hopes and fears of individuals, and "possess all the means, and have a right to resort to all the methods, of executing the powers with which it is intrusted" (Federalist 16: ML, 99; C, 103; R, 116). Those matters which could be separately provided would be subject to principles of self-government operative within each of the states. Those matters of common concern which could not be attained by the separate provisions of each state were subject to the concurrent operation of principles of self-government in a limited national government. Federal principles of organization provided a way of saving the advantages that Montesquieu had associated with a confederate republic while avoiding the conceptual errors that contributed to the failure of American confederation.

A major portion of *The Federalist* is preoccupied with a detailed examination of the powers assigned to the national government under the proposed constitution and how that assignment of authority would affect political relationships among the numerous governments in a federal system. Hamilton makes an extended analysis of the defense powers and of the powers of taxation. Madison's analysis examines each of the different powers assigned to the Federal government as to whether the grant of power was "necessary and proper." He is also concerned whether the aggregate powers—"the whole mass of them"—would be "dangerous to the portion of authority left in the several states" (Federalist 45: ML, 298; C, 308; R, 288). Their object was to maintain the essential legal and political independence of the states and of the Federal government so that each might govern in its sphere without being usurped by the prerogatives of the other. Their combined analysis indicates how they anticipate that a federal system of government would work.

THE USE OF MULTIPLE UNITS OF GOVERNMENT
TO PROVIDE FOR THE COMMON DEFENSE
AND INTERNAL SECURITY

The reasoning applicable to the assignment of authority to the national government to provide for the common defense has already been examined, in part (Chapter 2). While the states were denied authority to maintain a standing army or navy, they did retain authority to maintain a militia subject to such regulations as Congress might establish and subject to mobilization by the President as commander-in-chief in national emergencies. Even in matters of defense there were opportunities for concurrent exercise of political authority by both state and national governments although the national government was assigned the predominant weight of authority.

Constitutional Provision for the Common Defense

Provision for the common defense was a principal purpose of the Union; and Hamilton identifies as essential for that purpose the authority "to raise armies; to build and equip fleets; to prescribe rules for the government of both; to direct their operations; to provide for their support" (Federalist 23: ML, 142; C, 147; R, 153). Hamilton then emphasizes:

These powers ought to exist without limitation, *because it is impossible to foresee or define the extent and variety of national exigencies, or the correspondent extent and variety of the means which may be necessary to satisfy them.* The circumstances that endanger the safety of nations are infinite, and for this reason no constitutional shackles can wisely be imposed on the power to which the care of it is committed. (Federalist 23: ML, 142; C, 147; R, 153. Hamilton's emphasis.)

Hamilton argues that "the whole power" of making general provision for the common defense "was lodged in the *Legislature,* not in the **Executive**" (Federalist 24: ML, 148; C, 153; R, 158. Hamilton's emphasis). This power is limited by the condition that no appropriation of money to support an army can be made for a period of more than two years. The whole power to provide for the common defense is placed "in the hands of the representatives of the people" (Federalist 28: ML, 173; C, 178; R, 180).

The legislature of the United States will be *obliged,* by this provision, once at least in every two years, to deliberate upon the propriety of keeping a military force on foot; to come to a new resolution on the point; and to declare their sense of the matter, by a formal vote in the face of their constituents. They are not *at liberty* to vest in the executive department permanent funds for the support of an army, if they were ever incautious enough to be willing to repose in it so improper a confidence. (Federalist 26: ML, 163; C, 168; R, 171. Hamilton's emphasis.)

In addition, the proposed constitution would vest authority in the national legislature to regulate the militia since Congress would have power

to provide for organizing, arming, and disciplining the militia, and for governing such part of them as may be employed in the service of the United States, *reserving to the States respectively the appointment of the officers, and the authority of training the militia according to the discipline prescribed by Congress.* (Federalist 29: ML, 176; C, 181; R, 182. Hamilton's emphasis.)

Disposition of the forces provided by Congress (and of the militia of the several states when called into the service of the United States) was placed under the authority of the president as commander-in-chief. Exercise of executive authority by the president as commander-in-chief is subject to Congressional authority over defense policy and appropriation of funds to support a military establishment.

The Security Problem

Hamilton recognizes that "a wide ocean" separating the United States from Europe afforded significant protection to Americans, but he warned against "an excess of confidence or security" (Federalist 24: ML, 150; C, 155; R, 160). He calls attention to the dominions of two great European powers, Britain and Spain, on the North American continent. The "rear" was occupied by growing British settlements, and the remaining perimeter from Florida westward was occupied by Spain. These two European powers had a common interest in the maintenance of their dominions as against the Americans. In addition, "[T]he savage tribes on our Western frontier ought to be regarded as our natural enemies, their natural allies, because they have most to fear from us, and most to hope from them" (Federalist 24: ML, 151; C, 156; R, 161).

Britain and Spain were major maritime powers; and, in Hamilton's judgment, "[a] future concert of views between these nations ought not to be regarded as improbable" (Federalist 24: ML, 151; C, 156; R, 161). Apart from the potential threat of an alliance between Britain and Spain, the frontier required the maintenance of small garrisons to protect against Indian raids.

The Maintenance of Frontier Garrisons

Hamilton considers two alternatives for securing the frontier against sporadic Indian raids. Frontier garrisons might be maintained either by occasional detachments from the militia or by regular troops supported by the national government. The first alternative—use of the militia—is dismissed as "impracticable; and if practicable, would be pernicious" (Federalist 24: ML, 151; C, 156; R, 161). Men in the militia, Hamilton asserts, "would not long, if at all, submit to be dragged from their occupations and families to perform that most disagreeable duty in times of profound peace" (Federalist 24: ML, 151; C, 156; R, 161). The expense of a frequent rotation of service, the loss of labor, and the disruption of economic productivity would be among the costs of relying regularly upon the militia. This alternative would be "as burdensome and injurious to the public as ruinous to private citizens" (Federalist 24: ML, 151; C, 156; R, 161).

The second alternative—maintaining frontier garrisons by small corps of regular troops supported by the national government—would require a small standing army—"a small one, indeed, but not the less real for being small" (Federalist 24: ML, 151–152; C, 157; R, 161). Development of the western frontier depended upon the maintenance of posts for trade with the Indians and upon the security of settlers cultivating the resources of the frontier. Hamilton anticipates that as American strength and development in the frontier region increased, so would the British and Spanish efforts to augment their military establishments.

Similarly, a navy would be required to secure "our Atlantic side," and to protect American commerce, "[i]f we mean to be a commercial people" (Federalist 24: ML, 152; C, 157; R, 162). Dockyards, arsenals, fortifications, and garrisons would be required to defend those facilities from possible attack.

Separate Provision or Common Provision for the Common Defense

Hamilton characterizes these dangers as a *common* threat to the several states in the American Union:

The territories of Britain, Spain, and of the Indian nations in our neighborhood do not border on particular States, but encircle the Union from Maine to Georgia. (Federalist 25: ML, 153; C, 158; R, 163)

"The danger," he concludes, "though in different degrees, is therefore common" (Federalist 25: ML, 153; C, 158; R, 163).

Hamilton conceives "the primary principle of our political association" to require common measures to deal with common problems (Federalist 25: ML, 153; C, 158; R, 162–163). The means for guarding against a common danger "ought, in like manner, to be the objects of common councils and of a common treasury" (Federalist 25: ML, 153; C, 158; R, 163). Hamilton, in effect, argues that defense against a common threat requires a common enterprise based upon a general plan of action and supported by the common resources of a unit of government formed to tend to the common interests of the Union.

If each state acted separately in planning its own defense, some would find themselves more directly exposed than others. If required to act under "the plan of separate provisions, New York would have to sustain the whole weight of the establishments requisite to her immediate safety, and to the mediate or ultimate protection of her neighbors" (Federalist 25: ML, 153; C, 158; R, 163). Smaller states having less extensive commercial interests might in the short run rely upon the security afforded by the defense measures of a stronger neighbor. The short-term advantage of avoiding the costs of defense by relying upon the forces of a stronger neighbor would, according to Hamilton, be attended by various inconveniences which derive from a plan of separate provision. The states shouldering a disproportionately large share of the defense burden "would be as little able as willing, for a considerable time to come, to bear the burden of competent provision." If the larger states, then, acted to reduce their burden, insufficient provision for the common defense would follow. "The security of all would thus be subjected to the parsimony, improvidence, or inability of a part" (Federalist 25: ML, 153– 154; C, 158–159; R, 163).

If the interests of the people in each state were purely defensive, the stronger states, in providing for their own defense, would assume a large part of the burden to protect weaker neighbors. Weaker neighbors, taking advantage of the situation, would make little provision for defense and gain a comparative advantage by enjoying the protection of others without bearing a proportionate share of the costs. The people in the larger states perceiving their inequitable share of the burden would reduce defense expenditures. Thus, "the parsimony, improvidence, or inability" of each part to provide for the common good would lead to inadequate provision for the defense of the Union.

If two or three large states assumed a disproportionate burden for defending American interests against external threat, those states need not limit their strategic opportunities to purely defensive actions. A disproportionately large military force in the command of two or three states might cause the other states to "quickly take the alarm" (Federalist 25: ML, 154; C, 159; R, 163). Each would respond to the alarm by taking military countermeasures; and pretenses could easily be contrived to justify offensive action. And so, the logic of mutually destructive conflict would lead to the following situation:

[M]ilitary establishments, nourished by mutual jealousy, would be apt to swell beyond their natural or proper size; and being at the separate disposal of the members, they would be engines for the abridgment or demolition of the national authority. (Federalist 25: ML, 154; C, 159; R, 163)

This analysis led Hamilton to conclude that the proper constitutional solution is to leave provision for the common defense "to the discretion and prudence" (Federalist 24: ML, 152; C, 157; R, 162) of Congress. Congress would serve as a common council to authorize an appropriate force to assure the common defense of the American Union paid from a common treasury contributed to by people in each of the various states through uniform measures of taxation.

Insurrection or Disorder in Particular States

In addition to the common problems of continental defense, Hamilton also recognizes that disturbances to internal security may arise in any particular state. "If it should be a slight commotion in a small part of a State," Hamilton suggests that "the militia of the residue would be adequate to its suppression; and the natural presumption is that they would be ready to do their duty" (Federalist 28: ML, 171; C, 176; R, 178). The militia of a state would be adequate to such a task.

If, however, an "insurrection should pervade a whole State, or a principal part of it, the employment of a different kind of force might become unavoidable" (Federalist 28: ML, 171; C, 177; R, 178). The capacity of a state to supplement the use of its own militia by being able to draw upon the forces of the Union might be essential in preserving the public peace. Hamilton concludes that

> whether we have one government for all the States, or different governments for different parcels of them, or even if there should be an entire separation of the States, there might sometimes be a necessity to make use of a force constituted differently from the militia, to preserve the peace of the community and to maintain the just authority of the laws against those violent invasions of them which amount to insurrections and rebellions. (Federalist 28: ML, 172; C, 178; R, 179)

Hamilton argues that a mix of forces may be required for internal security and for the common defense. The authority to mobilize such forces should reside in the national legislature, and the means for securing the rights and privileges of the people are to be derived from placing "the whole powers of the proposed government . . . in the hands of the representatives of the people" (Federalist 28: ML, 173; C, 178; R, 180).

Hamilton's Preferred Solution to the Problems of Common Defense and Internal Security

Hamilton, in Federalist 29, takes a posture of advising a Federal legislator from New York about establishing an appropriate mix of forces if the proposed constitution were ratified. In considering "the proper establishment of the militia," Hamilton advises the prospective legislator that "[t]he attention of the government ought particularly to be directed to the formation of a select corps of moderate extent, upon such prin-

ciples as will really fit them for service in case of need" (Federalist 29: ML, 179; C, 184; R, 185). A well-trained militia would
then be available when the defense of a state requires such a
force. A select, well-trained militia available for service in each
of the states would lessen the need for regular military forces.
If an army of any magnitude should be required for the common defense, such an army "can never be formidable to the
liberties of the people while there is a large body of citizens,
little, if at all, inferior to them in discipline and the use of arms,
who stand ready to defend their own rights and those of their
fellow-citizens" (Federalist 29: ML, 179; C, 184; R, 185).

Thus, Hamilton's optimal solution is a mixed force of: (1) a
select corps of well-trained militiamen in each state available
for the defense of that state or for mobilization by the United
States for the common defense, and (2) a complement of national forces to man frontier garrisons and to provide for the
common defense of all of the states. The common defense
and internal security of the United States would thus be provided by a combination of forces maintained by the coordinated actions of the state and national governments operating
as concurrent units of government. This solution, Hamilton
concludes, "appears to me the only substitute that can be devised for a standing army, and the best possible security
against it, if it should exist" (Federalist 29: ML, 179; C, 184–
185; R, 185).

Hamilton's formulation of his preferred solution comes
after considering some of the costs that should be avoided in
a "project of disciplining *all* the militia of the United States"
(Federalist 29: ML, 178; C, 183; R, 184. My emphasis). Any
such "scheme of disciplining the whole nation must be abandoned as mischievous or impracticable" (Federalist 29: ML,
179; C, 184; R, 185). Hamilton anticipated some of the consequences from such a scheme:

[T]o oblige the great body of the yeomanry, and . . . other classes of
citizens, to be under arms for the purpose of going through military
exercises and evolutions, as often as might be necessary to acquire

the degree of perfection which would entitle them to the character
of a well-regulated militia, would be a real grievance to the people,
and a serious public inconvenience and loss. It would form an annual deduction from the productive labor of the country, to an
amount which, calculating upon the present numbers of the people,
would not fall far short of the whole expense of the civil establishments of all the States. To attempt a thing which would abridge the
mass of labor and industry to so considerable an extent, would be
unwise: and the experiment, if made, could not succeed, because it
would not long be endured. (Federalist 29: ML, 178; C, 184; R,
184–185)

Use of Military Force to Usurp Political Authority

Hamilton's analysis of the problem of common defense and
internal security also includes implied reference to the use of
militia in each state as security against a military coup or the
usurpation of national authority by a standing army. Both
Hamilton and Madison give explicit consideration to the possibility that military force might be used to usurp national political authority, and thus to destroy the American experiment
in constitutional government. Both of their analyses indicate
the significance of a federal system of government in extending people's control over their institutions of government.

In a unitary state, Hamilton contemplates that the usurpation of authority through military force by persons entrusted
with supreme political powers is a feasible undertaking. He
says that the people of different "parcels," "districts," or
"subdivisions,"

having no distinct government in each, can take no regular measures
for defence. The citizens must rush tumultuously to arms, without
concert, without system, without resource; except in their courage
and despair. The usurpers, clothed with the forms of legal authority,
can too often crush the opposition in embryo. (Federalist 28: ML,
173; C, 178–179; R, 180)

But, in a federal system with its concurrent structures of governmental authority, Hamilton anticipates a different outcome. The people can master their own fate, he concludes, by using one government to check the usurpations of the other.

[T]he people, by throwing themselves into either scale, will infallibly make it preponderate. If their rights are invaded by either, they can make use of the other as the instrument of redress. . . .

It may safely be received as an axiom in our political system, that the State governments will, in all possible contingencies, afford complete security against invasions of the public liberty by the national authority. Projects of usurpation cannot be masked under pretences so likely to escape the penetration of select bodies of men, as of the people at large. The legislatures will have better means of information. They can discover the danger at a distance; and possessing all the organs of civil power, and the confidence of the people, they can at once adopt a regular plan of opposition, in which they can combine all the resources of the community. They can readily communicate with each other in the different States, and unite their common forces for the protection of their common liberty. (Federalist 28: ML, 174; C, 179–180; R, 181)

With two overlapping sets of governments operating concurrently upon the same constituencies, people have a choice of one or the other in realizing their relative advantage. Instead of a monopoly of political authority, people in a federal system are confronted with a choice among political authorities. One can be used as a countervailing power in dealing with the other.

Madison also considers the prospect of military force being used to usurp political authority. On the one hand, he postulates the maximum size for a standing army given the conditions of that period. He juxtaposes the opposition of a militia "of citizens with arms in their hands, officered by men chosen from among themselves, fighting for their common liberties, and united and conducted by governments possessing their affections and confidence" (Federalist 46: ML, 310; C,

321; R, 299). He considers a successful military coup to be a highly improbable event under those circumstances. He then comments:

Besides the advantage of being armed, which the Americans possess over the people of almost every other nation, the existence of subordinate governments, to which the people are attached, and by which the militia officers are appointed, forms a barrier against the enterprises of ambition, more insurmountable than any which a simple government of any form can admit of. Notwithstanding the military establishments in the several kingdoms of Europe, which are carried as far as the public resources will bear, the governments are afraid to trust the people with arms. And it is not certain, that with this aid alone they would not be able to shake off their yokes. But were the people to possess the additional advantages of local governments chosen by themselves, who could collect the national will and direct the national force, and of officers appointed out of the militia, by these governments, and attached both to them and to the militia, it may be affirmed with the greatest assurance, that the throne of every tyranny in Europe would be speedily overturned in spite of the legions which surround it. Let us not insult the free and gallant citizens of America with the suspicion, that they would be less able to defend the rights of which they would be in actual possession, than the debased subjects of arbitrary power would be to rescue theirs from the hands of their oppressors. Let us rather no longer insult them with the supposition that they can ever reduce themselves to the necessity of making the experiment, by a blind and tame submission to the long train of insidious measures which must precede and produce it. (Federalist 46: ML, 310–311; C, 321–322; R, 299–300)

It is quite clear from these analyses that the authors of *The Federalist* use their political theory to be a tool for reasoning about hypothetical problems in order to draw inferences regarding likely or probable consequences. Given the same problem—the possibility of a military coup—they anticipated different consequences to be derived from varying structural characteristics in two different systems of government. The political structure of a compound republic permits the derivation of different solutions to the problem of a military coup than does the political structure of a simple or unitary republic.

Hamilton's analysis of the problem of defense and internal security reveals surprising parallels to the work of contemporary political economists like Mancur Olson (1965) and Thomas Schelling (1963). Hamilton's concept that a common danger should be met by common council through a common treasury is entirely congruent with the contemporary theory of public goods. Separate provision for the common defense is apt to lead to insufficient provision in the absence of a unit of government of appropriate size to deal with the common problem. He also recognizes that matters of internal security may require forces to deal with local matters and that local provision may be more responsive to those local needs. In the case of a military coup to usurp national political authority both Hamilton and Madison recognize that alternative units of government can facilitate the efforts of people to cope successfully with such a coup. A federal system of government affords distinct advantages over simple republics in providing for internal security and the common defense. The prevalence of military dictatorships in the world at large becomes more comprehensible.

CONCURRENT JURISDICTION IN TAXATION

In Federalist 30–36, Hamilton analyzes problems of public finance in a federal system of concurrent governments. These essays deserve careful study for what they have to say about federalism as a theory of overlapping governmental jurisdictions, and how such a system of government can be financed. My treatment of Hamilton's discussion is highly selective. Hamilton's analysis of public finance will be examined only as it applies to the operation of a federal system of government.

Predominant authority over foreign affairs, the common defense, interstate commerce, and related matters would, under the proposed constitution, be exercised by a national government. The supremacy of national law in matters of national affairs is essential if a limited national government is to manage those affairs that apply to the American Union.

"[I]n the article of taxation," Hamilton argues that "CON-CURRENT JURISDICTION . . . (is) the only admissible substitute for an entire subordination, in respect to this branch of power, of the State authority to that of the Union" (Federalist 33: ML, 202–203; C, 208; R, 205. Hamilton's emphasis. My parenthesis). This argument assumes that future demands for public revenue by the different governments in a federal system cannot be effectively anticipated. Assignment of exclusive authority to levy particular types of taxes would result in an inequitable imposition of tax burdens in the long run.

Hamilton assumes that the constitution of civil governments should not be based upon existing contingencies, but upon a calculation of "the probable exigencies of ages, according to the natural and tried course of human affairs" (Federalist 34: ML, 204; C, 210; R, 207). A constitution, thus, needs to provide for a capability to handle any exigency in its scope of authority. If warfare with its logic of mutually destructive conflict continues to reign in the affairs of nations, Hamilton anticipates that expenditures for national defense could dwarf other expenditures. He indicates that expenditures for warfare, defense, and related purposes absorbed fourteen-fifteenths of British national expenditures. Only one-fifteenth was devoted to the domestic welfare of the British people. Hamilton contemplates that comparable demands for national expenditures might, in the long run, significantly exceed the demand for state expenditures.

If the revenues of the national government were limited exclusively to import duties, Hamilton estimates that the states would have access to the largest share of potential revenue sources. In the long run, the national government might be burdened with the larger public expenditures. Hamilton then analyzes the consequences which would flow from levying excessively burdensome import duties to meet defense expenditures. Among the consequences he anticipates are the following:

One:

Exorbitant duties on imported articles would beget a general spirit of smuggling. . . . (Federalist 35: ML, 210; C, 216; R, 212)

Two:

(A general spirit of smuggling) is always prejudicial to the fair trader, and eventually to the (supply of) revenue itself. (Federalist 35: ML, 210; C, 216; R, 212. My parentheses.)

Three:

(Exorbitant duties) tend to render other classes of the community tributary, in an improper degree, to the manufacturing classes, to whom they give a premature monopoly of the markets. . . . (Federalist 35: ML, 210; C, 216; R, 212. My parenthesis.)

Four:

(Exorbitant duties) sometimes force industry out of its more natural channels into others in which it flows with less advantage. . . . (Federalist 35: ML, 210; C, 216; R, 212. My parenthesis.)

Five:

(Exorbitant duties) would be attended with inequality . . . between the manufacturing and the non-manufacturing States. (Federalist 35: ML, 211; C, 217; R, 212–213. My parenthesis.)

Six:

(The manufacturing States) would not, therefore . . . contribute to the public treasury in a ratio to their abilities. (Federalist 35: ML, 211; C, 217; R, 213. My parenthesis.)

Thus, Hamilton demonstrates that arbitrary allocation of tax sources is apt to cause exorbitant rates to be levied if supply cannot be apportioned to changing patterns of demand. Exorbitant rates, in turn, create incentives to violate the law, to affect adversely the supply of revenue, to alter the distribution of income in a society by giving quasi-monopoly advantages to some, and to place the burdens of payment upon those least able to pay. From this logic Hamilton concludes that "the most productive system of finance will always be the least burdensome" (Federalist 36: ML, 216; C, 222; R, 217).

Sound taxation would require that those responsible for the levying of taxes should have "a thorough knowledge of the principles of political economy" in order to anticipate the consequences of different taxing policies and have "a knowledge of the interests and feelings of the people" (Federalist 35: ML, 215–216; C, 221–222; R, 216–217). *The supply of revenue should be derived from those sources which involve the least cost in burdens imposed upon the people.* "The man who understands those principles best will be least likely to resort to oppressive expedients, or to sacrifice any particular class of citizens to the procurement of revenue" (Federalist 36: ML, 216; C, 222; R, 216–217).

If concurrent jurisdiction existed in the exercise of taxing authority, the question arises whether a dual authority would not give rise to the specter of "double sets of revenue officers" and "a duplication of their (the people's) burdens by double taxations" (Federalist 36: ML, 221; C, 227; R, 221. My parenthesis.). Hamilton pursues a careful analysis which dismisses the arguments raising the specter of duplicate effort and double taxation as representing "all the ingenious dexterity of political legerdemain (deception)" (Federalist 36: ML, 221; C, 227; R, 221. My parenthesis.).

Hamilton's analysis breaks revenue collection into a special case where Federal authorities have exclusive jurisdiction over collecting tariffs or import duties. A comparable control by states can be expected in those fields of revenue collected exclusively under state regulation. If the United States should enter a field of revenue already occupied by state regulation, Hamilton anticipates that "the United States will . . . make use of the State officers and State regulations for collecting the additional imposition" (Federalist 36: ML, 221; C, 227; R, 221). This solution, he suggests, "will best answer the views of revenue, because it will save expense in the collection, and will best avoid any occasion of disgust to the State governments and to the people" (Federalist 36: ML, 221; C, 227–228; R, 221–222). Instead of simply imposing an added expense for collecting Federal revenue upon state administrations, Hamilton clearly implies that such cooperative arrangements would depend upon mutual advantage when he observes:

[T]he most certain road to the accomplishment of its (the Union's) aim would be to employ the State officers as much as possible, and to attach them to the Union by an accumulation of their emoluments. This would serve to turn the tide of State influence into the channels of the national government, instead of making federal influence flow in an opposite and adverse current. (Federalist 36: ML, 222; C, 228; R, 222. My parenthesis.)

Hamilton clearly anticipates transfers of payment between state and Federal governments to facilitate coordinated arrangements among cooperating jurisdictions.

Rather than create a fully duplicate, separate administrative system, Hamilton suggests that the interests of national administration will be served by cooperative arrangements with state agencies so that both will gain the advantage of joint action and avoid the prospects of mutually exclusive rivalry. Thus, he anticipates that "[t]he national legislature can make use of the *system of each State within that State*" (Federalist 36: ML, 219; C, 226; R, 220. Hamilton's emphasis). Using the system internal to each state as an adjunct to national administration is readily available only when the state does not possess a formal veto on national programs and when the national legislature has authority to devise its own independent system of administration. Both are free to consider cooperative arrangements as long as each is free to consider alternative forms of action.

Responding to the double-taxation argument, Hamilton turns to the problem of proportioning the supply of revenue among the diverse units of government comprising a federal union. He assumes that the aggregate "wants of the Union are

to be supplied in one way or another" so that, "if to be done by
the authority of the federal government, it will not be done by
that of the State government" (Federalist 36: ML, 222; C, 228;
R, 222). Holding the aggregate supply of tax revenue constant, Hamilton considers whether an "advantage" or an
economy of scale will exist when provision is made through
the national government. He argues affirmatively that the
supply of tax revenues from commercial endeavors "can be
prudently improved to a much greater extent under federal
than under State regulation, and of course will render it less
necessary to recur to more inconvenient methods . . ." (Federalist 36: ML, 222; C, 228; R, 222). Local entrepreneurs may
be disadvantaged where high local taxes adversely affect their
competitive viability with other entrepreneurs who pay low
taxes and compete in the same market. Such disadvantage
can be avoided by levying taxes through an enlarged taxing
jurisdiction which would apply to all producers competing in
any given market. As the relevant market increases in domain, the larger jurisdiction will have an advantage in collecting tax revenues.

Hamilton also argues that a national administration has a
natural advantage in being able to tax the rich and

in making the luxury of the rich tributary to the public treasury, in
order to diminish the necessity of those impositions which might
create dissatisfaction in the poorer and most numerous classes of the
society. Happy it is when the interest which the government has in
the preservation of its own power, coincides with a proper distribution of the public burdens, and tends to guard the least wealthy
part of the community from oppression! (Federalist 36: ML, 222–
223; C, 229; R, 222–223)

In short, Hamilton anticipates that the larger unit of government will have an advantage in being able to levy commercial
imposts upon the more inclusive marketing area within a nation and thus better assure redistribution of income from the
most advantaged to the least advantaged classes of society.

An ability to benefit from the diverse scales of organization inherent in a federal system of government is based on the assumption that one unit of government can transfer fiscal resources to other units of government in order to realize a greater aggregate advantage for the people in such a political system. Hamilton clearly anticipates a cooperative federalism based upon joint administration of public services through intergovernmental agreements. Hamilton explicitly states the basic premise for a cooperative federalism in the following way:

As neither can *control* the other, each will have an obvious and sensible interest in . . . reciprocal forebearance. And where there is an *immediate* common interest, we may safely count upon its operation. (Federalist 36: ML, 221; C, 227; R, 221. Hamilton's emphasis.)

Thus, concurrent jurisdiction provides the foundation for a cooperative federalism among different units of government capable of exercising independent authority among overlapping jurisdictions.

Hamilton's treatment of defense and public finance examines two major problems of public administration in a federal system. Cooperation and coordinated action among various agencies at different levels of government is the hallmark of administration in a federal system. His emphasis upon cooperation among agencies at diverse levels of government clearly precludes any assumption that American public administration would become a centralized bureaucracy controlled from a single center of authority. His theory of executive organization in Federalist 66–77 is a special theory of administration concerned with the national executive establishment. His general theory of administration is elaborated in his consideration of defense and fiscal problems in Federalist 23–36.

A federal system of government with overlapping jurisdictions depends, then, not upon integrated hierarchy of command to gain coordination among diverse jurisdictions, but

upon a variety of different cooperative and joint arrangements. Again, the modern theory of public goods enables us
to understand that the primary difficulties requiring collective organization in a public economy occur on the consumption side of economic relationships. Powers of taxation and
the enforcement of rules and regulations among a community of users require recourse to powers of government. So
long as such powers are competently organized among diverse units of government it is possible for such units of governments to operate essentially as consumer cooperatives that
are capable of contracting with private vendors, nonprofit organizations, or other units of government to produce public
goods and services. Quasi-market structures can exist in public economies giving rise to different patterns of public administration than those that occur in highly centralized bureaucracies. A highly federalized system of administration
takes advantage of overlapping jurisdictions to generate competitive pressures toward increasing efficiency and responsiveness in the operation of service-delivery systems.[1]

POLITICAL REPRESENTATION IN A SYSTEM
OF CONCURRENT GOVERNMENTS

At numerous junctures in *The Federalist* both Hamilton and
Madison discuss the special effect that concurrent units of
government will have upon political representation. Madison
notes "the happy circumstance" in a federal constitutional system which permits "local and particular interest" to be represented in state legislatures while "the great and aggregate interests" of the people are represented in a national legislature
(Federalist 10: ML, 60; C, 63; R, 83).

Both Madison and Hamilton recognize circumstances
where persons occupying offices in state or local governments
may also represent and articulate national interests related to
national problems. In a military coup, for example. Madison

suggests that the representatives of the people acting through their offices in *local* government "could collect the *national* will and direct the *national* force" to resist the usurpation of national authority by a military regime (Federalist 46: ML, 311; C, 322; R, 300. My emphasis). In this case, local officials would come to the defense of the national interest and attempt to thwart an effort to usurp national authority by military force.

At another point, Hamilton indicates that "the support of a military force will always be a favorable topic for declamation" (Federalist 26: ML, 163; C, 168; R, 171–172). He anticipates that "the party in opposition" will arouse and attract public attention to the subject. If the majority should be disposed to exceed the proper limits in support of the military, Hamilton expects the party in opposition to warn the community against the danger. Apart from the parties in the national legislature, Hamilton also indicates,

the State legislatures, who will always be not only vigilant but suspicious and jealous guardians of the rights of the citizens against encroachments from the federal government, will constantly have their attention awake to the conduct of the national rulers, and will be ready enough, if anything improper appears, to sound the alarm to the people, and not only to be the VOICE, but, if necessary, the ARM of their discontent. (Federalist 26: ML, 163–164; C, 169; R, 172. Hamilton's emphasis.)

Persons holding state and local governmental office, thus, occupy positions of political authority to make decisions within the competence of that authority. At the same time, they can use their positions to represent the interests of their constituents in other matters within the competence of other governmental authorities. State governors, for example, have prerogatives as executive officers within the political structure of particular states; by virtue of those political prerogatives, governors are also free to speak out in representing the interests of their constituents in national political affairs. State offi-

cials perform significant political functions in representing
their constituencies within both the state political arenas and
the national political arena. The political independence of
governors or state legislators make them freer to speak out
than a senior Federal civil servant occupying a subordinate
position in a regional office of a national agency. A federal political system consequently gives fuller representation to a
greater diversity of interests than does a unitary state.

Madison, in defending biennial election of members to the
House of Representatives as against allegations favoring annual elections, indicates that the choice of a constitutional rule
for the Federal legislature must recognize that "the federal
legislature will possess a part only of that supreme legislative
authority which is vested completely in the British Parliament . . ." (Federalist 52: ML, 346; C, 358; R, 329). In addition, he argues that "the federal legislature will not only be
restrained by its dependence on the people, as other legislative bodies are, but that it will be . . . watched and controlled
by the several collateral legislatures, which other legislative
bodies are not" (Federalist 52: ML, 346; C, 359; R, 330). Collateral legislatures in a federal structure of government thus
safeguard republican principles of popular control by virtue
of the redundant set of representatives available to each
constituent.

The significance of concurrent jurisdiction is further indicated in Hamilton's discussion of the constitutional provision
prescribing the "times, places, and manner of holding elections for senators and representatives." This authority is initially extended to the legislatures of each state; but Congress
is assigned authority to "at any time, by law, make or alter
such regulations. . . . " The concurrent jurisdiction of Congress is considered essential by Hamilton on the assumption
that "*every government ought to contain in itself the means of its own
preservation*" (Federalist 59: ML, 384; C, 398; R, 362. Hamilton's emphasis). In other words, each unit of government in a
federal system should be able to maintain essential indepen-

dence within the scope of its prerogative as against any other unit of government. The point is further emphasized:

[A]n exclusive power of regulating elections for the national government, in the hands of the State legislatures, would leave the existence of the Union entirely at their mercy. They could at any moment annihilate it, by neglecting to provide for the choice of persons to administer its affairs. (Federalist 59: ML, 385; C, 399; R, 363)

With a system of concurrent governments giving each constituent a multiplicity of political representatives and with concurrent jurisdiction giving different units of government authority over times, places, and manners of holding elections, we might anticipate that the political practices in a compound republic will manifest a great diversity in political strategies. The conditions defining strategic opportunities for factions, parties, and coalitions to participate in the political process will vary widely. Thus, organizations can be expected to aggregate and disaggregate for different contests at different periods in time. Stable coalitions based upon a capacity to dominate a single center of authority will not be maintained in the long run.

CONCURRENT JURISDICTION OF THE STATE AND NATIONAL JUDICIARY

In considering the organization of the judiciary, Hamilton concludes, as he did in examining taxation, that significant areas of concurrent jurisdiction "would diminish the motives to the multiplication of federal courts, and would admit of arrangements calculated to contract the appellate jurisdiction of the Supreme Court" (Federalist 83: ML, 538; C, 557; R, 495). The original and appellate jurisdiction of the U.S. Supreme Court is defined to permit Federal courts to take cognizance of essential interests of parties in state courts involving controversies related to the U.S. Constitution and to Federal law. The judicial power of any court looks beyond

local and municipal law and examines the law relevant to the
dispute between the parties who are within its jurisdiction.
The Constitution and the laws of the United States require
state courts to give full faith and credit to the laws of other
states as well as the domestic law of their own state. As a consequence, Hamilton suggests that in the American judiciary
"the national and State systems are to be regarded as ONE
WHOLE" (Federalist 82: ML, 537; C, 556; R, 494. Hamilton's
emphasis). Again, people have access to justice in more than
one set of courts where they can assert their claims whenever
one set of officials may impair rights guaranteed by concurrent units of government in a federal system of government.

THE PURSUIT OF COMPARATIVE ADVANTAGE IN A
COMPOUND REPUBLIC

A federal political system implies that any individual is a
member of and able to function in the context of different
autonomous political communities. If account is taken of
what Hamilton calls "the *system of each State within that State*"
(Federalist 36: ML, 219; C, 226; R, 220. Hamilton's emphasis), several political structures are available to each individual. Each individual has diverse representatives, each of
whom is capable of participating in authoritative action in
the context of some one unit of government and of acting in
other units of government as a spokesperson for constituent
interests.

Each unit of government would be capable of taking collective decisions to provide public goods and services for
its political community. If mutual advantage can be gained
when two or more units of government act cooperatively to
provide a public good, Hamilton anticipates that such cooperative arrangements will develop. On the other hand, if
two or more such associations pursue interests detrimental
to each other, such conflicts presume a latent mutuality of
interests which can only be resolved by reference to a larger,

more inclusive political community. Thus, unresolved conflicts between two or more states require the development of incremental political structures for the government of national affairs involving the common interests of several states. The incremental unit of government would require authority to act on behalf of that common interest and to meet the costs of collective ventures from a common treasury.

Both Hamilton and Madison recognize that the general constitution of a federal political system can only be based upon the predominant authority of a more inclusive unit of government in dealing with problems transcending the affairs of existing units of government. Hamilton put this conclusion in the following way:

> If a number of political societies enter into a larger political society, the laws which the latter may enact, pursuant to the powers intrusted to it by its constitution, must necessarily be supreme over those societies, and the individuals of whom they are composed. It would otherwise be a mere treaty, dependent on the good faith of the parties, and not a government. . . . (Federalist 33: ML, 201; C, 207; R, 204)

This principle is, presumably, as applicable to the European Community in its relationship to member-nations as it was to a Federal government in its relationship to state governments.

As Hamilton's discussion of the problems of common defense so carefully indicates, constitutional assignment of authority providing for the common defense need not exclude the several states from defending their collective interests against insurrection and other disturbances. The states should not be free to war among themselves or upon the Union. Consequently, the political authority of the national regime must prevail in the *regulation* of state militia. The training and command of the militia was to be under the administration of state authorities except when called into Federal service. By implication, the states should not stand entirely dependent upon national authority in maintaining their peace and internal security. In the extreme case, the people should also be able to defend themselves through the agency of state and local authorities against military usurpation of national authority.

The constitution of the American federal system thus assumes that each political jurisdiction should be able to maintain an essential independence of action in tending to the collective interests of a political community, but to do so in a way that is congruent with the interests of its own constituents and of those in other jurisdictions. Madison's concern with whether the powers transferred to the Federal government would be dangerous to the authority left in the several states was one of maintaining an independent capability for each state to act on behalf of the collective interests of the persons comprising that state.

So long as such independence of action exists, people, as members of diverse units of government, are free to take best advantage of the diverse opportunities in each unit of government for advancing their collective welfare. People can look to different sets of authorities to provide them with the best combinations of public goods and services given their preferences and resources. People are thus confronted with several different purveyors of public goods and services, each offering somewhat different capabilities in the goods and services it can provide separately or cooperatively by joint action with other purveyors. So long as each unit of government remains essentially independent of the others, people have a choice as among alternative purveyors of public goods and services. They have a choice as among competing oligopolists rather than no choice in dealing with monopoly power. The power of a buyer is significantly enhanced if the buyer can act through the collective agency of an association in bargaining with a monopolist or with the freedom to choose from the services provided by several potential monopolists who compete with each other for the favor of a common clientele in overlapping markets.

Madison clearly anticipates that this rivalry by Federal authorities to provide services for the American people will in the long run affect the balance between the relative influence of national and state agencies. Thus, he concludes:

> If, therefore, . . . the people should in future become more partial to the federal than to the State governments, the change can only result from such manifest and irresistible proofs of a better administration, as will overcome all their antecedent propensities (to favor the states). (Federalist 46: ML, 306; C, 317; R, 295. My parenthesis.)

The opportunity to take advantage of the better alternative is a choice that ought to be available to people. "And in that case," Madison argues,

> the people ought not surely to be precluded from giving most of their confidence where they may discover it to be most due. . . . (Federalist 46: ML, 306; C, 317; R, 295)

However, the inherent advantage would not always be on the side of Federal authorities. "[I]t is only within a certain sphere that the federal power can, in the nature of things, be advantageously administered" (Federalist 46: ML, 306; C, 317; R, 295). To use contemporary language, it is "in the nature of things" to reflect *diverse economies of scale*. In the nature of *some* things the national government will realize a greater advantage in tending to large-scale problems. In the nature of *other* things, state and local instrumentalities of governments will realize a greater advantage in tending problems of smaller scale. A system of government organized through concurrent units of government will enable individuals to take best advantage of the opportunities afforded by each different unit of government. That advantage can occur only as long as one unit of government, or set of governments, cannot dominate all other units of government.

Authority in each unit of government must, as a consequence, be structured in a way that constrains decision making within proper limits and prevents anyone from usurping political authority in any one unit of government and endangering the independence of authorities in other units of government. The predominance of the most inclusive unit of government in a federal system of government implies that the constitutional distribution of authority of a *limited* national government is of special significance if limits are to be maintained. That problem is addressed in the next chapter.

NOTES

1. These potentials inherent in the logic of a federal system are more fully explored in V. Ostrom (1973; 1974).

CHAPTER SEVEN

The Distribution of Authority in the Organization of the National Government

THE NECESSARY CONDITION OF POLITICAL INEQUALITY

In discussing the principle of political constraint, we concluded earlier that any government depends upon an unequal allocation, exercise, and control of decision-making capabilities among the persons comprising its relevant political community. For any government to enforce law and act in the common benefit of its community, a rule of individual sovereignty must be relaxed. Any unit of government, thus, depends upon a capacity to take decisions which will be binding upon all persons in its jurisdiction. Madison's discussion of the principle of majority vote clearly articulates the presumption that a majority can take decisions which will bind a minority. Such a condition directly implies inequality in political authority and in the exercise of decision-making capabilities among those individuals who comprise a majority as against those who comprise a minority.

In response to a charge that the House of Representatives would be composed of "that class of citizens which will have least sympathy with the mass of the people, and be the most likely to aim at an ambitious sacrifice of the many to the aggrandizement of the few," the authors of *The Federalist* contend that such an argument, while "levelled against a pretended oligarchy, . . . strikes at the very root of republican government." Multitudes cannot deliberate and govern in the aggregate. A distinguishing characteristic of a republican form of government is its "elective mode of obtaining rulers" subject to "the most effectual precautions for keeping them virtuous whilst they continue to hold their public trust" (Federalist 57: ML, 370; C, 384; R, 350). In every large unit of government, the constraint of the size principle necessarily implies that a very small fraction of the population will make decisions that are binding upon others. All systems of government enable a few to exercise the extraordinary powers of government in relation to others.

Political inequality, as a necessary condition of any government, need not, however, be unconstrained or unlimited. The viability of a democratic republic depends upon a capacity to limit and constrain the conduct of the few who exercise the extraordinary prerogatives of governmental authority. All "free governments," as Hamilton characterizes democratic republics, would indeed be "inconsistent with the order of society" (Federalist 9: ML, 48; C, 51; R, 72) if the conduct of political officials could not be limited and constrained by the scrutiny and actions of other public officials and the authority of individual persons. Thus, "[t]he constant aim is to divide and arrange the several offices in such a manner as that each may be a check on the other—that the private interest of every individual may be a sentinel over the public rights" (Federalist 51: ML, 337; C, 349; R, 322). "These inventions of prudence," Madison asserts, "cannot be less requisite in the distribution of the supreme powers of the State" than in the subordinate positions of a society (Federalist 51: ML, 337–338; C, 349; R, 322).

The principle of political inequality is accepted by the authors of *The Federalist* as a necessary condition in the organization of any government. For societies of men to establish good government from reflection and choice, they must be able to devise ways and means for constraining and limiting the authority of those who are vested with the prerogatives of government. The resolution of this problem depends upon the general theory of a limited constitution (Federalist 81: ML, 524; C, 543; R, 482). The doctrine of the separation of powers, and the related concept of checks and balances, is an essential part of the American theory of constitutional choice. This doctrine is especially important in constituting a *limited* national government.

CONSTITUTIONAL RULE AND THE SEPARATION OF POWERS

The American theory of constitutional choice, as indicated in Chapter 3, assumes that the basic constitutional rules governing the exercise of governmental authority are *not alterable* by those exercising the immediate prerogatives of government. The alteration of basic constitutional rules, instead, depends upon extraordinary processes of constitutional decision making which lie beyond the legal and political competence of regular governmental authorities. The acts of persons exercising political authority under a constitution are governed by the provisions of that constitution. Thus, the exercise of prerogative by governmental authorities is subject to juridical determination of its validity in light of constitutional law. If invalid, official acts are held to be null and void. Officials, in that case, act without authority. They are potentially liable as individual persons for the wrongs they may have committed when acting beyond the bounds of their authority. The legal integrity of a constitution can be maintained so long as there are individuals willing to challenge unconstitutional acts of officials, and there are judges of sufficient independence to render judgments in accordance with the principles of a limited constitution.

When supreme authority is vested in a single center of authority, distinctions between constitutional decision making and governmental decision making can no longer be made. Such a supreme authority would both enact legislation and judge its constitutional validity at one and the same place. A limited constitution cannot be enforced unless the juridical claims of those who challenge the validity of legislative action can be determined by some authority other than those who enact legislation. Consequently, a political system organized in accordance with the principles of a limited constitution *must necessarily* separate power among different decision structures if limits are to be enforceable as constitutional law. The concept of separation of powers, thus, is a logically necessary element of a general theory of *limited* constitutions.

The organization of decision-making arrangements in a limited constitutional system of government requires ways and means for taking collective action that limits the exercise of discretion by all public authorities. Madison is well aware that "in every political institution, a power to advance the public happiness involves a discretion which may be misapplied and abused" (Federalist 41: ML, 260; C, 269; R, 255–256). He is also aware that "parchment barriers" are insufficient to prevent "the encroaching spirit of power" (Federalist 48: ML, 321; C, 333; R, 308). If discretion could be misapplied or abused, "parchment barriers" are insufficient security against the usurpation of political authority to the advantage of a ruling elite. "A dependence on the people is," Madison contends, "no doubt, the primary control on the government; but experience has taught mankind the necessity of auxiliary precautions" (Federalist 51: ML, 337; C, 349; R, 322).

Madison pursues a carefully reasoned analysis regarding the dispersion of decision-making authority among three great "departments" of government—the legislative, the executive, and the judicial. To Madison, "[T]he accumulation of all powers, legislative, executive, and judiciary, in the same hands . . . may justly be pronounced the very definition of tyranny" (Federalist 47: ML, 313; C, 324; R, 301). Those three departments are instruments for taking authoritative action on behalf of a political community. The separate departments must each act independently to take and enforce collective decisions; but collective action depends upon the concurrent exercise of authority through legislative, executive, and judicial instrumentalities of government. Any one department must be prevented from usurping the authority of the others lest a ruling faction gain dominance over the exercise of all authority and abuse its discretion to the detriment of "other citizens, or to the permanent and aggregate interests of the community" (Federalist 10: ML, 54; C, 57; R, 78).

By separating the formulation of law from the enforcement of law, and the determination of the appropriate application of law both from the formulation and enforcement of law, the language of law presumably acquires a public character where its meaning is determinable by independently acting officials. Establishing such publicness of meaning by providing independent opportunities to challenge the application of law helps to safeguard the interests of those who are subject to the enforcement of law. Law acquires a public integrity when its meaning can be independently established as a separate basis for executive action and for judicial determination. Opportunities to test and establish the public meaning of law occur when authority for formulating law, enforcing law, and determining the propriety of its application is separately and independently exercised by different decision structures that share definable and limited responsibilities in the governance of society.

Madison's analysis of the separation-of-powers doctrine first demonstrates that an exclusive and complete separation of powers is not possible. He construes Montesquieu's maxims that "there can be no liberty where the legislative and executive powers are united in the same person, or body of magistrates" or "if the power of judging be not separated from the legislative and executive powers" to mean that "where the *whole* power of one department is exercised by the same hands which possess the *whole* power of another department, the fundamental principles of a free constitution are subverted" (Federalist 47: ML, 314–315; C, 325–326; R, 302–303. Madison's emphasis).

Madison, thus, contends that Montesquieu "did *not* (my emphasis) mean that these departments ought to have no *partial agency* in, or no *control* over, the acts of each other" (Federalist

47: ML, 314; C, 325; R, 302. Madison's emphasis). Examining the constitutions of the several states, Madison concludes that "there is no single instance in which the several departments of power have been kept absolutely separate and distinct" (Federalist 47: ML, 314; C, 325; R, 302). The New Hampshire constitution expressed the need for partial interdependency among decision structures when it indicated that the separate departments

ought to be kept as separate from, and independent of, each other *as the nature of a free government will admit; or as is consistent with that chain of connection that binds the whole fabric of the constitution in one indissoluble bond of unity and amity.* (Federalist 47: ML, 316; C, 327; R, 304. Madison's emphasis.)

Instead of an absolute separation of powers, Madison contends that partial interdependence among separate decision structures is necessary. A separation of powers implies a sharing of powers in taking collective action, as Daniel Elazar often emphasizes.

To secure the necessary degree of independence, each department must be able to exercise potential veto positions in relation to the others so as "to give each a constitutional control over the others . . . " (Federalist 48: ML, 321; C, 332; R, 308). Each department has its constitutional prerogatives defined by authority to discharge essential prerogatives; but such authority is also limited by the formulation of potential veto positions which can be exercised by other departments. Each decision structure acts within appropriate latitudes defined by constitutional rules, but other decision structures hold potential veto positions and thus establish limits upon each of those who exercise the political prerogatives of government.

Maintenance of a limited constitutional order can only be assured, in Madison's analysis, by "contriving the interior structure of the government as that its several constituent parts may, by their mutual relations, be the means of keeping each other in their proper places" (Federalist 51: ML, 336; C, 347–

348; R, 320). A set of potential veto positions requires those exercising the political prerogatives of any one department or branch of government to take account of those in other departments in attempting to reach agreeable and workable decisions for the government as a whole. Thus, each is governed within the limits of the potential veto positions which can be exercised by the others. The capacity of such a system to govern depends upon the capacity of each part to reach agreement within the potential veto positions of each other part. Where a part has a power of veto in relation to the whole, the operation of the whole requires that all of the parts be in concurrence.[1]

When a government is constituted so that several decision structures are limited by the veto positions of each part, Madison insists that "each . . . should have a will of its own" (Federalist 51: ML, 336; C, 348; R, 321). If any one department is to be free to exercise a potential veto, it must maintain essential independence from each other department. Thus, Madison concludes, members of each department should have as little dependence as possible upon the tenure of persons serving in other departments. The members of each department should derive their tenure from different constituencies. Those constituencies depend, directly or indirectly, upon the citizenry of the Union. The principal exception to this rule applies to the judiciary; and Madison anticipates that the permanent tenure of judges will destroy their dependence upon the authority conferring appointment. Similarly, "the members of each department should be as little dependent as possible on those of the others, for the emoluments annexed to their offices" (Federalist 51: ML, 337; C, 348; R, 321). Those who administer each department must have "the necessary constitutional means and personal motives to resist encroachments of the others" (Federalist 51: ML, 337; C, 349; R, 321–322) if the system of government is to be governed in accordance with the decision rules of a limited constitutional order.

THE DISTRIBUTION OF AUTHORITY FOR LEGISLATION
IN THE GOVERNMENT OF NATIONAL AFFAIRS

Approximately one third of *The Federalist* papers are an analysis of the principal decision structures designed to govern national affairs in the American Union. These arrangements
comprise the portion of the American political formula most
familiar to students of American government. I see no purpose in dwelling upon those familiar features except briefly to
illustrate the essential points in Madison's argument regarding: (1) the conditions for assuring the independence of each
decision structure and (2) the use of potential veto positions
for establishing limits to the authority of any one decision
structure.

   Hamilton, at a much earlier juncture, had indicated that
"[g]overnment implies the power of making laws" (Federalist
15: ML, 91; C, 95; R, 110). While the *execution* of law is essential in any government, determining the scope and limits of
government authority depends especially upon the scope and
limits of *legislative* authority. Legislative authority establishes
the basic decision rules for authorizing executive action. In
the following discussion consideration is, therefore, given
only to the exercise of legislative authority for the United
States as a national political community. If the two houses of
Congress are considered separately, three of the four principal decision structures provided for in the U.S. Constitution
are based upon three different modes of representation,
three distinct sets of constituencies, and three distinctly different terms of office.

Modes of Representation

Representation in the House of Representatives was to be assigned on the basis of population. Representatives were to be
elected in each state by electors having the same qualifications
as the electors of the most numerous branch of that state's legislature. Two Senators were to be elected from each state by

the legislature of that state. The President was to be selected by a number of electors, equal to the number of Representatives and Senators from each state, to be appointed in each state in such manner as the legislature of that state might decide. *No member* of the U.S. Senate or of the House of Representatives and *no person* holding an office of profit or trust from the United States was eligible to serve as an elector for purposes of electing a president of the United States.

Representation of Diverse Constituencies

The three sets of constituencies would permit the representation of diverse sets of interests in developing national policies. The House of Representatives was constituted on the assumption that "the representative ought to be acquainted with the interests and circumstances of his constituents" (Federalist 56: ML, 365–366; C, 379; R, 346). Such a deliberative body would be composed of members representing the disparate and discrete interests of the American electorate. The deliberation of such representatives would be derived from "a local knowledge of their respective districts" (Federalist 56: ML, 367; C, 380; R, 348).

The Senate affords equal representation to the different states and an opportunity to articulate the interests of the smaller as well as the larger states. On population alone, the four largest states would have had a voting majority in the House of Representatives. "[A] coalition of a very few States" would have been sufficient to "overrule the opposition" without the concurrent operation of the Senate as a legislative body (Federalist 58: ML, 378; C, 392; R, 357).

The president, on the other hand, would be elected by electors where no single state nor any permanently organized body of men—the members of the national legislature or the national administration—could directly dominate the selection. As a consequence of these precautions, Hamilton anticipates that the electoral arrangements for selecting a president would require such talents and merits as will "establish him in

the esteem and confidence of the whole Union, or of so considerable a portion of it as would be necessary to make him a
successful candidate for the distinguished office of President
of the United States"[2] (Federalist 68: ML, 444; C, 460–461;
R, 414).

Rather than consider local interests as selfish interests and
therefore to be ignored, the designers of the U.S. Constitution consider such interests essential to the formulation of national policy and allow for those interests to be specifically articulated in the House of Representatives. The interests of
small states are as essential as the interests of large states in
the organization of the Senate. On the other hand, election
of the President was devised to articulate interests that can
win the esteem and confidence of the Union as a whole.

The three sets of interests can be articulated with equal
merit only so long as a coalition is prevented from using the
authority of one decision structure to preempt the selection of
personnel and to dominate the decisions of those occupying
positions of authority in other decision structures. The essential condition for national legislation is the concurrence of decision makers representing these three sets of constituent interests—local, state, and national—in the formulation of
national policy. Arrangements internal to the national government are constituted to take account of the interests of
other political associations and constituencies forming essential elements in a compound republic.

Tenure in Office

Variations in the terms of office also minimize the prospect
that an election for one office will dominate elections to other
offices. Attention to "the happiness of the people" and knowledge appropriate to the objects of national legislation and foreign affairs are essential for selecting appropriate terms of
office (Federalist 62: ML, 404; C, 419; R, 308). A two-year
term for members of the House of Representatives reflects a
priority for responsiveness to the changing opinions and sen-

timents of the population. A six-year term for Senators reflects a greater priority upon the importance of a knowledge in foreign affairs and a continuity in public policy. A four-year term for President, with opportunity for re-election, is considered appropriate for a due dependence upon the people and for an informed competence in national affairs.

The structural components incorporated into the constitution of each separate decision structure in the national government are designed to represent disparate sets of interests and assure that each is capable of exercising an independence from the other. Different sets of constituencies, different modes of election, and varying terms of office contribute to structural differences reflected in the House of Representatives, the Senate, and the presidency. In short, the internal constitution of decision structures in the national government must take account of a great diversity of interests in a compound republic. A disparate constitution for each different decision structure provides increased opportunity for representing more diverse interests.

Separate and disparate decision structures can express distinctive interests only to the extent that each is taken into account in formulating any particular course of action. Each has a "voice" only if each can say "no" in the course of making a decision. Thus, we must examine the conditions that give each decision structure a "voice" or "say" in the enactment of legislation.

Decision Rules and Veto Positions

In the constitutional assignment of authority for *legislative* action, each department is assigned special prerogative. The president, as chief executive, for example, is specifically assigned legislative prerogatives in advising Congress on the state of the Union and in recommending for legislative consideration such matters as are deemed necessary. Congress can exercise an independent capability for ascertaining the state of the Union and for considering its own and other recommendations for legislative action. A president can recommend an agenda for legislative considerations; but each house of Congress is free to set its own agenda.

Constitutional provisions for the proceedings of each house of Congress permit legislative action to be taken by less than a majority of all members. A simple majority of the members of each house constitutes a quorum for general legislative purposes; and a majority of a quorum meets the minimal constitutional requirement for enacting legislation. If more than a majority were required for a quorum, a minority would exercise an effective veto by absenting itself from legislative deliberations. Action by a majority of a quorum encourages each member to be present and to cast a vote to influence the course of a decision. Thus, majority votes will tend to prevail although only a majority of a quorum meets the constitutional requisites for enacting legislation.

Legislation approved by each house of Congress must, in turn, be presented to the president for approval before it can become law. If the president disapproves, the legislation must be enacted by a two-thirds majority of each house of Congress before it becomes law. The Presidential veto thus gives the president a voting strength in the legislative process approximately equivalent to one sixth of the membership of each house in Congress. A president on his own authority can execute a suspensive veto and require Congress to reconsider its previous action; a president supported by one member more than one third of the members of *either* house of Congress can sustain an absolute veto over an act of Congress.

In addition to the Presidential veto, Hamilton, in discussing the constitutional authority of the judiciary, recognizes that "there is not a syllable in the plan under consideration (i.e., the U.S. Constitution) which *directly* empowers the national courts to construe the laws according to the spirit of the Constitution" (Federalist 81: ML, 524; c, 543; R, 482. Hamilton's emphasis). However, "the general theory of a limited constitution" (Federalist 81: ML, 524; C, 543; R, 482) implies such authority: "[W]henever a particular statute contravenes the Constitution, it will be the duty of the judicial tribunals to adhere to the latter and disregard the former" (Federalist 78: ML, 507; C, 526; R, 468). Thus, an independent judiciary can render judgment upon any infraction of the Constitution by any governmental authority established under a limited constitution. The judicial department can, on behalf of a constitutionally valid argument advanced by any plaintiff, exercise a potential veto position in relation to legislation which goes beyond the bounds of explicit constitutional authority. Each individual, through such exercise of judicial prerogative, has access to a potential veto of governmental authority.

The structure of American national government is so contrived, to paraphrase Madison, that (1) its constituent parts reflect disparate, but not mutually exclusive, sets of interests essential to the consideration and realization of the general welfare; (2) each part is organized to have a will of its own; and (3) each part, by its constitutional relations with the other parts, supplies means for keeping each in its proper place. Thus, the separation of powers is an "auxiliary precaution" for the control of government in addition to "a dependence on the people" derived from the "elective mode of obtaining rulers."

The capacity of each department or branch of government to check or veto the other implies that no one department or branch can dominate the rest, but that the processes of government occur within bounds of discretion established by the respective veto positions. Instrumentalities of government can then make decisions within the decision space that is bounded by respective veto positions. The task in creating and maintaining the political feasibility of any program is that of searching out those conditions that are mutually agreeable to the diverse decision structures that can exercise potential veto capabilities. Decisions may be delayed for some time if strong veto positions exist. This is why a system of separation of powers entails both "checks" and "balances." Power is shared within the limits of veto positions as check points. Governance occurs within an equilibrating system that has recourse to many decision points and processes.

A compound republic, then, is not only a compound of multiple, autonomous units of government in a federal system of government; it is also a compound of decision structures within each unit of government. Such a system would fail if any one decision structure or unit of government gained dominance over the rest and maintained that dominance through time. Maintaining such a compounding of structures in conjunction within a multitude of veto positions depends essentially upon the operation of constitutions as enforceable law. So long as people understand the basic concepts that are inherent in the logic of such relationships and have the appropriate structures available for properly using such concepts to implement and bind relationships with one another and with those who exercise the prerogatives of government, we might expect such a system of organized complexity to work in practice. A compound republic is one where principles of constitutional choice are reiterated to regulate and control relationships both among units of government and among decision structures within units of government. The viability of such a system turns critically upon the authority exercised by persons in the governance of political relationships.

Reciprocity in political relationships also depends upon the claims which individual persons can make and enforce upon public authorities. We shall turn to the issue posed by the concept of inalienable rights, or authority of persons, inherent in a general theory of the limited constitution, before we assess the general significance of this "auxiliary precaution" for the maintenance of a republican system of government.

THE AUTHORITY OF PERSONS IN THE GOVERNANCE OF POLITICAL RELATIONSHIPS

In discussing the judicial department, Hamilton finds it necessary to define the concept of a limited constitution as a condition requiring "[t]he complete independence of the courts of justice." A limited constitution is defined as "one which contains certain specified exceptions to the legislative authority; such, for instance, as that it shall pass no bills of attainder, no *ex-post-facto* laws, and the like" (Federalist 78: ML, 505; C, 524; R, 466. Hamilton's emphasis). Hamilton then observes:

Limitations of this kind can be preserved in practice no other way than through the medium of courts of justice, whose duty it must be to declare all acts contrary to the manifest tenor of the Constitution void. Without this, all the reservations of particular rights or privileges would amount to nothing. (Federalist 78: ML, 505; C, 524; R, 466)

Hamilton's reference to the term "legislative authority," in this context, should probably be construed broadly to mean governmental authority in general. "Government," as we have already noted, is defined by Hamilton as "the power of making laws" (Federalist 15: ML, 91; C, 95; R, 110). Thus, the scope of governmental authority can be defined by the scope and limitations placed upon the exercise of legislative authority.

Since, in Hamilton's political science, "the persons of the citizens" (Federalist 16: ML, 98; C, 102; R, 116) are "the only proper objects of government" (Federalist 15: ML, 91; C, 95; R, 109), his theory of the limited constitution implies that limitations upon the law-making powers of a government involve the rights of persons. The courts are obliged to uphold the rights of persons in the face of legislative action which exceeds the constitutional limits of legislative authority. "No legislative act . . . contrary to the Constitution," Hamilton insists, "can be valid" (Federalist 78: ML, 505; C, 524; R, 467).

If political representatives are to be bound by the limits of authority delegated to them, the practical question in any political system is: Who can be a competent judge of constitutional authority? Hamilton rejects the assumption that a legislative body can be a competent constitutional judge of its own powers. In such a case, the representatives of the people could substitute their will for the will of the people. Instead, he concludes:

It is far more rational to suppose, that the *courts* were designed to be an intermediate body between the *people* and the *legislature,* in order, among other things, to keep the latter within the limits assigned to their authority. The interpretation of law is the proper and peculiar province of the courts. A constitution is, in fact, and must be regarded by the judges, as a fundamental law. It therefore belongs to them to ascertain its meaning, as well as the meaning of any particular act proceeding from the legislative body. If there should happen to be an irreconcilable variance between the two, that which has the superior obligation and validity ought, of course, to be preferred; or, in other words, the Constitution ought to be preferred to the statute, the intention of the *people* to the intention of their *agents.* (Federalist 78: ML, 506; C, 525; R, 467. My emphasis.)

The critical question in this analysis turns upon *who is entitled to speak for "the people"* when there is a conflict of law arising between the "intention of the people" expressed in a constitution and "the intention of their agents" expressed in a statutory enactment. Hamilton does not directly answer this question. The primary thrust of his analysis is to justify "[t]he complete independence of the courts of justice" (Federalist 78: ML, 505; C, 524; R, 466).

The only answer I can derive from Hamilton's reasoning, or from the political theory of a compound republic more generally, is that *every individual person, or every association of individuals* recognized as having legal personality is entitled to exercise a claim to right under constitutional prerogative in challenging the validity of actions taken by governmental authorities pursuant to the Constitution. In other words, *any person* is entitled to claim rights reserved to the people and not granted to a government under a limited constitution when one's individual interests are adversely affected. In a conflict between the provisions of a constitution and the provisions of a statute, a court is obliged to hear the claim of *any person*

whose interest is adversely affected and to render judgment
adhering to the provisions of the constitution and disregard-
ing the statute if it is contrary to the Constitution.

Hamilton also suggests:

> Until the people have, by some solemn and authoritative act, an-
> nulled or changed the established form, it is binding upon them-
> selves collectively, as well as individually; and no presumption, or
> even knowledge, of their sentiments, can warrant their represen-
> tatives in a departure from it, prior to such an act. (Federalist 78:
> ML, 509; C, 527–528; R, 470)

If a constitution binds a people both in their collective capacities and in their individual capacities, then each individual is
entitled to exercise a right derived from his authority as a person to claim benefits to which he is entitled as an individual
member of a collectivity. Such authority derives from the
terms of a constitution; and constitutional provisions defining
the rights of persons are a matter of constitutional prerogative binding upon those who assume responsibility for the exercise of governmental authority.

Constitutional provisions specifying limits upon the exercise of governmental authority and other constitutional provisions specifying the right of persons are thus correlative legal
propositions. A right of *any person* implies a limitation upon
the authority of those who exercise governmental prerogative;
a prohibition against governmental action implies that a commensurate constitutional authority is reserved for exercise by
any person. A definition of the authority of persons can derive from a correlative formulation of limitations on the authority of a government (see Commons, 1959: 65–117).

Thus, a general theory of limited constitutions implies that
a constitutional definition of the authority of persons is a necessary condition for imposing limits upon the condition of political inequality. The exercise of governmental prerogatives
on behalf of members of a political community by a relatively
few persons in such a community is a necessary condition in

the government of any society. *The critical question in a constitutional republic turns upon the authority that* ANY PERSON *can exercise in making and enforcing lawful claims upon governmental authorities regarding the proper discharge of their governmental prerogatives.* The authority which any person can claim, or the inalienable rights which any individual can assert, is an essential element in the structure of a system of constitutional government where the conduct of rulers is to be subject to the rule of law. Individuals have access to potential veto capabilities through the judiciary that can be used to impose limits upon those who exercise governmental prerogatives.

Conclusions about the constitutional standing of the individual authority of persons poses a serious dilemma. For individuals to test the limits of governmental authority requires that they be willing to refuse to obey those authorities and seek a determination by a court of law about the propriety of such actions. A person must determine to his or her own satisfaction that an official action was improper and then be willing to submit his or her determination to the independent judgment of the courts. The maintenance of limits upon governmental authority turns critically upon the willingness of citizens to refuse to obey ordinary law when they are convinced that such laws violate the basic terms of constitutional law and to be willing to pay the price of an adverse decision that may well entail fines, imprisonment, or both.

The maintenance of a system of constitutional law, thus, depends upon the willingness of citizens to exercise the basic judgments about what are the proper limits of governmental authority. Citizens must be willing to pay the price of challenging the improper exercise of authority in a lawful way so that the issues can be determined first in courts of law and secondly, in the larger political arena that pertains to the capacity of people to function in processes of constitutional decision making. Civil disobedience, then, is a fundamental part of the political processes of a constitutional system of government. Terror and violence are not justified. Refusal to obey ordinary law contrary to fundamental precepts of justice and constitutional law is justified. Processes afforded by judicial remedies and reasoned efforts to persuade one's fellow citizens are the appropriate methods for justifying one's refusal to obey ordinary law. It is only then that human beings can aspire to live in a lawful society where governmental officials are themselves subject to a rule of law. Martin Luther King's "Letter from Birmingham Jail" properly presents the burden of citizenship in a constitutional republic if the representatives of the people are not to become superior to and masters over the people, to paraphrase Hamilton's discussion of the implications that follow from the general theory of limited constitutions.

A further issue arises with regard to the authority of persons to act positively in procuring the enforcement of law and commanding the services of officials under the general terms of public law. The peace of the community, for example, may depend upon the capacity of political authorities to take collective action in defining lawful relationships among the people of a community, and to take coercive measures against persons who may act to injure others and thus threaten the peace of the community. The capability of any individual to partake in the peace of the community will depend upon one's authority to command officials to act on behalf of one's lawful claims when those interests are threatened by the unlawful actions of others. If police, for example, are not available upon the command of anyone to enforce laws for the common benefit of all members of the community, then a common benefit is not being provided for everyone. If *anyone* can command the provision of a common good or service then *everyone* adhering to lawful standards of conduct can benefit. Otherwise, governments will provide *selective* benefits for only *some* members of the community; favoritism and corruption will then reign.

The authority or political prerogatives of persons, thus, rests upon two grounds. The first derives from the constitutional prerogatives of persons as defined either in a bill of rights or in limitations upon the exercise of governmental authority. Several essential formulations of the rights of persons derive from: (1) limitations contained in Article I, defining Federal legislative powers, (2) the constitutional limits placed upon the exercise of governmental authority by the states in Article IV, and (3) the provisions included in the several constitutional amendments which formed the Bill of Rights. In addition to these constitutional sources defining the rights of persons, grounds for the authority of persons may also derive from a right to make claims upon public officials for services which are to be rendered by law to all persons in like circumstances who are entitled to the provision of any particular public good or service.

Entitlements under general rules of law are not subject to exclusive determination by executive officials. Persons entitled to benefits under general rules of law may also function in an executive capacity and invoke judicial authority to command the services of officials. Writs of mandamus and of injunction can be used either to compel official action or to enjoin official action. Individual persons can, in these circumstances, function in executive capacities as well as governmental officials.

In either case, whether the political prerogative of persons derives from constitutional authority or from statutory authority entitling persons to the provision of a public service, the authority of persons can be expressed as a claim asserted by any one person. In this sense, we can speak of an any-one rule as being requisite to the maintenance of a rule of law in a constitutional republic. An any-one rule is as essential to political choice in a democratic society as any other decision rule including that of majority rule.

Substantive powers inherent in the authority of persons pertains to the capacity of persons to govern their own affairs and to participate in an open public realm that is not subject to dominance by governmental authorities. In a democracy, each individual can be viewed as first his or her own governor. Prerogatives associated with constitutional guarantees of individual rights pertain to the individual standing of persons, their capacity to enter into contractual relationships with other persons, and to undertake joint activities in voluntary association with others. There is a realm where individuals assume primary responsibility for the governance of their own affairs.

Constitutional provisions establishing an individual's entitlement to due process of law implies that those who exercise governmental authority are obliged to conduct themselves and discharge their prerogatives in nonarbitrary ways. Due process implies that the procedures and processes of government are required to meet specifiable conditions for rendering decisions in the exercise of governmental authority. These conditions relate to standards of impartiality and justice that are assumed to apply in the discharge of governmental prerogatives.

In addition, provisions that bear upon freedom of speech, press, and assembly, have the effect of guaranteeing that individuals in a democracy can maintain an open public realm that is not subject to governmental domination. Citizens are free to communicate with one another about public affairs and reach conclusions that provide a basis for independent judgments about matters of common concern. Informed citizenship depends upon the maintenance of a public realm where people can freely communicate with one another.

Constitutional prerogatives also establish the authority of persons to participate directly or indirectly in the processes of government. Election of officials to discharge the prerogatives of government involves an indirect participation in governmental decision making. Citizens participate directly in processes of judicial decision making when they serve as members of juries and grand juries. In many state constitutions, citizens also directly participate in processes of legislation and constitutional revision through processes of initiative and referendum. All of these circumstances enable citizens to monitor the discharge of public trust on the part of those who exercise the prerogatives of government.

THE STRATEGIC OPPORTUNITIES FOR
DUE DELIBERATION

The organization of governmental authority based on separate decision structures, with disparate constitutions for each part, provides a variety of opportunities for persons, acting individually and collectively, to express their preferences and to make demands upon governmental authorities. Political remedies are available through the limited tenure of office held by members of Congress and by the President and Vice-President. Legislative remedies are available through the redundant representation offered by members of the House of Representatives and the Senate. Administrative remedies are available through the executive obligation to take care that the laws be faithfully executed. Judicial remedies are available under the requirements of due process of law entitling any person to a consideration of his bill of complaint and a plea for judgment to redress a wrong. Finally, constitutional remedies may be available in the form of action to alter and revise a constitution itself.

The accessibility of diverse decision structures to the demands of persons acting individually or collectively provides an increased probability that grievances will become known and taken into account in public deliberation. Hamilton states the basic assumption bearing upon the efficacy of such decision-making arrangements when he observes that:

the oftener . . . [a] measure is brought under examination, the greater the diversity in the situations of those who are to examine it, the less must be the danger of those errors which flow from want of due deliberation, or of those missteps which proceed from the contagion of some common passion or interest. (Federalist 73: ML, 477; C, 495; R, 443)

Hamilton concedes that "the power of preventing bad laws" also involves the power of "preventing good ones" (Federalist 73: ML, 478; C, 496; R, 443). But where disagreements prevail to such an extent that people will avail themselves of alternative remedies, we can only infer that those who disagree perceive the consequences flowing from the adoption of a "measure" to be more costly than the expenses entailed in seeking alternative solutions. It is often better to risk delay in the presence of substantial disagreement than to risk failure to calculate the costs of precipitous action.

A corollary of Hamilton's proposition and one of equally general application is asserted by Madison when he states, "[W]here there is a consciousness of unjust or dishonorable purposes, communication is always checked by distrust in proportion to the number whose concurrence is necessary" (Federalist 10: ML, 61; C, 64; R, 83). Madison implies that unjust and dishonorable purposes are most likely to succeed where open and public scrutiny is *not* assured by an opportunity to require examination of such schemes in a diversity of situations. The capacity of any person to claim remedies as a lawful exercise of his constitutional prerogative in relation to diverse decision structures is a means for assuring open and public scrutiny of unjust and dishonorable schemes.

The risk inherent in acting too quickly compared to the risk of acting too slowly depends in part upon the danger involved and the element of potential surprise. The appropriateness of decision rules contained in a constitution thus depends upon the capability of taking and implementing decisions under varying contingencies. The one area where precipitous action can be undertaken without significant constitutional constraint is in the discharge of the prerogatives of the president as commander-in-chief of the armed forces. The rationale for so little constitutional constraint in mobilizing forces essential to national security has already been examined in terms of the logic of organized warfare. To impede a quick response to a forceful military adventure by an adversary is to court disaster.

The prerogative of commander-in-chief also enables a president to precipitate military adventures through his own initiative. Such a possibility cannot be foreclosed, but the wisdom of such a measure is subject to reconsideration in al-

ternative decision-making arrangements in a compound republic. A president's tenure is limited. His reelection or the
election of another to the presidency provides opportunity to
reconsider the merit of his actions. Congress may make its own
assessments and is free to consider the merit of presidential
actions. Opportunities are afforded to elect new representatives to Congress every two years. Finally, the judiciary may also
consider the lawfulness of official actions wherever individuals may be prepared to challenge those actions as violating
the requirements of due process of law in the taking of life,
liberty, or property as instruments of warfare. In short, the
one-person rule inherent in the prerogatives of commander-
in-chief permits presidents to act with great dispatch. The
remedies applicable to presidential fallibility can be invoked
only after the fact. The costs may be very high. But, even a
president is not a proper judge of his own cause except in the
very short run.

When disagreement prevails, Hamilton concludes: (1) the
more frequently a measure is examined and (2) the greater
the diversity in the situations of those who examine it, the
greater the opportunities for exercising reason and justice in
governing human affairs. To the extent these conditions are
met, he anticipates a diminution of error derived from human fallibility and a reduction in the opportunities available
to a majority faction to realize preemptive advantage at the
expense of others by usurping the political process.

A basic puzzle remains. Drawing upon the principle of opposite and rival interests to create a system of government
where the several offices are arranged in such a manner that
each can be a check upon the other creates a potentiality for
stalemate and immobility on the part of governments rather
than due deliberation and a reduction of propensities to err.
Such possibilities exist and cannot be foreclosed simply by the
way that institutions of government are designed. The resolution of this puzzle depends upon the shared level of understanding held by citizens in a democracy about the methods of

inquiry that are appropriate to the processing of conflict and the attainment of conflict resolution.

It is entirely possible for societies to exist where relationships are ones of latent, if not manifest, warfare among different elements of the society. Politics becomes a struggle of one faction to gain dominance over another faction. Each views the other either as an oppressor or as a fundamental threat to stability. Veto capabilities with opportunities for due deliberation can then be a prelude to stalemate and to violence. A system of constitutional rule cannot be maintained under such conditions.

By contrast, it is also possible for people in human societies to recognize conflict as a manifestation of an interdependency of interests that have reference to implicit or inchoate communities of interest. The occurrence of conflict is then recognized as inviting inquiry about the nature of the contending interests, the nature of the interdependent relationships, and the conditions where those interests might become complementary to one another within a larger community of interests. Such a community of interests would then be characterized by reciprocity in a system of mutually productive relationships. Conflict is viewed as an occasion for invoking processes of inquiry that lead to conflict resolution. From this perspective, political structures are, as Hamilton suggests, but diversely structured situations for due deliberation in the processing of human conflicts and in the attainment of conflict resolution.

Madison's conception of using opposite and rival interests in building structures of human governance will not suffice to prevent people from warring upon one another where the other is viewed as the enemy with whom one shares no potential community of interest. Nor is the conception of opposite and rival interests one where competing interests simply cancel one another out. Rather, a structure of opposite and rival interests is a prelude to methods of inquiry that enable human beings to use the exigencies of conflict to explore possibilities and to move toward resolutions that are the basis for fashioning mutually productive communities of relationships. Federalism, thus, implies a method of inquiry for developing and maintaining diversely structured communities of relationships in which the relationships of both rulers and ruled are bounded by rules of law and commonly accepted standards of judgment. Federal systems of government can only be expected to work when those who use instrumentalities of government also *know how* to make ***proper*** use of them.

CONCLUSION

The political theory of a compound republic, thus, is based upon an assumption that the principle of political constraint can be used to minimize the prospects of a preemptive advantage on the part of some, especially a majority faction, to dominate decisions and exploit others. Such arrangements permit anyone to use both time and diversely structured institutional facilities to articulate essential interests. No single structure dominates. Instead, the assumption is made that any decision may be based upon erroneous conceptions without proper calculation of both individually relevant consequences and community relevant consequences. The prospects for error-correcting strategies are enhanced when decision makers and interested parties have the opportunity to challenge prevailing assumptions, to propose alternative conceptions, and to participate in processes of reasoned deliberation.

These are but some precautions for assuring members of a political community that "leading individuals in the communities," who comprise the ruling elite, would *not* "[abuse] the confidence they possessed; and assuming the pretext of some public motive . . . sacrifice the national tranquillity to personal advantage or personal gratification" (Federalist 6: ML, 28; C, 29; R, 54). "[G]eneral or remote considerations of policy, utility, or justice" can prevail only if "momentary passions, and immediate interests" are not to have "a more active and imperious control over human conduct" (Federalist 6: ML, 30; C, 31; R, 56). Constraint is requisite for the application of reason and justice in human affairs. The principle of political constraint must, in short, apply to the conduct of rulers as well as to the ruled.

A properly designed constitution can specify the structural conditions where all exercises of authority are subject to the limits of constitutional law and no one can exercise unlimited authority. No one is allowed to be the ultimate judge of his or her own cause in relation to the interests of others. Each exercise of authority is subject to an accountability to others. But, the ultimate burden for maintaining such limits turns upon the willingness of citizens to resist the improper exercise of authority by governmental officials, to know the grounds for making such judgments and using appropriate methods for seeking redress. The necessary and sufficient conditions for maintaining a system of constitutional government where governmental officials are themselves subject to a rule of law depends not only upon a proper structure, but upon a knowledge of what is improper and unjust and a willingness to act upon that knowledge. When these conditions are reiterated in a federal system of government, we can understand how the improbable becomes possible. It is possible, albeit improbable, that people might establish and maintain "good government from reflection and choice." We increase the probability of that possibility when we have a knowledgeable awareness of those terms and conditions.

NOTES

1. This restates the general veto theorem formulated by W. Ross Ashby in *Design for a Brain* and in *An Introduction to Cybernetics*. Ashby's veto theorem and his analysis of adaptation in a multistable system is surprisingly congruent with Hamilton and Madison's formulation of the political theory of a compound republic.

2. Criticism of the electoral arrangement for selecting the president of the United States rarely takes account of the essential argument advanced in *The Federalist* to justify that device. Care was taken to prevent members of Congress or of the Federal executive from

dominating the line of succession to the presidency. Long-term instability of the congressional caucus in determining presidential succession should have been anticipated.

It is also reasonable to expect that no one could have been elected president without prior consultation and prior candidacy of particular persons if electors are elected by states and are expected to assemble and cast their votes in each separate state.

A revolution had been organized and conducted by committees of correspondence and by a government organized by various congresses and conventions composed of persons representing the different states. In light of such extended experience in organizing coalitions of interests on continental proportions, I infer that Madison and Hamilton expected candidacies to be organized and consultations to occur in the selection of the president and vice-president. Their principal concern was that such selections not be dominated by any permanently established body, such as the Congress or the Federal executive.

We can then ask whether the convention system is congruent with the electoral formula established for selecting the president; or whether the conventions are to be considered as "any preexisting bodies of men, who might be tampered with beforehand to prostitute their votes" (Federalist 68: ML, 442; C, 459; R, 413). If the systems of state law arranging for the nomination and election of the president have provided for a succession of men who hold "the esteem and confidence of the whole Union," and are capable of discharging the prerogatives of office without being dependent upon a preexisting body of men, then the electoral formula would appear to have served its purpose.

CHAPTER EIGHT

CHAPTER EIGHT

Two Centuries Later: Some Reflections on the American Experiments in Constitutional Choice

INTRODUCTION

The American experiments in constitutional choice have persisted through two centuries. Given the improbable nature of those experiments, a duration of two centuries represents an important achievement. The conditions in which the experiments occurred have themselves been subject to radical transformation. American society in the 1980s is vastly different from American society in the 1780s. Yet, the American constitutional system bears a strong resemblance to that which was conceptualized and formulated at Philadelphia in 1787 and in the American states at both earlier and later junctures. A reader can still make meaningful associations between the words written in 1787 and the institutions of a national government, their relationships to one another and to entities referred to as states.

In making a general assessment of the American experiments in constitutional choice, we need to address the question of whether the system of government created by those experiments has performed in a way that is consistent with constitutional theory. Has it performed as we would anticipate from the theoretical explanation offered by Hamilton and Madison in 1787 and 1788 before the Federal constitution was authorized to create the American federal Union? Has it allowed for the autonomous operation of concurrent systems of government where people have been capable of maintaining multiple self-governing communities of interest? Has the system performed in accordance with principles of federalism and constitutional rule? Has it maintained the essential values of stability, safety, justice, freedom, and the pursuit of mutually productive relationships?

In seeking general answers to these questions, we can look for manifestations of institutional weaknesses and institutional failures. Have the equilibrating tendencies of a polycentric, or many-centered, political order foreclosed dominance by any single decision structure or by any single political coalition that has gained long-term dominance over all decision structures? When problems of basic institutional weaknesses and failures manifest themselves, as in the beginning era of confederation, have institutional facilities existed at the constitutional level to search out arrangements for correcting those sources of weakness or failure? Have the essential characteristics of the American constitutional system maintained themselves despite radical changes in technologies and productive capabilities in both the private and public sectors?

These questions involve a shift in level and type of analysis. In Chapters 2 through 7, I focused upon the explanation offered by Hamilton and Madison about the way the American constitutional system was conceptualized and how it was expected to work. I now assume that it was roughly put together to embody the design principles explained in their theoretical arguments, and I examine how the system has generally worked in the course of two centuries of experience.

It is presumptuous to attempt such an analysis, which requires going beyond the reasonable bounds of human perception and cognition. Yet, an initial speculative effort needs to be made if we are to begin to conjecture about the meaning and significance of experiments in constitutional choice in human societies. I make such an effort, despite its vulnerability, because any reader who has a general familiarity with American history can critically scrutinize my assessment. We can learn from a critical dialogue only if we make the effort.

My analysis will be highly selective and limited in the range of the problems addressed. I first turn to the assessment made by Alexis de Tocqueville in his *Democracy in America*. I do so to correct the limited perspective of *The Federalist*, which was confined to the U.S. Constitution. Tocqueville treats the Federal constitution in the context of a more general analysis of the American constitutional system as a whole. He has reference to townships, counties, and states as units of government in the more general frame of government. Further, Tocqueville provides a critical assessment of the performance characteristics of that system, a concern that is relevant to the particular issues I shall address.

After reviewing Tocqueville's assessment, I shall turn to the fundamental contradiction posed by the institution of slavery for basic constitutional principles. I shall indicate how this issue has been addressed. I then turn to the other great constitutional challenge, the growth of machine politics and boss rule that came to fruition in the nineteenth century and was addressed through constitutional reforms in the Progressive reform movement. I then turn to a more fundamental challenge by some of the leading Progressives, including Woodrow Wilson, who rejected the theory of *The Federalist* and expounded the theory of a unitary republic, governed by principles of parliamentary supremacy and bureaucratic administration, as the true principles that reflect the essential characteristics of any system of democratic government. This is the theory that has contributed to the nationalization of American societies and the challenges of nationalization for the American system of constitutional government. How these challenges are resolved remains on the future agenda of American democracy.

TOCQUEVILLE'S ASSESSMENT

Alexis de Tocqueville, as a young citizen of France, was preoccupied with a basic puzzle in the governance of human societies. He was persuaded that the long-term trend in human society was toward increasing equality among human beings. This is what he meant by the term "democracy." The key issue, as he saw it, was whether human beings could resolve increasing tendencies toward equality with the maintenance of liberty. From his point of view, the passion for equality gains expression in envy and an intolerance of conditions that deviate from uniformities that become associated with equality. Human creativity depends, in turn, upon freedom and innovation; and these pose threats to equality and uniformity. Equality expressed as uniformity is a threat to freedom and creativity.

Tocqueville was further aware that the governance of human societies depends upon a fundamental inequality among human beings. Rule-governed societies necessarily imply rulers and ruled; and the distinction between rulers and ruled necessarily implies inequality. A passion for equality with its emphasis upon uniformity is likely to be expressed as a demand for increasing centralization of authority which creates increasing uniformity under law *and* an increasing inequality between those who function as rulers in society and those who are subject to law. He was fearful that this tendency would yield a new despotism more pervasive than any that had occurred before in human societies. He had observed these tendencies in the French Revolution and the French efforts to design and create republican institutions. However, he recognized these tendencies to be more broadly characteristic of human societies in general.

Tocqueville's task in *Democracy in America* was to understand the American efforts to organize a republican system of government and to determine whether it offered a promise of maintaining liberty under conditions of equality. This task is closely related to questions that have been a central focus in our inquiry about the political theory of a compound republic: Can people exercise basic control over their institutions of government so that governmental officials are themselves limited by a rule of law while people both individually and collectively maintain an autonomy which allows for the

exercise of freedom and for an imposition of limits upon governmental authorities? Tocqueville's problem, thus, has critical
relevance to the basic issues inherent in the political theory of
a compound republic.

Tocqueville begins his analysis by focusing upon the origins
of Anglo-American society, which he viewed as containing
"the germ of all that is to follow and the key to almost the
whole work" (Tocqueville, 1945: I, 28). He finds this germ in
the covenantal theology of the Puritans, which was not only a
religious doctrine but "corresponded in many points with the
most democratic and republican theories" (Tocqueville, 1945:
I, 32). The first act of the Pilgrims after departing from Europe was to constitute themselves as a political community by
covenanting with one another in what has come to be known
as the Mayflower Compact. As Tocqueville observed:

> The new settlers did not derive their powers from the head of the
> empire, although they did not deny its supremacy; they constituted
> themselves into a society, and it was not until thirty or forty years
> afterwards, under Charles II, that their existence was legally recog-
> nized by a royal charter. (Tocqueville, 1945: I, 36–37)

The code of laws adopted in Connecticut in 1650 owed its inspiration more to the Old Testament than to the common law
of England.

The methods of government that germinated and developed in the New England townships became the basis of a system of democratic self-government which Tocqueville characterized as the "sovereignty of the people." In the American
revolution, Tocqueville argues,

> [t]he doctrine of the sovereignty of the people came out of the town-
> ships and took possession of the state. Every class was enlisted in its
> cause; battles were fought and victories were attained for it; it be-
> came the law of laws. (Tocqueville, 1945: I, 56)

The law of the laws was the principle of government by
covenantal or constitutional methods in a federal system. In
this process, "the township was organized before the county,

the county before the state, the state before the nation" (Tocqueville, 1945: I, 40). As the last to be adopted, the form of
the Federal government was "in fact nothing more than a
summary of those republican principles which were current
in the whole community before it existed and independently
of its existence" (Tocqueville, 1945: I, 59). Political and administrative life was focused around four different arenas of
action: the township, the county, the state, and finally, the nation. The system was to be understood by looking at it from
the bottom up.

Tocqueville was much struck by what he called the system
of "decentralized administration." Day-to-day activities in the
maintenance of schools, provision of roads, and many other
public services were organized in local communities with basic
standards and requirements set in general provisions of law
formulated by state legislatures. There was no single hierarchy of administrative authority in the United States, in contrast to France. Administration was conducted by a multitude
of hands where there were almost as many different elected
functionaries as there were functions. However, Tocqueville
found that the system worked both in conformity to law and
in conformity to the preferences of the community.

Most administrative functionaries were elected by citizens
of the community. In New England this was done through the
direct participation of citizens in town meetings. But all officials were also accountable to law. Any citizen could seek a
remedy in a court of law to hold officials accountable to standards of performance required by law. Instead of being accountable to superiors in an administrative hierarchy, each
official had substantial discretion that was bounded by processes of democratic control through elections and public
scrutiny and by processes of judicial control. This led Tocqueville to generalize:

The extension of the judicial power in the political world ought to be
in the exact ratio of the extension of the elective power; if these two

institutions do not go hand in hand, the state falls into anarchy or into servitude. (Tocqueville, 1945: I, 74)

America had developed a system of democratic administration that could be contrasted with the French system of bureaucratic administration. Citizens were actively involved in tending to community problems and in providing public services. While the American system was prone to error, it was also characterized by great animation and effort:

> In no country in the world do the citizens make such exertions for the common weal. I know of no people who have established schools so numerous and efficacious, places of worship better suited to the wants of its inhabitants, or roads kept in better repair. (Tocqueville, 1945: I, 91)

The federal system, thus, combines the advantages that accrue from being able to organize activities in self-governing communities on a small scale, while at the same time giving access to much larger communities of interest. The states are free to turn to internal improvement because they do not need to maintain the engines of war to resist ambitious neighbors. "The Union is happy and free as a small people and glorious and strong as a great nation" (Tocqueville, 1945: I, 165). This result is attainable through principles of federalism that permit people to function through self-governing institutions among local, regional, and national communities of interest in organizing collective endeavors.

The weakness that Tocqueville sees in such a federal system is its complexity:

> The federal system . . . rests upon a theory which is complicated at best and which demands the daily exercise of a considerable share of discretion on the part of those it governs. (Tocqueville, 1945: I, 166)

The system is workable by a people who are sufficiently well informed and experienced in governing their own affairs:

The whole structure of government is artificial and conventional, and it would be ill adapted to a people which has not been long accustomed to the conduct of its own affairs, or to one in which the science of politics has not descended to the humblest classes of society. (Tocqueville, 1945: I, 167)

The opportunities that citizens had to participate directly in the governance of their own affairs provided both a schooling in a science of politics and a practice that became essential for making the American system of government work. Tocqueville viewed municipal institutions as constituting the strength of a free nation:

Town meetings are to liberty what primary schools are to science; they bring it within the people's reach, they teach men how to use and how to enjoy it. A nation can establish a free government, but without municipal institutions it cannot have the spirit of liberty. (Tocqueville, 1945: I, 61)

Yet without power and independence a town may contain good subjects, but it can have no active citizens. (Tocqueville, 1945: I, 67)

Tocqueville observed much the same effects arising from citizens directly participating in the governance of their own affairs through the jury system and through voluntary associations organized to deal with shared concerns. Citizens as jurors directly participate and share in making decisions within the formal institutions of the judiciary rather than electing representatives to act on their behalf. The science and art of association is what enables people in a democratic society to pool their resources and capabilities and accomplish tasks that they could not otherwise accomplish by acting alone. This again leads Tocqueville to conclude:

In democratic countries the science of association is the mother of science; the progress of all else depends upon the progress it has made. (Tocqueville, 1945: II, 110)

If men are to remain civilized or to become so, the art of associating together must grow and improve in the same ratio that the equality of condition is increased. (Tocqueville, 1945: II, 110)

In his critical assessment of American democracy, Tocqueville viewed the greatest dangers as arising from the unlimited power of the majority in the American states. This is the danger that Hamilton and Madison had associated with majority faction and the reason for the exercise of limited authority in a federal constitutional system with multiple checks and balances. Tocqueville viewed the state constitutions as affording fewer checks than the Federal constitution with the possibility that popularly elected legislatures, executive officials, and judges would all be dominated by a majority coalition that had little regard for minority interests and individual opinion. He saw a danger that anything could be justified in the name of the majority. Law is made and sanctioned in the name of justice; and the exercise of all authority should be "confined within the limits of what is just" (Tocqueville, 1945: I, 259). So long as governmental powers are exercised within appropriate limits, Tocqueville shares the opinions of Hamilton and Madison that governments can be democratic or republican in nature while incurring little risk of tyranny.

However, democracy has the danger of presuming that a majority can do no wrong. Such power has an apparent moral justification in the presumption that the interests of the many should prevail over the interests of the few. The greater good of the greater number can be used as a moral precept to dominate all other moral considerations and justify an unlimited exercise of public authority in the name of democracy. But such a precept can also be used to justify the most extreme tyranny.

The lack of limits to legislative authority in the government of the American states was viewed by Tocqueville as creating the greatest vulnerability to a tyranny of the majority.[1] Majorities could wield the instruments of unlimited power, dominate the exercise of public opinion, and silence those who are not of the dominant opinion. The danger was less in the practice of tyranny at the time when Tocqueville visited America than "the existence of no sure barriers against it" (Tocqueville, 1945: I, 262). The temper of the legal profession, trial by jury, the place of local government in the execution of laws, and many other factors tended to mitigate the tyranny of the majority; but the danger remained.

Tocqueville's explicit consideration of the U.S. Constitution and the implications that follow for the organization and conduct of the American national government is confined to a single chapter on "The Federal Constitution." His presentation reveals a detailed knowledge of the Constitution, *The Federalist*, and the leading legal commentaries by Chancellor Kent and Justice Story. He viewed the Federal constitution as being better balanced than those of the states.

However, the workability of this system of separated powers depended critically upon what Tocqueville refers to as the accidental circumstances of America being separated from the rest of the world by an extended ocean and the absence of powerful neighbors on the North American continent. The president was commander-in-chief of the armed forces and responsible for the conduct of foreign relations. These powers were distinctly limited when the U.S. army was composed of only 6,000 men. In these circumstances Tocqueville recognized,

[t]he President of the United States possesses almost royal prerogatives, which he has no opportunities of exercising; and the privileges which he can at present use are very circumscribed. The laws (i.e., the Constitution) allow him to be strong, but the circumstances keep him weak. (Tocqueville, 1945: I, 126. My parenthesis.)

If circumstances were otherwise, the President could be expected to exercise a much more powerful position.

Tocqueville anticipated that regular elections and the separation of powers in the American system of government would produce such vulnerability for a European nation that it would prove to be a fatal exposure to external aggression by hostile neighbors. For any people to follow the American example amid the great monarchies of Europe would pose a grave danger to its own existence. Europe, Tocqueville anticipated, might consider a federal system of distributed authority only if the great nations of Europe were prepared to undertake such an experiment at the same time.

The slavery of blacks in America was viewed by Tocqueville to be the "most formidible of all the ills that threaten the future of the Union" (Tocqueville, 1945: I, 356). A distinctive non-European people had been forcibly brought to America to function as slaves and to be denied an existence as free and equal members of the human community. The basic moral precept of a covenantal community—Do not that to another which thou wouldst not have done to thyself—was violated in a most fundamental way.

Tocqueville viewed slavery as a great moral offense that yielded a tragic harvest of evil from which he could not imagine a constructive resolution. Free labor, Tocqueville was convinced, is more productive than slave labor. Slavery makes labor demeaning both for the slave and for the master. There is little incentive to produce, except the threat and use of force, when individuals do not derive a yield from their own labor. The master who scorns labor is trained to be a "domestic dictator from infancy" (Tocqueville, 1945: I, 394), lives in "idle independence," and excels in a passionate love for the hunt, sports, individual combat, and military exercises (Tocqueville, 1945: I, 364). The slave is brutalized, learns to keep his place, and to deny aspirations and ambitions (Tocqueville, 1945: I, 364). The slave codes in America sought to deny education and skilled employment to blacks and access to the achievements of civilization.

The climate and geography of the South was more conducive to the practice of slavery than in the North. As slavery was abolished in the North, it became more concentrated in the South until the number of slaves exceeded the number of nonslaves in some southern states. This circumstance created another puzzle. If slavery were eliminated under circumstances where blacks comprised the majority of the population, institutions of democratic government created the possibility that blacks might now become the dominant faction and control the destiny of those societies. Yet, they had been de-

nied both the education and experience necessary to exercise
responsibility for managing economic enterprises or governing public affairs. In the West Indies, Tocqueville expected
slave revolts to be successful. In the southern states, slave revolts posed a potential threat that reinforced oppressive tendencies. Slavery was a cancer in American society for which
Tocqueville could not anticipate a constructive resolution.

In light of this assessment, Tocqueville was not optimistic
about the longer-term survival of the American federal Union.
He anticipated that the time would come when the American
Union would comprise at least 40 republics and a population
of 130 million people. But he had serious doubts that the
American federal Union could survive the basic tensions in
American society that were produced by the way that the institutions of slavery affected the character and manners of
people and how they related to one another.

THE AUTHORITY OF PERSONS AND THE INSTITUTION
OF SLAVERY

The most serious deficiency in the Constitution as formulated
at Philadelphia in 1787 was its failure to address the authority
of persons. As indicated in Chapters 3 and 7, this problem
was, in part, addressed in the first ten amendments which
were formulated as a Bill of Rights during the course of constitutional deliberations. These "rights" were technically formulated as limitations on the authority of Congress and not as
rights of persons *per se*. A serious deficiency remained in the
failure to define citizenship and the status of persons who
comprised the new national political community formed by
the United States of America. Qualifications for voting were
to be established by the states by taking those qualifications
used in each state for electing the most numerous branch of
the state legislature unless Congress provided otherwise. Explicit reference is made in the U.S. Constitution to apportion-
ing representation in the House of Representatives "by adding

to the whole number of free persons, including those bound to service for a term of years, and excluding Indians not taxed, three fifths of all other persons" (Article I, Section 2). The allusion to "all other persons" is to slaves who were considered as property and denied legal personality under the laws of those states where the institution of slavery was practiced.

The defense of the formula for representation allowing slaves to be calculated as three fifths of a person is not argued directly in *The Federalist*. Instead, a literary device is used to attribute a hypothetical argument to "one of our Southern brethren" (Federalist 54: ML, 354; C, 367; R, 336). This hypothetical southerner contends that the national Constitution views slaves in "the mixed character of persons and of property" (Federalist 54: ML, 355; C, 368; R, 337). One can only conclude that this formula represented an expedient and *unprincipled* compromise which neither Hamilton nor Madison could defend in good conscience.

The problem they faced was a perplexing one. The Constitution would never have been ratified by the southern states had citizenship in the United States been extended to all individuals including slaves. The failure of several states to ratify would have posed the threat of war among separate confederations of free and slave states which would then have existed on the North American continent. A primary purpose of the Constitution was to avoid that contingency. Yet the failure to address the issue of slavery meant that it remained as a fundamental threat to the future development of American society. No agreeable basis could be devised for treating all individuals as having political personality and being entitled to exercise the political prerogatives of persons within the U.S. Constitution as amended. The failure to extend the logic of the constitutional formula to all human beings in the United States was clearly an insufficient solution for tending to the interests of those who were excluded. They were the object of one of the cruelest tyrannies ever sustained by any faction anywhere. No black in America could agree that the "'tyranny of the majority' has been a term to scare little children with" (Burns, 1963: 40).

The institution of slavery remained a cancer in American society and continued to fuel the debate over confederation until the Civil War. The contention at that time that the states could nullify national legislation was a revival of arguments about principles of confederation. John C. Calhoun's *Disquisition on Government* is an attempt to restate the case for confederation. The Civil War was fought over the issue of whether the Federal government could maintain its concurrent authority within the domain of states that sought to deny that authority. In the aftermath of the Civil War, three additional amendments were added to the United States Constitution to extend the fundamental statement of constitutional rights to include a definition of citizenship, deny involuntary servitude, and extend the scope of U.S. constitutional rights as binding upon the states in addition to Congress.

The attainment of a constitutional "settlement" that was in substantial part a result of the coercion of arms posed a problem that was not easy to resolve. The adoption of constitutional amendments had the immediate effect of only adding words on paper. The maintenance of military occupation in a democractic society could only be a temporary expediency that did not foreclose the possibility of forceful resistance through secret societies on the part of a population trained to become "a sort of domestic dictator from infancy," skilled in the hunt, and experienced in warfare (Tocqueville, 1945: I, 394). The potential beneficiaries of the words on paper were members of a population that had been systematically deprived of education and the experiences of governing their own affairs in a free society. The subsequent struggle was a prolonged and unequal one carried out under adverse circumstances and plagued by gross injustices.

That struggle was marked by the creation of educational institutions, like Tuskegee Institute, and the development of schools and colleges that began the fundamental tasks of education. Blacks also exercised options to vote by their feet and to gain access to better opportunities. The basic aspirations of a free society informed by principles of justice made the burdens of injustice the more intolerable to bear.

The basic structure of institutional facilities in a compound republic afforded a variety of remedies that became increasingly available to blacks as they acquired both the education and the skills necessary to gain access to those remedies and press their claims under constitutional law against the abusive exercise of discretion by governmental officials at all levels of government. The critical issue remained that of individuals knowing what is improper and taking actions that are respectful of proper relationships with others in human societies.

The exercise of the basic constitutional prerogatives of persons and citizenship has only gradually opened opportunities for blacks to assume increasing responsibility in the governance of affairs among the diverse communities of people in a compound republic. While the process has been excruciatingly slow, American blacks have made great achievements in gradually converting words on paper into enforceable rules of law where a greater semblance of justice is coming to apply to the ordering of human relationships among blacks and whites in American society. The effectiveness of the system depends upon the capacity of people to make it work for themselves in accordance with the basic rules of constitutional law that apply to all persons alike. Americans can now have some measure of confidence in constructive resolutions to the so-called race problem, where Tocqueville had none. The principles embodied in constitutional formulations and the forms of governmental arrangements have had the long-term effect of biasing decisions in the right direction. The merit of a system turns upon the capacity of individuals to make it work in advancing their legitimate claims against the unjust demands and actions of others. No set of words on paper is sufficient to right wrongs in human societies.

THE CHALLENGE OF MACHINE POLITICS AND
BOSS RULE

Tocqueville's warning about the dangers of majority tyranny inherent in state constitutions came to fruition in the latter part of the nineteenth century. Radical transformations in American society, deriving from technological developments, industrialization, urbanization, and new claims to authority, contributed to these developments. A new era of constitutional reform brought new developments in the American constitutional system.

Industrial applications of new technologies brought new sources of energy, new modes of communication and transportation, and a whole array of new and different goods and services. Railway, telegraph, and telephone lines soon spanned the continent. Large new cities developed as great industrial centers. The westward movement was replaced by a movement of population from rural areas to urban centers. New immigrants became industrial workers in urban centers rather than settlers and developers of open land.

A key element in these new patterns of development was the relationship of population size to patterns of political organization. Principles of majority voting inherent in a democratic system of government create opportunities for the winners to dominate the subsequent decisions of government. Where the opportunities for payoffs are high, incentives are created for some to use political processes to gain dominance over others. The task of appealing to an electorate and canvassing votes requires an expenditure of time and effort that increases with population size.

The American constitutional system with its separation of powers necessarily means that different legislative, executive, and judicial officers are subject to election. If several candidates develop a joint slate and then work together as a team in the conduct of their election campaign, they can gain an advantage over individual candidates who work only on their own behalf. This advantage is negligible when constituencies are sufficiently small for each voter to have a personal knowledge of each candidate. The advantage increases significantly as voters lack personal knowledge about each candidate. If slates are more successful than unslated candidates, competing slates will form among other potential candidates. The unslated candidate is likely to have minimal success in large electorates unless he or she has had a high level of public visibility through prior experiences.

Since elections for local governments were often held on an annual or biennial basis, a further advantage could be gained if a campaign organization were established on a regular basis and used from one election to the next. If organization contributes significantly to winning elections and the payoffs to be derived are of sufficient magnitude, then incentives exist for someone to undertake, on a full-time basis, the entrepreneurial initiative of slating candidates, canvassing voters, and maintaining a party organization. A political machine develops as a result of these incentives.

When carried through to its full potential, political organizers have incentives to slate candidates for all of the numerous legislative, executive, and judicial offices in their relevant political jurisdictions; to procure positions on public payrolls for those assisting in organized efforts to conduct campaigns, canvass votes, and deliver voters to the polls; to control the decisions made by the public officials elected as a part of the organization's slate; and to receive contributions from those who benefit from the decisions taken. The successful organizer becomes a "boss" in control of the different offices where his candidates have been successful. He has the potential of functioning as a monopolist capable of controlling the relevant governmental decisions to maximize his return as an entrepreneur. By virtue of his control over legislative, executive, and judicial offices, the boss manages the diverse centers of authority as though his were a fully integrated system of command. The dominance of boss rule posed a basic threat to constitutional principles of separation of powers with checks and balances. A boss's control is facilitated by secrecy; and it is in his interest to minimize his exposure to public scrutiny.[2]

Changes in technology also facilitated the emergence of boss rule. The development of new techniques in metallurgy, new forms of energy resources including natural gas, petroleum, and electricity, new modes of transportation such as railroads and electrical street cars, and electronic communication created opportunities for entrepreneurship in a wide range of utility enterprises to supply the basic requirements of large aggregations of people. Each of these utility enterprises, whether railroad, telephone, electrical power, natural gas, or water supply, depends upon the use of facilities to supply a continuous flow of services from central sources through distributional networks that reach to ultimate users. Such facilities require the use either of public rights-of-way for pipes, transmission lines or tracks along public streets, alleys, and thoroughfares or access to the power of eminent domain to acquire such rights-of-way across the properties of owners who would not otherwise willingly grant them. The power of eminent domain is the power of a government to acquire property by forced sale upon compensation for "fair market value" as established by a court of law. Such powers can be extended to privately owned utility companies on the assumption that they provide essential services to the public. Furthermore, utility enterprises are considered to be natural monopolies in the sense that the cost of a fully duplicate set of facilities to assure an alternative source of supply would be extremely high. Such enterprises are typically subject to public regulations so that their profitability is determined by governmental authorities.

With the construction of railroads and the development of electrical, gas, water, and telecommunication utility companies in the nineteenth century, substantial incentives existed for such enterprises to gain favorable decisions by local, state, and national governments to grant franchises, extend powers of eminent domain, secure favorable regulatory decisions, and obtain grants of public lands and public funds. These incentives, reinforced by very large accumulations of wealth invested in such ventures, created entrepreneurial opportunities of substantial magnitude for political bosses who could deliver favorable decisions by the relevant governmental authorities. In many instances the railroads, as the dominant monopolists among a community of natural monopolists, and political bosses joined together to dominate governmental decisions.

These developments were reinforced by the formulation of legal doctrines which held that the residual authority not granted to the Federal government in the U.S. Constitution rested in state legislatures. Subject to the terms of the state constitution, a state legislature was presumed to be sovereign and thus to exercise supreme law-making authority within each state. When applied to the affairs of local units of government, this doctrine was articulated as Dillon's rule, which held that

[m]unicipal corporations owe their origins to and derive their powers and rights wholly from the (state) legislature. It breathes into them the breath of life, without which they cannot exist. As it creates, so it may destroy. If it may destroy, it may abridge and control. Unless there is some constitutional limitation on the right, the legislature might, by a simple act, if we can suppose it capable of so great a folly and so great a wrong, sweep from existence all of the municipal corporations of a state and the corporation could not prevent it. We know no limitation on this right so far as the corporations themselves are concerned. They are, so to phrase it, the mere tenants at will of the legislature. (City of Clinton v. Cedar Rapids and Missouri Railroad Co., 24, Iowa 455, 475, 1868. My parenthesis.)

Dillon's rule was subsequently affirmed by most state courts and by the U.S. Supreme Court.

Absolute and unlimited sovereignty on the part of state legislatures over municipal corporations and other units of local government made state legislatures the focus of attention for controlling local governments. State legislatures under this authority enacted special charters and laws that applied to specifically named cities rather than formulating general rules that applied to general categories of local units of government. Such charters and enactments became instruments for detailed legislative interferences in local affairs. As one student of this period has observed:

Not only are charters amended, superseded and repealed with great abandon, but frequently other special acts, not purporting to amend or repeal existing charters and not otherwise referring to such charters, very drastically interfered with the local affairs of particular cities. Only in a relatively few instances did it appear that the wishes of the cities or of their inhabitants were made a prerequisite to the operation of such laws. (Peppin, 1941: 10–11)

Political bosses who exercised control over a state legislature could dominate local governmental affairs for a state as a whole. Legislators having "no acquaintance with, interest in, or responsibility to the people of the locality affected" (Peppin, 1941: 2) were free to exploit the opportunities available with no limitations on their rights so far as the local corporations themselves were concerned. Dillon's rule made legal the rape of the cities by the bosses and so-called robber barons of the late nineteenth century.

Since members of the U.S. Senate were elected by the state legislatures, political bosses could also secure their own election to the Senate without having to stand for popular election and exposing themselves directly to the electoral process. As a result, the U.S. Senate became a club of bosses that epitomized the control of machine politics in the latter part of the nineteenth century. Through a tradition of "senatorial courtesy," this club of bosses was able to gain effective dominance of national affairs as well as dominance over the affairs of state and local governments. Political bosses operating at the local, state, and national levels of government put together coalitions that enabled them to gain dominance over different decision structures both in particular units of government and over different levels of government.

The initial response to the corruption of machine politics and boss rule became manifest in sporadic reform movements that swept through city after city and state after state in the late nineteenth century. But spontaneous reform movements were at an inherent disadvantage in a long-term struggle with professionally organized political machines in which political entrepreneurs made a business of conducting and winning elections. Successful reform candidates either faced defeat at the next election or were required to devote themselves to the task of creating a new political machine. The viability of any new organization depended upon the same types of accommodation that were inherent in machine politics and boss rule. Political bosses could dismiss reformers as "morning glories" that blossomed and faded after election day (Roirdon, 1963: 17).

Another avenue of reform was available through processes of constitutional decision making. By changing the provisions of state constitutions, reformers could hope to modify the structure of government so as to constrain the opportunities for political machines to dominate the slating process. These changes altered the terms and conditions of government so that decisions could less easily be dominated by a political machine. A major response to machine politics and boss rule was an effort in virtually every state to undertake major changes in state constitutions. These general reform efforts have been identified with the Progressive reform movement.

Constitutional revisions during the Progressive reform movement almost uniformly placed restrictions upon state legislatures making it unlawful for legislatures to enact local legislation that applied to a specifically named locality or to a specifically designated situation (e.g., the conveyance of property) and requiring that legislation pertaining to local affairs be formulated as general legislation applicable to all localities in like circumstances. Other constitutional requirements placed limits upon public indebtednesses, required competitive bidding in the awarding of public contracts, and prohibited public expenditures for private purposes. Constraints

upon special legislation and requirements of general legislation significantly reinforced the tradition that general rules of
law operate in the organization of human conduct rather than
the discrete granting of favors by political patrons to political
clients.

Some of these requirements were circumvented by legislatures that adopted a strategy of classifying cities so that
some classes contained only a single city. Through such devices, legislation applicable to the largest city in a state often
assumed the proportions of special legislation formulated in
the language of general legislation as applied to "cities of the
first class." Even with this strategy, however, the requirement
that legislatures proceed under terms of general legislation
significantly constrained the opportunities for political corruption for most cities in most states.

A companion set of constitutional provisions gave a commensurate increase in opportunities for local communities to
control their own local affairs subject to the general laws of
the state. In more than one half of the American states, constitutional authority was extended to local communities to formulate their own local municipal charters to govern local affairs. These "home-rule" charters extended the prerogatives
of constitutional decision making to citizens of local communities. Citizens in home-rule cities could stipulate their own
constitutional terms and conditions that would apply to the
governance of a local community. Home-rule charters could be
revised or amended by the actions of local citizens where processes of the initiative and referendum were made applicable.

The California constitutional convention of 1879, for example, quite clearly proclaimed its efforts to create a "new system of local self government." Cities and towns were explicitly
recognized as having a right of local self-government in the
conduct of their own local affairs subject to the terms of general laws. Larger municipalities were extended authority to
formulate their own home-rule charters that were subject to
approval or disapproval as a whole without amendment by

the state legislature. In several states, including California, counties were also extended "home rule" and thus were able to undertake a wider variety of experimentation in the development of local governmental institutions.

The rationale used in the development of this new system of local self-government was to apply principles of federalism in the relationships of a state to its local units of government. The Progressive reform movement thus extended the principle of federalism that had applied to organization of the national and state governments downward so that this principle also applied to the organization of local units of government. State constitutional provisions authorizing home-rule charters recognized a constitutional right of local self-government among local communities.

A wide variety of electoral reforms for state and local government was also adopted as a consequence of the Progressive reform movement. Because the U.S. Constitution recognized state electoral laws applicable to the most numerous branch of the state legislature as applying to national elections, reform at the state level automatically applied to national elections. Public conduct of local, state, and national elections was uniformly established in all states by state constitutional and legislative enactments. Standard election ballots were supplied by public authorities rather than relying upon ballots supplied by political parties. Registration laws were formulated, requiring that lists of registered voters be publicly available prior to elections. The impetus behind this reform was to thwart the political boss's appeal to party faithful to "vote early and often." The U.S. Constitution was amended to elect senators by popular election in each state.

Most states also established direct primary elections where party nominations for public offices were made through a publicly conducted election, and where all voters registered as party members were entitled to vote in determining a party's slate of candidates. The political machine could no longer exercise direct control over the slating of party candidates. Any party member might challenge any other party member for nomination as the party candidate in a publicly conducted primary election.

Several of the states provided for nonpartisan local and judicial elections on a presumption that local and judicial affairs had little relationship to partisan politics in state and national elections. Many states scheduled local elections so that they would not coincide with state and national elections. Again, this was an effort to maintain the autonomy of local governments and reduce the opportunity for political coalitions at the state level to exercise control over local affairs.

The extensive revision of state and local constitutional authority undertaken as a part of the Progressive reform movement had the effect of reducing the dominance of machine politics and boss rule in American politics. This reduced the danger of majority tyranny that was the subject of Tocqueville's critical commentary. Processes of constitutional reform were an integral part of the American effort to refashion institutions of government to meet the changing conditions of the nineteenth century. The reforms undertaken built new constitutional constraints into state constitutions and extended principles of constitutional choice to local governments in the form of home-rule charters. The general theory of limited constitutions gained wider application.

THE BREAK WITH THE FEDERALIST TRADITION IN THE TWENTIETH CENTURY

Another response to the era of machine politics and boss rule was to question the theoretical grounds that served as the basis for the American experiments in constitutional choice. These challenges took many different forms. Charles A. Beard, for example, attacked the economic motives of those who played leading roles in framing the American constitutional system and thus cast doubts upon the system as anything other than a self-serving arrangement for a propertied class (Beard, 1965). Others, like Frank J. Goodnow, rejected

constitutions as meaningless formalisms that had little significance for the way that governments worked (Goodnow, 1900).
For Goodnow, a system of government organized on the basis
of a separation of powers with checks and balances was an obstacle to collective action that could only be overcome by the
leadership of a political boss who exercised disciplined control through a political machine to *make* the system work.
From his perspective, the American system of constitutional
government could only be made to work by a coalition that
could exercise dominance over the different decision structures and override constitutional limits.

Still others, like Woodrow Wilson, held that the design of
the American constitutional system represented misguided
efforts on the part of people who failed to understand the essential nature of the political process. In effect Wilson was arguing, as Hamilton had argued before about confederation,
that principles of federalism and separation of powers were
based upon fallacious concepts and that the true nature of
government was dominance by a single center of ultimate authority. Wilson's argument has been the most influential in the
twentieth century; and I shall use it to indicate the nature of
the break with *The Federalist* tradition.

Wilson viewed his own generation as the first that was capable of taking an objective view of the American constitutional system. Earlier generations, he argued, had been so
possessed of an adoration for the Constitution that they could
not be objective. Wilson saw his generation to be free from the
shackles of infatuation and, thus, had the privilege and responsibility to speak out in "the first season of free, outspoken,
unrestrained constitutional criticism" (Wilson, 1956: 27).

Wilson's view was strongly influenced by the earlier publication of Walter Bagehot's *The English Constitution*. Bagehot rejected earlier interpretations of the English constitution as
being based upon a separation of powers and argued that the
Cabinet was the link that tied the British government into a
unitary whole. This was the efficient part of the British government that needed to be distinguished from the formal

constitutional facade that concealed the realities of British politics.

Wilson followed the basic Bagehot theses by arguing that the constitutional structure designed in the eighteenth century had become little more than a facade that concealed the basic realities of American politics. The title of his book, *Congressional Government*, first published in 1885, anticipated his thesis that "the actual form of our present government is simply a scheme of congressional supremacy" (Wilson, 1956: 28) that could no longer be squared with traditional constitutional theory.

Wilson wrote in the era when the Senate was still a club of bosses. As he saw developments,

All niceties of constitutional restriction and even many broad principles of constitutional limitation have been overridden, and a thoroughly organized system of congressional control set up which gives a very rude negative to some theories of balance and some schemes of distributed powers, but which suits well with convenience, and does violence to none of the principles of self-government contained in the Constitution. (Wilson, 1956: 31)

Wilson rejected what he refers to as the "literary theories" and "paper pictures" of the Constitution as reflected in the writings of John Adams, Alexander Hamilton, and James Madison: "These checks and balances have proved mischievous just to the extent to which they have succeeded in establishing themselves as realities" (Wilson, 1956: 187). He further asserted, "This balance of state against national authorities," inherent in a federal system, "has proved, of all constitutional checks, the least effectual" (Wilson, 1956: 34).

Wilson viewed a system of checks and balances as contrary to the essential nature of government. Instead, he assumed that there is always some single center of authority that exercises the ultimate prerogative of government. The task of a scholar, Wilson argued, is to determine "where in this system is that centre? In whose hands is self-sufficient authority lodged and through what agencies does that authority speak and act?" (Wilson, 1956: 30). If one looks behind formalities and identifies the real center of authority, Wilson contended, "the predominant and controlling force, the centre and source of all motive and of all regulative power, is Congress" (Wilson, 1956: 31).

The controlling principle in Wilson's political theory—"the more power is divided the more irresponsible it becomes" (Wilson, 1956: 77)—is in basic contradiction to Madison's principle that opposite and rival interests hold those who exercise the prerogatives of government accountable to a public trust. Wilson's preferred solution was the British parliamentary model of government where Parliament exercises the supreme authority of government. The requirement of self-government could be met for Wilson if Parliament (or Congress) as the representative legislative body was raised "to a position of absolute supremacy" (Wilson, 1956: 203). Wilson thus asserts:

No one, I take it for granted, is disposed to disallow the principle that *the representatives of the people are the proper ultimate authority in all matters of government,* and that administration is merely the clerical part of government. Legislation is the originating force. It determines what shall be done; and the President, if he cannot or will not stay legislation by the use of his extraordinary power as a branch of the legislature, is plainly bound in duty to render unquestioning obedience to Congress. And if it be his duty to obey, still more is obedience the bounden duty of his subordinates. The power of making laws is in its very nature and essence the power of directing, and that power is given to Congress. (Wilson, 1956: 181. My emphasis.)

Adherence to principles of democratic control of Congress was, in Wilson's view, sufficient to maintain principles of self-government without having recourse to a federal system, or a separation of powers in the constitution of the national government. Self-government, for Wilson, was a "straightforward thing of simple method, single, unstinted power and clear responsibility . . . " (Wilson, 1956: 215). Wilson was prepared to accept Congress as "the proper ultimate authority in

all matters of government . . ." (Wilson, 1956: 181). He considered it intuitively obvious that the more authority is concentrated, the more responsible it becomes.

Wilson's thesis that Congress is the proper ultimate authority in *all matters of government* is the antithesis of the position taken in *The Federalist*. Madison considered it to be the
very definition of tyranny to vest all matters of government in
a single body of men. Representatives of the people are themselves fallible, prone to error, and susceptible of corruption.
Any numerous legislative body is subject to oligarchical tendencies such that a mere handful of individuals will dominate
and direct its proceedings because only one person can speak
at a time in any deliberative group. This yields counterintuitive
implications in the governance of democratic societies. Only
by having recourse to numerous units of government and by
placing effective limits on all exercises of governmental prerogative could the capacity of mankind for self-government
be realized.

To presume that Congress is supreme in all matters of government would have meant for Hamilton that "the representatives of the people are superior to the people themselves"
(Federalist 78: ML, 506; C, 524; R, 467). If the principle that
Congress is the proper ultimate authority in all matters of
government is accepted, it is not clear that limits can be maintained on the exercise of governmental authority. Only by
placing limits upon legislative, executive, and judicial authority is it possible to maintain the power of the people as
superior to each. Wilson did not address the question of how
it is possible to maintain an enforceable system of constitutional law and for people to exercise choice and maintain control over the terms and conditions of government. He accepts
Bagehot's argument as being intuitively true without coming
to terms with the essential contradictions between that argument and the arguments advanced in *The Federalist*. Those arguments are dismissed as "literary theories" and "paper pictures" without sympathetically examining their merit and
establishing specific grounds for their rejection.

On the occasion of the fifteenth printing of *Congressional Government* in 1900, Wilson wrote a new preface where he found it necessary to call attention to the extensive changes that had taken place in "our singular system of Congressional government" (Wilson, 1956: 19). The war with Spain had resulted in important changes in the exercise of power in the Federal government. The increasing power of the President was bringing a fundamental change in the American system of government. Reflecting upon these changes, Wilson concludes his preface with the following observation:

> It may be, too, that the new leadership of the Executive, insomuch as it is likely to last, will have a very far-reaching effect upon our whole method of government. It may give the heads of the executive departments a new influence upon the actions of Congress. It may bring about, as a consequence, an integration which will substitute statesmanship for government by mass meeting. It may put this whole volume hopelessly out of date. (Wilson, 1956: 23)

The representatives of the people in Congress had become "government by mass meeting." Instead of viewing Congress as the proper ultimate authority in all matters of government—as the "people's parliament" (Wilson, 1956: 203)—Wilson now anticipated that the "new leadership of the Executive" would "substitute statesmanship for government by mass meeting." We have no indication of whether Wilson came to regard the president as the proper ultimate authority in all matters of government. When fifteen years can make a book hopelessly out of date, we might assume that it is impossible for a people by "reflection and choice" to determine the fundamental terms and conditions of government. Governments, presumably, evolve as a matter of historical happenstance.

In an essay on "The Study of Administration" published in 1887, Wilson also exercised a profound influence on the study of American public administration. In that essay he wrote that constitutional considerations are of an ideological nature and influence the general form of government as a monarchy or a republic. But when it comes to the organiza-

tion of administration, Wilson argued that the same principles of good administration apply to all governments alike.
These were the principles of administration which had been
most highly perfected in France by Napoleon and in Prussia
by Frederick the Great and his successors. The French system
of bureaucratic administration, which Tocqueville had contrasted to the American system of decentralized or democratic
administration, was accepted by Wilson as the model of good
administration applicable to all governments alike, including
the American system of government (V. Ostrom, 1974).

For all of its limitations, the approach taken by Wilson became the prevailing mode of analysis in addressing problems
of governmental organization in the twentieth century. Its
presumption of modernity and its claim to be addressing political realities had a profound appeal in an era when methods
of the natural sciences were assumed to be the proper method
for the development of a value-free political science. Processes of constitutional choice were viewed as pertaining to institutional formalities rather than political realities. The parliamentary model was assumed to be the appropriate model
for the organization of political processes culminating in legislative formulation of public policy. The French and Prussian
systems of bureaucratic administration were assumed to provide an appropriate model for the organization of executive
implementation of public policy. Both models—parliamentary and bureaucratic—presume a single center of ultimate
authority for all matters of government.

While there has been a great deal of intellectual support
for the parliamentary model, the constitutional constraints of
the American system of separation of powers with its checks
and balances has been particularly intractable in allowing for
any radical reorganization of the national legislature. The
more important change has been congressional neglect of legislative prerogatives and the extension of increasing rule-
making authority to executive instrumentalities. The organization of the executive has been more tractable to efforts

to introduce principles of bureaucratic control through administrative reorganization. These measures have served to strengthen greatly the administrative, legislative, and political powers of the president. In the course of the twentieth century, it has become commonplace to refer to the American *system* of government as one of "presidential government" rather than "congressional government." The term "American government" has come to refer increasingly to the American national government and not to the federal system of government. Students in the latter part of the twentieth century can study American government in courses that focus exclusively upon the national government with a presumption that the proper ultimate authority in all matters of government resides in Washington, D.C.

THE NATIONALIZATION OF AMERICAN GOVERNMENT
AND ITS LIKELY SOURCES OF FAILURE

As Americans approach the end of the second century in their experiments with constitutional choice, those experiments manifest patterns of increasing dominance by the national government over all aspects of life. In turn, the American national government is subject to an increasing dominance of the executive. So long as Federal funds are being appropriated, few limits are recognized in the exercise of prerogatives by the American national government. Wherever Federal funds are used to finance some activity of a state, local, or private nature, Federal rules and regulations become mandatory in the operation of state, local, or private concerns. Even the conduct of research by faculty and students in colleges and universities is potentially subject to Federal regulation whether or not the particular research effort is being supported by Federal funds.[3] So long as a college or university receives some Federal funds, then the Federal government is asserting jurisdiction to enforce its rules and regulations in any aspect of college or university affairs.

Congress cannot be expected to establish relevant standards of legislation that are appropriate to all matters of government in a country that ranges across a continent and includes the arctic and subarctic regions of Alaska and the
subtropical regions of Hawaii, Florida, and California. As a
result, congressional standards have become increasingly ambiguous with reference to "pure water," "clean air," "public
safety," and the "general welfare." Within the scope of such
ambiguous references, authority is delegated to administrative instrumentalities to develop rules and regulations which
will have the force of law in carrying out programs to realize
those objectives. Anonymous administrative employees with
minimal awareness of the diversity of circumstances in which
Americans live, rather than elected representatives, have the
task of formulating rules and regulations with the force of
law. These rules and regulations fail to take account of vari-
able environmental and cultural conditions.

Once legislation has been brought within the domain of
executive competence, the president has substantial authority
under the Administrative Reorganization Act to change the
basic configuration of priorities, interests, and structures by
proposing "reorganization plans" that have the force of law
unless vetoed by a resolution of either the House of Representatives or the Senate within 60 days of its publication in the
Federal Register. Such reorganization plans may take the form
of transferring the basic authority involved to the president to
allocate under such terms and conditions as he sees fit. No
further public notice is required to exercise such discretion-
ary authority.

The administrative reorganization plan creating the Office
of Management and Budget and the Domestic Council in the
Executive Offices of the President contained such language
giving the president authority to delegate or assign responsibilities as he sees fit. Under these circumstances, presidential
instructions are being given the force of law [4] and the exercise
of congressional authority is being largely confined to the formulation of slogans that have more the import of positive mo-

rality than positive law. Presidential government is becoming a reality because of the failure to insist upon essential limits in maintaining a system of constitutional rule.

The fuller potential for developing a system of presidential government is indicated by proposals that executive authority be used to "manage" intergovernmental relations. The reorganization plan creating the Office of Management and Budget, for example, anticipated the development of "Washington-based coordinators" who would coordinate interagency and intergovernmental relations throughout the country (U.S. *Codes*, Congressional and Administrative Laws 91st Congress, 2nd Sess. 1970, Vol. III: 6,316). James L. Sundquist of the Brookings Institution anticipates in *Making Federalism Work* "the final burial" of traditional doctrines of American federalism and the development of a new model of "federalism" that will be run from the Executive Offices of the president (Sundquist, 1969: 31). Sundquist anticipates that the guidance of the whole system of Federal, state, and local relationships can only "come from a single source of authority—the President" (Sundquist, 1969: 278). Direction by a bureaucracy of presidential functionaries is presumably necessary to *manage* intergovernmental relations and *make* federalism work.

Others, like Congressman Henry S. Reuss in his book, *Revenue Sharing*, call for Congress to use revenue sharing as a "catalyst" to reorganize the structure of state and local government. Congressman Reuss assumes that revenue sharing serves as a "crutch" to support what he alleges to be a bankrupt and inefficient system of state and local government. Instead, he argues, revenue sharing ought to be used as a "catalyst" to modernize state and local governments and make them more efficient. He presumes that the elimination of smaller units of local government, which he refers to as "wasteful Lilliputs" (Reuss, 1970: 143), and the creation of larger units of local government with greater management capabilities will yield increased efficiency. Still others urge the simplification of local government structures in order to enhance management capabilities on the part of the Federal government to exercise greater control over local government in the implementation of national policies. The Federal government is viewed as the proper authority to make constitutional decisions about the basic structure of state and local governments; and the president is being viewed as the proper authority to direct and manage the whole systems of national, state, and local governments.

At this juncture in American history, we cannot anticipate whether American government has become presidential government and whether the American people have lost control over their system of government. Various authors have written books on congressional government, presidential government, and judicial supremacy. So long as the search for a single ultimate center of authority has drawn competing analyses, some measure of confirmation has been given to the independent viability of the different decision structures in the national government. However, continued expansion of presidential government poses a potential threat to the viability of democratic institutions in American society unless effective limits can be reestablished.[5]

In his book on *The End of Liberalism,* Theodore J. Lowi advances the argument that the "First Republic" has already been succeeded by a "Second Republic" because of a failure to maintain constitutional limits in the 1960s and 1970s. The center of all government, Lowi contends, is the presidency. Congress has, in effect, become a part of the formal facade of government with little influence upon its operation. But Lowi's polemical argument is intended to provoke Americans into serious reflection about what is happening to the American system of government. Time may still be available to exercise some measure of reflection and choice about the structure of American government.

If the logic of a compound republic has merit, we might expect the nationalization of American government to yield increasingly serious problems of institutional weakness and institutional failure. We might expect that modern reform efforts to eliminate fragmentation of authority and overlapping jurisdictions will yield poorer performance rather than better performance. As the national government concerns itself with all matters of government, we might also expect serious neglect of those problems that are clearly of national importance. In addition, we might anticipate the existence of still other problems, particularly those affecting multinational communities of interest, to be intractable to resolution by unitary nation-states. In relation to each of these circumstances, the political theory of a compound republic may provide important conceptual tools for exploring a range of options that are of importance to the future of human civilization.

The Likely Failures of Increasing Consolidation of Governmental Authority

According to the precepts of the Wilsonian models of parliamentary government and bureaucratic administration, the basic sources of failure in the American system of government are fragmentation of authority and overlapping jurisdictions. Fragmentation of authority is assumed to confuse political responsibility in a democratic society. Overlapping jurisdictions are viewed from the Wilsonian perspective as pathological because they imply duplication of services and therefore create waste and inefficiency in government. The appropriate method for political reform and governmental reorganization is assumed to be one of creating a single center of ultimate authority to which a system of bureaucratic administration can be held accountable in discharging the prerogatives of government. Yet these characteristics of fragmentation of authority and overlapping jurisdictions are essential attributes of constitutional rule and of a federal system of government. A constitutional separation of powers entails fragmentation of authority. A federal system of government necessarily involves, as an essential defining characteristic, the existence of overlapping jurisdictions. Eliminating fragmentation of authority and overlapping jurisdictions would necessarily eliminate structures which are conducive to constitutional rule and a federal system of government.

The anomaly in contemporary American society is that the largest, most unified units of local government are the ones that are experiencing the most serious problems of failure to supply essential public goods and services. It is the largest cities that cannot control crime in the streets, maintain elementary standards of sanitation in public places, and prevent whole neighborhoods from being demolished. Public housing projects that win architectual awards are destroyed and subject to demolition within a decade. By contrast, the "Lilliputs," whether in black, white, or mixed communities manage to cope and at least avoid demolition.

Bureaucracies, which are assumed to be the embodiment of efficiency and rationality, have increasingly been observed to be characterized by rigid rules and lax enforcement, indifference to the problems confronting people in their particular circumstances, and gross inefficiency. Governments relying upon highly centralized bureaucracies promise more than they can perform. And the conditions of life confronting people are radically at variance with the expectations created by those who exercise the prerogatives of government.

So long as formulations like the Wilsonian views on fragmentation of authority and overlapping jurisdictions are accepted as intuitively obvious, there appears little reason to be sceptical and demand that those formulations be justified. What is intuitively obvious to common sense seemingly requires no further justification. However, it is a fundamental error for human beings, as fallible creatures, to make such an assumption. The important steps in the development of any science turns upon the discovery of counterintuitive relationships that call commonsense intuitions into question.

The problem can be illustrated by the observation that the sun always "rises" in the east, moves across the sky, and "sets" in the west. It is intuitively obvious that the sun rotates around the earth. It is only in the course of time that a counterintuitive explanation about the earth spinning in daily rotation and orbiting around the sun in an annual ellipse has been accepted as a plausible explanation. This explanation is counterintuitive to initial commonsense impressions.

Any effort to investigate the efficiency of administration in a federal system of government cannot turn upon presumptions that overlapping jurisdictions necessarily imply wasteful duplications of effort. Administration in a federal system of government must instead be considered in relation to multiorganizational structures that are coordinated through nonbureaucratic methods. Plausible concepts that allow overlapping jurisdictions to be treated as variables, not as evils, need to be formulated. The performance of differently structured administrative systems might then be compared with reference to criteria such as efficiency and justice.

The closest analogy to overlapping jurisdictions in a federal system of government is the structure of multiorganizational arrangements in a private "industry." Industries are typically composed of differently sized firms where relationships among firms are coordinated by processes of negotiation and exchange under conditions involving competitive options. Firms are often differentiated to perform complementary, as well as competing, services. Some firms operate as large-scale producers, others as intermediate suppliers, and still others as smaller retail and maintenance enterprises. Industries *without* "overlapping jurisdictions" have the characteristics of being vertically *integrated monopolies*. Industries with a large number of firms would be expected to perform differently than an integrated monopoly; and their performance would be expected to vary with the type of good or service being supplied.

We can anticipate problems in applying the concept of an "industry" to the public sector because public goods and services have different characteristics than private goods and services. A key difference is that units of government function as collective consumption units having to do with collective goods and services. They are constituted to take account of people's preferences, levy taxes, regulate patterns of use, and monitor the performance of producers. Units of government in a public economy perform their essential role by being the equivalent of consumer cooperatives. Making allowances for these differences, it is possible to view relationships in a federal system of administration as having the characteristics of "public-service industries" (V. Ostrom and E. Ostrom, 1965; 1977). This is a more "realistic" conception than assuming that all public sector activities must be viewed as internal to a single unit of government.

A federal system of administration viewed as industry structures would be composed of diverse, independent agencies, collaborating in supplying and arranging for the availability of different bundles of collective goods and services. A water industry, for example, might include large-scale producers like the U.S. Corps of Engineers or Reclamation Service, intermediate agencies like state departments of natural resources, and a combination of local public, cooperative, and private distributors supplying services directly to individual water users and serving many other communities of users who make diverse uses of water resource systems. Once one begins to think in this way, one can imagine the possibility of an education industry, a police industry, a fire-protection industry, a trash and garbage disposal industry, a welfare industry, a health-services industry, and many other public-service industries that would appropriately characterize a *federal* system of public administration. When such a concept is introduced, it is no longer intuitively obvious that overlapping jurisdictions yield duplication of services entailing waste and inefficiency (V. Ostrom, 1974).

Once different structural arrangements are conceptualized in theoretically meaningful ways and measured operationally, then it becomes possible to test hypotheses about the relationship of structures to performance inherent in different proposals for political reform and governmental reorganization. The assumption that eliminating multiple overlapping jurisdictions will yield increased efficiency is not supported by empirical research (E. Ostrom, 1972). The "wasteful Lilliputs," condemned by Congressman Reuss, stand critical scrutiny in efficiently providing *some* services for neighborhood-type communities. They function best when appropriately complemented by other differently sized (and overlapping) public-service agencies. Conversely, large police forces accountable to a single command structure, for example, perform poorly in responding to the needs of different neighborhoods in large cities. Interagency agreements and collaborative working arrangements mean that very little duplication exists in an initial response to calls for services among overlapping police jurisdictions; but back-up services are available if supplementary response capabilities are required.

Counterintuitive explanations for the superior performance of systems of administration characterized by overlapping jurisdictions point up the relevance of the political theory of a compound republic for addressing contemporary problems. As Americans experience increasing frustration with the operation of presidential government, a wide variety of options may be available if the premature rejection of federal theory is reconsidered.

The Neglect of Essential National Problems

The propensity to view every problem as a national problem subject to a national solution will predictably yield frustration and a neglect of those problems that are genuinely national in character. Problems of aging, health, housing, crime in the streets, poverty, urban affairs, and the environment derive from many different conditions. Some elements of these problems may have aspects that require national action; but they may also have many other dimensions of an individual, local, regional, or international character. There is no reason to assume that national considerations should dominate all other considerations. Instead, the task is one of working out arrangements that take proper account of diverse communities of interest. Some problems, such as aging, may be fundamentally intractable to political "solutions."

The propensity to view any problem as a crisis that can be appropriately addressed with the expenditure of public funds has made members of Congress into active collaborators in the game of raiding the national treasury. Everyone competes with everyone else to get as much as he can from Federal funds; and the expenditure of national public funds increasingly serves the private interests and needs of individuals and families rather than the public interests shared in common by a national community. The playing of this game, in turn, seriously interferes with the discharge of national responsibilities for regulating the national economy. Fiscal irresponsibility becomes a major factor potentially contributing to inflation, which contributes to the erosion of economic welfare, and everyone is left worse off.

A particularly perverse structure of incentives exists in assuming that any political crisis can appropriately be addressed by spending Federal funds. Political incentives exist to provoke a crisis mentality. The expenditure of money is then justified as a political imperative. Spending money to "solve" problems means that people are being employed to give more emphatic attention to "crises," not less. If expenditures get out of control and too many dollars are available to procure too few goods and services, inflation is stimulated.

Since a progressive income tax yields greater tax returns with higher incomes, inflation drives people into higher tax brackets even though their dollars are worth less. This means a proportionately greater tax yield for the national treasury with a declining proportionate tax yield for local and state treasuries when localities and states rely upon less elastic sources of revenue. This in turn creates increased incentives for state and local governments to play the game of raiding the national treasury. In the meantime, the national economy has the possibility of spiralling out of control with escalating national expenditures amid increasingly anxious proclamations of crises, when reflective inquiry is required. Measures such as indexing the income tax may alleviate some pressures; but fiscal accountability in a democracy depends upon the costs of services being borne by the relevant communities of beneficiaries.

Treating all problems as national problems contributes to an erosion of the ability of the national government to address those problems that are of fundamental national importance. The more modest presumptions of a national government confining its attention to problems of national affairs in a compound republic is more sound than the presumption that the national government is the proper ultimate authority in all matters of government. When politics becomes a game of everyone competing with everyone else to get as much as possible from the U.S. Treasury, we can expect a serious erosion in the quality of public life.

CONSTITUTING MULTINATIONAL COMMUNITIES

The presumption that national governments are the proper ultimate authorities in all matters of government also stands in the way of tending to multinational communities of interest. This is a problem that Woodrow Wilson lived to see as a central preoccupation in his presidency when he became involved in constitutional efforts to create a League of Nations. If he had given careful consideration to Alexander Hamilton's critical analysis of confederation and had considered Hamilton's formulation of the minimal conditions for developing viable political instrumentalities for tending to a multinational community of interest, Wilson would have recognized the precarious nature of a League of Nations and the high probability of its failure. We can sympathetically appreciate the nature of the problem that President Wilson confronted and recognize that a viable political resolution was not politically feasible. A misconceived step along the way may have been better than none.

Yet, Wilson's political science was a fundamental obstacle to

conceptualizing appropriate measures. One cannot have national governments that exercise ultimate authority in all
matters of government and at the same time create multinational instrumentalities of government capable of making
binding decisions pertaining to multinational communities of
interest. A theory of unlimited sovereignty drives to mutually
exclusive possibilities: sovereign nation-states or unlimited
world government. Instead, we need reference to a general
theory of limited constitutions where multiple units of government can exercise concurrent authority subject to enforceable limits of constitutional law. World government assumes
absurd proportions, unless one begins with Madison's perspective that the capacity of mankind for self-government can
only be realized with a proper structure of limited and concurrent governments where principles of self-government
can be applied to each community of interest.

The effort to fashion a multinational political community is
today being more realistically confronted among the peoples
of the European Community. The Treaty of Rome was of constitutional significance and a first step toward fashioning a political community in Western Europe. Europeans are cognizant of the fragile structure of the instrumentalities which
they are fashioning. The political theory of a compound republic as formulated in early American experiments in constitutional choice is relevant to tasks confronting Europe. In
turn, we have reason to hope that Europeans in confronting
their challenge will contribute to the further development of
a theory of constitutional choice for multinational communities. Achieving constitutional solutions in creating multinational communities is an alternative to imperialism and the
dominance of executive authority. The future development of
human civilization turns critically upon the resolutions that
are attained in Europe. Models of government that rely upon
presumptions that there must always be a single center of ultimate authority in all matters of government are not adequate
to that task.

The problem of fashioning political solutions to interde-

pendencies in human societies that recognize the legitimacy
of diverse communities of interest is by no means confined to
Europe. This is the critical problem in the Middle East where
communities of people of diverse cultural traditions have co-
existed for millenia. Creating new sovereign states in the
Middle East can be expected to exacerbate problems. The
task is one of working out mutually productive ways for resolving problems among different communities of people
living as neighbors in the same land. Federal approaches
offer, at least, a promise that is an alternative to struggles for
dominance and survival. In the Third World, the formula of
national independence and unlimited government is unlikely
to succeed among former colonies when it has failed in Europe. Increasing the capacity of mankind for self-government
depends upon fashioning alternatives both to imperialism
and to the use of unlimited authority to dominate social relationships in particular societies. Unlimited governments
are too inclined to treat people as subjects and then to use
instruments of violence to defend official exercise of governmental prerogative and to war upon subjects. This is why re-
iterating principles of constitutional choice in federal systems
of government enhances the prospect of democratic self-
government.

CONCLUSION

As Americans enter the third century of their experiments in
constitutional choice, they confront basic problems in reflecting upon what has happened in the twentieth century and
what it means to create and maintain a system of government
by reflection and choice. In principle, the challenges of the
twentieth century are no more difficult than those of machine
politics and boss rule and the continuing struggle of blacks
for human dignity. The most serious difficulty arises from
the basic rejection of the theory that was used to design the
American system of constitutional government. Without an
appropriate theory, people cannot hope to maintain systems
of government designed from reflection and choice. Theory

provides people with a basic understanding about the criteria, methods, and structures that apply to the proper conduct of government. Without an appropriate theory, people become the subjects of apparently uncontrollable forces where their fate is determined more by accident and force rather than reflection and choice.

We might anticipate that problems of institutional weakness and institutional failure associated with the excessive nationalization of American government will be the occasion for increasingly serious reflection about the organization of political processes in American society. Reliance upon any single authority for all matters of government presents serious difficulties for coping with increasingly complex patterns of interdependency in contemporary societies. The political theory of a compound republic presumes the concurrent existence of multiple communities of interest. Such a theory is open to the conceptualization of new communities of interest that can fashion new constitutional settlements where decisions can be taken with a limited exercise of governmental prerogative. This openness to new possibilities can range from considerations involving neighborhood communities in urban agglomerations to multinational communities of continental and global proportions. Where each community of interest exercises limited authority to govern its own affairs, each can proceed simultaneously to tend to its own affairs, leaving each other political community free to proceed independently in a similar way. Simultaneity of action among independently constituted and overlapping political communities allows for constructive responses to complexity. Diversity can exist in accommodating to different environmental conditions; and the formulation of public policies and the provision of public services can vary with different cultural aspirations and patterns of demand. Conducting concurrent experiments in constitutional choice offers a prospect of increasing the capacity of mankind for self-government.

NOTES

1. Tocqueville uses the expression "American republics" in referring to the states in Chapter XV on the unlimited power of the majority. He makes his intention explicit in Footnote 6 where he observes:

I presume that it is scarcely necessary to remind the reader here, as well as throughout this chapter, that I am speaking, not of the Federal government, but of the government of the individual states, which the majority controls at its pleasure. (Tocqueville, 1945: I, 269)

2. The best commentary on boss rule and machine politics is found in Moisei Ostrogorski, *Democracy and the Organization of Political Parties*. Volume II: The United States.

3. I write "potentially subject" because various drafts of proposed Federal regulations have been circulated that would make all research using "human subjects" depend upon prior approval by administrative authorities. The term "human subjects" has been construed sufficiently broadly to include reference to all historical and social scientific research. The protection of human subjects was conceived so as to require that anonymity be extended to anyone who was involved in the inquiry. Had such regulations been in effect, the study which I did as a doctoral dissertation, relying only upon my own resources and subsequently published as *Water and Politics*, would have required prior approval by an administrative committee. The method which I used of factually reporting events in relation to specifically named persons would have been in violation of proposed regulations. Regulations designed to protect "human subjects" can easily entail censorship to protect those engaged in political corruption and the abuse of political authority.

4. The creation of the so-called "plumber's unit" in the Domestic Council was pursuant to the authority vested with the president under the reorganization plan creating the Domestic Council. This was the unit involved in bugging the headquarters of the Democratic National Committee during the Nixon administration, an event that

gave rise to the so-called Watergate affair. So far as I know, no one has questioned the authority of President Nixon to create such an office at his own initiative and without public notice in the *Federal Register* even though some of the persons involved, including the director of the Domestic Council, were subsequently convicted for criminal offenses in obstructing justice in connection with the Watergate affair.

5. To assert, as I have done, that presidential government poses a threat to the viability of democratic institutions does not mean that it is the only threat. Presumptions of legislative supremacy pose a threat in failing both to recognize limits upon legislative authority and to exercise legislative authority in a proper manner. Failure to establish proper standards in legislation contributes to the general erosion of a rule of law.

Presumptions of judicial supremacy contribute to the abandonment of due process in the operation of the judicial process itself. When courts provide judicial remedies for *de facto* wrongs without engaging in a judicial inquiry to establish the *de jure* basis for the *de facto* wrong, they have abandoned the most fundamental element in the methodology of judicial due process. Racial segregation, for example, is treated as a *de facto* wrong without judicial inquiry to establish the *de jure* basis for the wrong. Remedies are then formulated without addressing the fundamental source of the wrong. Innocent third parties are mandated to provide remedies that have no essential causal relationship to the wrong. Unless schools are engaged in *de jure* segregation, there is no ground for assuming that they committed the wrong being alleged. Providing remedies to *de facto* segregation treats the symptom without identifying the source of the problem and providing an appropriate remedy when a wrong has been established.

As I indicated in the introduction to this chapter, my analysis is highly selective and limited. I am concerned to address some basic issues of constitutional importance without having addressed all such issues. When legislators, executive officials, judges, and citizens address themselves to "problems" of collective action without being cognizant of the proper methods and limits that apply to the processes of government, there is a serious danger that "accident and force" rather than "reflection and choice" will prevail in human relationships. When that happens, efforts to right wrongs lead to the compounding of wrongs, and the offices of justice become the instruments of injustice.

CHAPTER NINE

The Constitutional Level of Analysis: A Challenge

THEORIES, LIVING REALITIES, AND BRUTE FACTS

In the essays published as *The Federalist*, Alexander Hamilton, John Jay, and James Madison addressed the constitutional level of analysis. That is, they conceptualized, analyzed, and explained the provisions of the U.S. Constitution by drawing upon a general theory of limited constitutions. This is the intellectual apparatus that I call the political theory of a compound republic. It is a logic that might be used to design constitutional rules for other units of government and collective decision-making arrangements. The theory is as relevant to the contemporary world as it was to the world of 1787.[1]

Before one can begin to appreciate the logic of a compound republic, any scholar or analyst must make a much more extended inquiry about the constitutional level of analysis. In my own inquiry, I have found Thomas Hobbes's analysis in *Leviathan* and *De Cive* to be especially helpful. He establishes the foundations for the constitutional level of analysis with great care. Hobbes's own political theory leads him to expound a unitary theory of sovereignty as the only way to constitute government in a commonwealth. Hobbes's theory of sovereignty is the antithesis of a general theory of limited constitutions. One does not have to agree with his prescriptions to acknowledge the importance of his work for analysis conducted at a constitutional level.

Montesquieu's *The Spirit of the Laws* is also helpful in clarifying constitutional foundations. Montesquieu's work enabled me to understand how one could take Hobbes's account of democracy in *De Cive*, add to it the concept of a constitution (the rules that apply to the conduct of an assembly), have recourse to a compound system of republics, and thereby transform a theory of sovereignty into a theory for the governance of a democratic society. Hobbes's concept of democracy, so transformed, meets Madison's condition for basing "all our political experiments on the capacity of mankind for self-government." Rousseau poses important puzzles, and one might conceive his general will as the shared common understanding that applies to the constitutional level of analysis. Locke added important calculations in thinking about the differentiation of governmental authority with reference to legislative and executive powers. David Hume adds great depth to the problem of normative inquiry at the constitutional level of analysis as does Adam Smith in *The Theory of Moral Sentiments*.

There are others whose work, acclaimed in other contexts, is seriously deficient at the constitutional level of analysis. Jeremy Bentham, in moving to a summary concept of utility, made important contributions to modern economic analysis; but the concept of utility has greatly impoverished constitutional inquiry. Summarizing all values on a single scale called "utility" sweeps aside considerations of mutual respect, justice, and liberty which are basic to constitutional analysis. John Austin's analysis of the place of constitutional law as positive morality rather than positive law enables one to appreciate the intellectual achievement attained in *The Federalist* and Austin's failure to understand that achievement. Hegel and Marx offered alternative explanations for human social and cultural evolution which render constitutional choice largely irrelevant. Lenin, on the other hand, develops a theory of revolution in *What Is To Be Done?* that brings one back to the equivalent of Hobbes's theory of sovereignty for fashioning the leadership for a revolutionary movement. In *State and Revolution*, Lenin follows Marx in anticipating the withering away of the state; but his revolutionary party becomes the new sovereign in the Soviet state, as Hobbes would have anticipated. Milovan Djilas (1957: especially 37–38) recognizes that the Communist party's monopoly of the state apparatus has created a new ruling class in the socialist societies of Eastern Europe. We have as much to learn from failures as from successes in addressing the constitutional level of analysis; but we do need to know how to address that level of analysis.

Political analysts in the nineteenth century were preoccupied with "living realities," not with the design and formulation of experiments in constitutional choice. Walter Bagehot, in *The English Constitution,* first published in 1867, describes his effort as portraying "living reality" in contrast to "paper descriptions." Constitutional formulations were associated with "paper descriptions." Bagehot, Wilson, and others in that tradition never confronted the irony that they too put words on paper and thus rendered paper descriptions. Generations of legal and political analysts, who became known as "realists," were inspired by Bagehot's efforts to come to terms with "living realities" rather than "paper descriptions."

In his efforts to represent the living reality of the English constitution, Bagehot viewed the task of the analyst as breaking through the facade of the dignified parts to describe the efficient parts of a constitution. The Cabinet was, for Bagehot, the efficient core of the English system. It tied the working parts together into a single unitary whole. Anomalies arise in his analysis because Bagehot also viewed human governance as based upon methods of discussion (Cf. Bagehot, 1908). He thus retained a fundamental concern for basic criteria at the constitutional level of analysis. Due process of government, viewed from a constitutional perspective, is one that enables discussions to occur where contestable arguments can be advanced to inform deliberations about governmental policies.

A careful reading of Bagehot reveals a concern for checks and balances that facilitate a proper order of debate and deliberation. In the introduction to the second edition published in 1872, Bagehot anticipated that the voice of the people could become the voice of the devil under the perverse circumstances where ignorant masses are manipulated by po-

litical demagogues and wirepullers. Checks become necessary
to rationality in order to provide a structure that enables each
participant in a political process to listen to "the reasons of
others," to compare "them quietly with one's own reasons,"
and then to be "guided by the result" (Bagehot, 1964: 297).
The extension of voting to masses of people by the Reform
Act of 1867 meant that the dignified parts of the constitution
were no longer there to shield the quality of parliamentary
discussion that informed the efficient parts of the constitution. Demagogues and wirepullers could be expected to transform Parliament into a new form of public theater.

Woodrow Wilson's efforts to reveal living reality were inspired by Bagehot without being troubled by the possibility of
Vox populi becoming *Vox diaboli*. Wilson saw his task of portraying the living reality of the American constitution as one
where an observer would

escape from theory and attach himself to facts, not allowing himself
to be confused by a knowledge of what that government was intended to be, or led away into conjectures as to what it may one day
become, but striving to catch its present phases and to photograph
the delicate organism in all its characteristic parts exactly as it is today; an undertaking all the more arduous and doubtful of issue because it has to be entered into without guidance from writers of ac-
knowledged authority. (Wilson, 1956: 30)

This conception of a political observer's task suggests a calculated effort to turn one's back upon the cumulative efforts of
others to inquire about the nature and constitution of order
in human societies. Instead, the observer is represented as
painting word pictures about institutions of government as
living realities. Considerations of what government were "intended to be" or what they "may one day become" were to be
set aside as theoretical conjectures. We must instead rely upon
human vision as though one could see everything in pristine
clarity without a conceptual apparatus to suggest what to look
for, how to discern potential difficulties, and how to evaluate
performance.

We do not "see" the conceptual apparatus that enables us to make sense of the world when attempting to portray living realities. The logic of any artifactual creation is to be understood in large part by what it was intended to be. Conjectures about what it "may one day become" provide grounds for testing how design characteristics can be expected to affect conduct and performance. Wilson's rejection of theory ran the risk of dismissing the prior accumulation of knowledge as irrelevant, without trying to sort out and distinguish the merit of different efforts to think about the governance of human societies. Thus, we observe sweeping tendencies to reject "all niceties of constitutional restriction" and "broad principles of constitutional limitation." These had presumably been swept aside or overridden by "a thoroughly organized system of congressional control." The "facts," then, gave "a very rude negative to some theories of balance and some schemes of distributed power" (Wilson, 1956: 31).

Wilson's conclusion, that a thoroughly organized system of congressional government dominated the living reality of American politics, poses a deep puzzle in light of Hobbes's analysis of democracy in *De Cive*. Hobbes argues that there are essential conditions which frame a democracy. Exigencies may arise in a democratic society where the extraordinary prerogatives of government are assigned to particular officials who act as agents on behalf of the people who govern in assembly. A possibility always exists that those agents may usurp authority and assume the full prerogatives of government. If they do so, and a people acquiesces in such a usurpation of authority, Hobbes asserts that the "death" of democracy has occurred. Was Wilson's vision of congressional government a preliminary manifestation of pathologies that might eventuate in the death of democracy? Might "presidential government" be the terminal stage in that process?

The essential condition for the survival of democracy in Hobbes's analysis is that the people maintain limits with respect to the exercise of governmental authority. If constitutions specify the terms and conditions of government, then "constitutional restrictions" and "broad principles of constitutional limitations" are of fundamental importance. The failure to maintain limits will mark the death of democracy.

A system of popular or democratic government can be maintained so long as people continue to exercise the basic prerogatives of constitutional choice and hold those who exercise governmental prerogatives accountable to constitutional limits and standards of performance inherent in a general theory of limited constitutions. This is the appropriate foundation for civic education and for critical discussions about the living reality in any system of democratic government. The proper discharge of the prerogatives of citizenship and of public office can be judged only with reference to the constitutional level of analysis.

Conjectures about discrepancies between "living realities" and constitutional formalities have an important place at a constitutional level of analysis. When the working parts in a system of governance fail to perform as intended, we have reason to believe that design concepts may have been inadequate. Problems of institutional weakness or institutional failure may exist. The rise of machine politics and boss rule in the nineteenth century did pose a fundamental challenge to constitutional government in the United States. Tocqueville had assessed the possibility that such a development might occur in his chapter on the unlimited power of the majority. Moisei Ostrogorski, in the second volume of his *Democracy and the Organization of Political Parties,* goes a long way in helping us to understand the constitutional character of political parties in governmental processes. A great deal can be learned about processes of coalition formation and the function of political parties in light of both American and European efforts to maintain party rivalry as a way of exploring alternative possibilities without falling victims to boss rule. Those problems need to be understood at a constitutional level of analysis.

The critique of the legal and political realists strongly emphasized that constitutional provisions can become mere formalities without much bearing upon what happens in the workings of government. This difficulty was well recognized by both Hamilton and Madison. Mere words on paper do not become operable in human conduct. Parchment barriers to the usurpation of authority are never sufficient. The problem is how to build structures and processes of governance so that individuals as actors are led to give force and effect to conceptions symbolized as words on paper in ordering their relationships to one another. But, a critical consciousness of what was intended and what possibilities might occur are necessary to maintain the integrity of any set of rule-ordered relationships. If words were self-formulating, self-applying, and self-enforcing, we might conceive of a word-ordered universe where governments were unnecessary. Giving effect to words on paper is a general problem which applies to all rules as word-ordered relationships and is not confined to constitutions.

If we dismiss constitutions as words on paper without meaningful significance, the same problem can apply to the enactments of legislatures. Legislatures, too, can put words on paper that have no particular significance for ordering relationships in human societies. Under such circumstances, legislatures, including Congress, can become the ceremonial facade of government. Responsibility for formulating rules and regulations may be passed along to someone else, such as subordinate officials in the bureaucracy. Rules and regulations sprout everywhere. Any pretense of maintaining a rule of law can be abandoned. Laws can instead become little more than occasional traps for money when bribe bargains become the price for getting one's own way. Everyone can end up bribing everyone else. Tragedies arise when conditions of scarcity impose constraints. Many wind up being oppressed and exploited by others; and few have incentives to do more than is minimally necessary to meet the exigencies of life.

Efforts to describe the "living reality" of government often take on the characteristic of describing machines without seeing what they do. The machine works, but we do not see its effects upon the conditions of life in society. Some of the

descriptions of the more confined machinery of local government were accompanied by portraits of corruption as
perverse relationships between officials and others in the
community. Such studies were called muckraking. Outside
the context of local communities, efforts to portray the living
reality of government were usually devoid of such links to the
living reality that occurred in the lives of ordinary people. An
image of what was missing is indicated by Harold Lasswell's
title of a book, *Politics: Who Gets What, When, How*. If only we
could see connections between the machinery of government
as a living reality and who gets what, when, and how, we
might come to a better understanding of government as a
living reality. There would then be a link between "government" and something else.

While Lasswell proposed to take the "working attitude of
practicing politicians" (Lasswell, 1958: 7) as the basis for his
study, he was never able to present a portrait of politics as a
living reality. The institutions of the national government
were presumed to be a supergame. A stratum of population
characterized as "elites" were presumed to be players in that
supergame. Lasswell's *Politics,* however, is not a portrait of a
living reality that enables one to see who gets what, when, and
how. Rather, it indicates the means used and the results
achieved in a topical presentation devoid of the living reality
that occurs in the play of the game of politics.

Anyone who has witnessed a game of football will appreciate the great difficulty of rendering an effective portrait of
that "living reality" in all its phases and characteristic parts.
An effort to portray the living reality of a system of governance and its operation in a society, without a knowledge of
what is intended and conjectures about what may occur, exceeds the limits of human cognition. John Searle, a contemporary scholar in the philosophy of language, indicates how
we understand the facts of games as living realities. We can
understand those living realities only if we have an implicit
understanding of how rules are "constitutive" of social facts as
"institutional" facts (Searle, 1969: 51). The living reality of a

football game becomes comprehensible only when we understand the rules of the game, which are based on an understanding of what the game was intended to be and what types
of play might occur in it.

Searle argues that the living reality of human institutions
can never be understood as "brute facts." To illustrate his
point, Searle suggests that a group of highly trained scientific
observers be asked to formulate the basic scientific law that
could be used to describe the game of American football. He
suggests that these scientific observers might discover a "law
of periodic clustering." Searle states the law of periodic clustering in the following way:

> [A]t statistically regular intervals, organisms in like colored shirts
> cluster together in a roughly circular fashion (the huddle). Further-
> more, at equally regular intervals, circular clustering is followed by
> linear clustering (the teams line up for the play) and linear clustering
> is followed by the phenomenon of linear interpenetration. (Searle,
> 1969: 52. Searle's parenthetical observations.)

Having discovered the law of periodic clustering, our scientific observers presumably have provided us with a scientific
understanding of the living reality represented by the game
of football.

Our response to Searle's conjecture is to be struck by its absurdity. The irony is that Searle's conjecture is no more absurd
than suggesting that anyone who wants to understand the
living reality of politics should "escape from theory and attach
himself to facts, not allowing himself to be confused by a
knowledge of what government was intended to be, or led
away with conjectures as to what it may one day become . . ."
(Wilson, 1956: 30). When this happens, observers cut themselves off from essential considerations that might enable
them to understand the point of the game, the range of
strategies appropriate to a fair game, and what constitutes
foul play.

We can understand the structures and processes of government, or other aspects of human social reality, only as institu-

tional facts. Institutional facts exist because rules are constitutive of human social relationships. We understand the games of life by the way that they are constituted according to rules and standards of propriety and fairness. Rules assign both capabilities and limitations for the actions that can be taken. We understand rules and the meaning of rule-ordered relationships with reference to what was intended to be and in light of conjectures about what may occur.

If people intend to create a system of government where those who make rules, enforce them, and judge their application are themselves subject to enforceable rules of constitutional law, it is absurd to ignore constitutional restrictions and principles of constitutional limitations in playing the game that we call democracy. People who play that game need to be especially cognizant of conjectures about what may occur if some players pursue strategies to rig the game by dominating the choices of officials and judges. A fair game cannot be maintained without careful attention to particular restrictions and to principles for formulating essential limitations.

When people in a democratic society consider rules that establish the terms and conditions of government as mere words on paper, they are in deep trouble. Rules may need to be revised; but revisions need to be made in light of some fundamental criteria for what is required to maintain the basic integrity of a game (a complexly configured multigame) that we call democracy. There may be counterintuitive circumstances, such as the oligarchical tendencies that arise in all deliberative assemblies, which require special safeguards. In such circumstances, people may find themselves trapped by preemptive moves where a few players learn how to set the agenda and dominate the play of the game. All of these contingencies require cautious regard for rules that establish appropriate restrictions. The integrity of a fair game cannot be maintained without an awareness of basic principles of constitutional limitations. When human beings abandon the possibility of creating and maintaining a system of enforceable rules that apply to the conduct of government, they put them-

selves at the disposal of those who govern. This has been the
fate of most people through the course of human history. The
rule-ruler-ruled relationship has usually been a simple dominance relationship where some—rulers—dominate and exploit others—their subjects.

COPING WITH BRUTE FACTS AND BRUTE EMPIRICISM

Efforts to understand American politics as a living reality
have generated an intellectual odyssey of almost unbelievable
proportions. Much of my life has been involved in that odyssey. My account is, ironically, my effort to understand that odyssey as a living reality. My conjectures should be treated as
contestable. My reference is to an explicit literature and historical experience which anyone else can study and interpret
independently. We can understand what occurred only in
light of inquiry informed by conjectures about the meaning
of that experience.

I regard Harold Lasswell as one of the intellectual giants in
American political science during the twentieth century. His
Politics: Who Gets What, When, How was a serious effort to
understand politics as a supergame. Instead of resting there,
Lasswell found it necessary to go back to fundamentals and
begin to build a theoretical framework for political inquiry. By
fundamentals, I mean basic elements and relationships represented by such terms as actors, acts, environment, response,
symbol, identification, and personality. Lasswell built a technical language for disciplined inquiry and discourse about the
complex structures and processes that occur in political reality.
These efforts are expounded in *Power and Society,* coauthored
with Abraham Kaplan, a distinguished philosopher. *Power
and Society* had an important role in my own intellectual development. I mastered the language and transformational logic
expounded by Lasswell and Kaplan. I worked with colleagues
who had also learned that language. Errors were challenged
and differences clarified so that we knew what we were saying

to one another. This was probably the most fundamental step I took in becoming a political scientist.

We need to discipline our use of language if we are to know what we hear and what we say when we talk to one another. Too much of the ordinary language of political discourse is filled with words that can mean anything, everything, and nothing. We talk to one another, but we do not communicate with one another. Human communication depends upon having a shared community of understanding about what words mean. Mere words as such do not have meaning. I know of no one who has seen "the" government.[2] Bagehot trapped himself into believing that he could use words to portray a "living reality" that could be contrasted to "paper descriptions" while offering no more than a paper description himself. Wilson and other legal and political realists caught themselves in this same trap. Words depend upon conceptions imbedded in logical constructions expressed as elements and relationships associated at diverse levels of consideration.

In the course of time, I went on to learn the basic language and transformational logic used by economists, especially as that language and logic was applied to the study of collective choice, including its application to constitutional choice as expounded by James Buchanan and Gordon Tullock in *The Calculus of Consent*. Having learned Lasswellese and Economese, I acquired some rudimentary skill in unravelling the language and computational logic inherent in the work of other political theorists, as I have attempted to do in this book. Other thinkers, including Thomas Hobbes, had developed frameworks for political inquiry that have strong parallels to the efforts of Lasswell and Kaplan. Once one comes to appreciate the intellectual apparatus that scholars use as their frameworks for political inquiry, it also becomes possible to read descriptive studies with an awareness of how words are used, not in standard English but in a technical language with its own computational logic. The English language is rich enough in its miscellaneous terms and definitions that it can be used to articulate many different technical languages with specialized terminologies and logics. I have found the work of Tocqueville, both in *Democracy in America* and *The Old Regime and the French Revolution,* to be especially important when read this way. Tocqueville thoroughly understood the political theory of a compound republic and the basic logics that apply to other types of political regimes.[3]

These intellectual efforts on my part presented me with a strange puzzle. I accepted the basic contention in Lasswell and Kaplan that a theoretical framework was necessary to empirical inquiry. I accepted their argument that "brute empiricism" was an unsatisfactory way to proceed with political inquiry. However, I was presented with the anomaly of Lasswell and Kaplan pointing to Tocqueville as coming dangerously close to "brute empiricism" in his descriptive studies. "Brute empiricism" consisted of "the gathering of 'facts' without a corresponding elaboration of hypotheses" (Lasswell and Kaplan, 1950: x). However, I had come to see Tocqueville's work as carefully informed by a theoretical framework.

In the author's introduction to *Democracy in America,* Tocqueville posed a basic issue in political theory: Can human beings aspire to increasing equality in human societies without great risk to aspirations for freedom? Hobbes would have recognized that the liberty of subjects is constrained by the requirements of sovereignty. Sovereignty meant, in Hobbes's formulation, that those who rule are the source of law and, as such, are above the law and cannot be held accountable to law. The general theory of limited constitutions meant, by contrast, that the terms and conditions of government can be specified as fundamental law and systems of government constituted where all authority is subject to limits and no one exercises unlimited authority.

In the concluding paragraph to Chapter 1, on the geography of North America, Tocqueville wrote:

In that land the great experiment to construct society upon a new basis was to be made by civilized man; and it is there, for the first time, that theories hitherto unknown, or deemed impracticable, were to exhibit a spectacle for which the world had not been prepared by the history of the past. (Tocqueville, 1945: 25)

Tocqueville was suggesting that an intellectual development of Copernican proportions had occurred and that the "theories hitherto unknown or deemed impracticable" had been used to conduct a "great experiment." That experiment exhibited "a spectacle for which the world had not been prepared by the history of the past." Great societies in the history of the past had all been constituted as empires. A general theory of limited constitutions had enabled a people on the North American continent to reiterate principles of democratic self-government to reach from the little traditions of townships to a great society of continental proportions. Was this an introduction to a political narrative grounded in brute empiricism?

In a brief chapter on "The Sovereignty of the People of America," Tocqueville expounded the basic principle used in organizing that "great experiment." Sovereignty was conceived as "the right of making laws" (Tocqueville, 1945: 123) in contrast to the way that Hobbes conceived sovereignty. Constitutions are fundamental laws. People who exercise the basic prerogatives of constitutional choice formulate the fundamental laws that apply to the conduct of governments.

In concluding that chapter, Tocqueville indicated the relevance of these circumstances. "In some countries," he observed "a power exists which, though it is in a degree foreign to the social body, directs it and forces it to pursue a certain track" (Tocqueville, 1945: 57). In those countries, it would be appropriate to speak of states which rule over societies. "In others," Tocqueville continued, "the ruling force is divided, being partly within and partly without the ranks of the people." In such circumstances, we might speak of the powers of government being shared by a "king-in-parliament" with aspects of local self-government. To this, Tocqueville contrasted the American situation: "But nothing of the kind is to be seen in the United States, there society governs itself for itself" (Tocqueville, 1945: 57). A system of governance existed where a society had become self-governing and did not depend upon a state to rule over society.

Such a possibility was of revolutionary importance in a world where great societies had existed only as empires. Liberty had existed among the petty warring city republics of Greece, and in other self-governing city republics; but no great society of continental proportions had existed as a compound system of self-governing republics. The closest approximations were two confederations: the United Provinces and Switzerland. France, in Tocqueville's lifetime and that of his father, was first an absolute monarchy, a constitutional monarchy, a republic, then an empire, a restored monarchy, a second republic, and a second empire, if I have the succession correct.

In his concluding assessment of the institutions of governance in American democracy, Tocqueville identified the key institutions contributing most to self-governing capabilities as: (1) the federal form of government, (2) township institutions, and (3) the constitution of the judiciary. More important than these institutional arrangements, however, were the habits of the heart and mind of the American people, because individuals are first their own governors in democratic republics and because citizens use a common understanding based upon shared habits of the heart and mind to formulate fundamental law and hold officials accountable to it. There are, however, dangers that this shared understanding might erode if people "fall to denying what they cannot understand" (Tocqueville, 1945: II, 4), neglect the importance of the utility of form and the science of association upon which an appreciation for the utility of form is based, and act upon natural inclinations stimulated by anxiety and envy. In those circumstances, democratic societies can be expected to give way to increasing centralization of authority and the abandonment of self-governing capabilities. Tocqueville, in his analysis, gives relatively little attention to Congress. In his view, the federal system, townships, religion, the judiciary, voluntary associations, and the press occupy places of more fundamental importance in the governance of American society.

We are now confronted with the circumstance that visions of the "living reality" adopted by the legal and political realists overwhelmingly involve a search for some single ultimate center of self-sufficient authority to direct the machinery of government and to rule over society. Wilson initially saw Congress as that supreme authority in a system of congressional government. But he later saw the "new leadership of the Executive" as promising to "substitute statesmanship for government by mass meeting" (Wilson, 1956: 23). Presidential government had promise of being an alternative to congressional government. Others have had visions of judicial supremacy where a Supreme Court was the ultimate authority which had the last say.

A basic proposition, characteristically asserted as a self-evident truth by these realists, is that "the more power is divided the more irresponsible it becomes" (Wilson, 1956: 77). The logical correlary is: The more power is unified the more responsible it becomes. At this point we can contrast this presupposition with the basic conceptualization in Hobbes's theory of sovereignty: a sovereign, as the ultimate source of law, is above the law, and cannot be held accountable to law. Those who exercise ultimate authority and have the last say are not legally and politically responsible to other human beings. They are, in some fundamental way, outlaws (outside the reach of law) in relation to the rest of society. Persons who occupy such positions are the ultimate judges of their own interests in relation to the interests of others. This violates a basic precept of justice that "no one is a fit judge of his or her own cause in relation to the interest of others."

Those who presume to see systems of government as "living realities," without the benefit of an explicit analytical language to serve as an intellectual tool for enquiring about that "reality," commit an added error of assuming the existence of self-evident truths. What appears to be intuitively obvious may not be true. As I indicated in Chapter 8, it is intuitively obvious to me that the sun rises in the east, moves across the sky, sets in the west, and rotates around the earth each day. I have come to appreciate that my intuitive perception of earthly and heavenly realities is false. There is a better way of conceptualizing that reality. That alternative conceptualization is counterintuitive, requires a more complex explanation, and offers a better understanding of earthly and heavenly events. We cannot build a political science upon intuitively obvious, commonsense observations of human institutions as "living realities." There are many counterintuitive and counterintentional contingencies that need to be taken into account if a political science is to be a science of human institutions rather than paintings presented in words. Every counterintuitive or counterintentional contingency is a potential trap for the naive realist, who presumes to see the whole picture of living reality with its self-evident truths.

In such circumstances, those who escape from theory and attach themselves to facts in portraying the living reality of American government can be observed, like Wilson, making clean sweeps of "constitutional restrictions" and "broad principles of constitutional limitations" for a thoroughly organized system of central-government control. A "rude negative" is given to the American theory of constitutional government (Wilson, 1956: 31). When a logic of limited constitutions is abandoned as "literary theories" and "paper pictures," and correlative limits upon government are abandoned while making increasing demands upon "the" government to tend to all problems in life, we run the risk of also abandoning the conditions for maintaining a self-governing society. The death of democracy occurs when limits no longer apply to those who presume to exercise the prerogatives of government. We may have become a nation, to paraphrase Tocqueville, where freedom was not torn from our grasp by foreign conquerors, but where freedom was trampled under foot (Tocqueville, 1945: II, 47).

When we cut ourselves off from understanding the constitutive nature of rules in creating the institutional facts of life in human societies, we can leave ourselves, like Searle's scientific observers, casting around for scientific generalizations. Those who speculate about strategic implications of the game of politics view the whole point of the game as winning and reaping the fruits of victory. Pulling the wool over people's eyes, lying, and cheating are useful strategies if you get away with them. Elections, debate, and deliberation are aspects of a theater for creating public images that have no necessary connection to solving problems shared by communities of people and developing shared communities of understanding of what it means to live in a self-governing society.

This strange intellectual odyssey can be viewed as the plausible result of presupposing that human beings can somehow "see" human societies and systems of governance as "living realities." No human being can "see" that reality, much less paint word pictures which accurately portray that reality. We simply cannot see the whole picture of that living reality. To assume that we can see the whole picture is to create gross illusions about human capabilities. We fantasize; we deny what we cannot "see"; we trample under foot; and we acquiesce in the death of democracy. We praise greatness; we hail progress; but we fail to read the signs of decay in our own civilization.

THE CONCEPTUALIZATION OF
ALTERNATIVE POSSIBILITIES

An alternative to presuming that we can directly see human societies as living realities is to learn how to use the languages and computational logics that are appropriate to the study of human societies as rule-ordered relationships. The constitutional level of analysis is the foundation for building analytical capabilities. We use the logics of alternative possibilities to come to a basic understanding about how systems of governance work both in relation to what they were intended to be and in light of conjectures about what may one day occur. This is the method of competing hypotheses that stands at the foundation of the experimental sciences. We observe what occurs in relation to what was intended to be and come to a better understanding about the basic linkages that exist in human societies as aggregations of simultaneous and sequential games that work themselves out in continuities of space and time. We need to understand the concepts and the computational logic that inform experiments in constitutional choice. We can learn from the puzzles and difficulties that arise. But we can understand the meaning of particular experiments only in light of a more general understanding of the problems of governance in human societies and how human beings have coped with these problems through history.

It is also possible to use the intellectual apparatus afforded by the languages and computational logics appropriate to political inquiry to conjecture about the future—about what may one day occur, to paraphrase Wilson. In *Democracy in America,* Tocqueville closed the first volume with a conjecture that the United States and Russia, whose principles of collective action rely, respectively, upon freedom and obedience, will each come "to sway the destinies of half the globe" (Tocqueville, 1945: 434). Elsewhere he despaired that France could ever break the shackles of centralization (Tocqueville, 1959: 189–190).

Today I am led to conjecture that the United States, snared in a morass created by the increasing nationalization of American society, will be forced to draw back and explore ways to free itself from the central-governmental trap. I shall not be surprised if France frees itself from excessive centralization and moves forward at the forefront of European development. Spain will not be far behind. Italy, the home of the free cities that gave birth to the Enlightenment, may experience a new renaissance. In these circumstances, Germany will abandon its anxieties, generate new levels of achievement, and again turn outward in relating its own cultural achievements to the cultural achievements of other peoples. The British will continue to ponder about the puzzle of whether Parliament can reform itself.

Europe may again spark intellectual developments, create new configurations of institutional arrangements in the European Community, and achieve material and cultural advances that carry human civilization far beyond present thresholds. We may again move forward toward a new era in human civilization where peoples learn to base their political experiments upon the capacity of mankind for self-government. Acquiring that capacity depends upon learning how to use theoretical conjectures, reflections, and choice to conceptualize, conduct, and construe the meaning of diverse experiments in constitutional choice. In such a world, liberation theologies, if they are to contribute to human liberation, will have close intellectual and spiritual kinships to political theories of compound republics.

NOTES

1. This does not imply that citizens in modern times or other lands would produce a document exactly like the U.S. Constitution if they were to use the political theory of a compound republic. The product of an application of a theory should not be confused with the underlying theory used in design. This would be like confusing the blueprints for the Brooklyn Bridge with the theory underlying the design of bridges. The same theories used by the designers of the Brooklyn Bridge can be used in other circumstances to conceptualize dramatically different blueprints. Nor does this statement imply that the theory used in 1787 was complete. Major increments have been added, including a better understanding of processes of coalition formation and the function of political parties, institutions of local government, systems of public administration, and international organization.

2. John Dewey once observed:

The moment we utter the words "The State" a score of intellectual ghosts rise to obscure our vision. Without our intention and without our notice, the notion of 'The State' draws us imperceptibly into a consideration of the logical relationship of various ideas to one another, and away from facts of human activity. (Dewey, n.d.: 8–9)

Dewey's comment is interesting because he neglects the possibility that societies might be organized by reference to different theoretical conceptions. The logical relationships of various ideas to one another inherent in the concept of "the State" may not be appropriate to understanding the facts of human activities that are organized by the logical relationships of various ideas to one another inherent in a self-governing society. Dewey's effort to address the problem of governance in *The Public and Its Problems* was not well grounded in the general theory of limited constitutions used to design the American experiments in constitutional choice. He does come to some interesting generalizations in his efforts to generate hypotheses about the "facts of human activity" in that system of governance. He could have gone much further if he had built upon Tocqueville's conjectures about a "great experiment" on the North American continent and the way that experiment might be viewed as being based upon theories that were radically at variance with the theory of "the State."

3. Different types of political regimes may require different logics in the same way that the design, construction, operation, maintenance, and repair of gasoline and electrical motors require recourse to different logics.

References

Ashby, W. Ross. 1956. *An Introduction to Cybernetics*. New York: John Wiley and Sons.

————. 1960. *Design for a Brain: The Origin of Adaptive Behavior*. New York: John Wiley and Sons.

Austin, John. 1955. The *Province of Jurisprudence Determined*. H.L.A. Hart, ed. London: Weidenfeld and Nicolson.

Bagehot, Walter. 1908. *Physics and Politics*. New York: D. Appleton.

————. 1964. *The English Constitution*. R.H.S. Crossman, ed. London: C. A. Watts.

Beard, Charles A. 1965. *An Economic Interpretation of the Constitution of the United States*. New York: Free Press.

Bentham, Jeremy. 1948. *The Principles of Morals and Legislation*. New York: Hafner Press.

Bish, Robert. 1971. *The Public Economy of Metropolitan Areas*. Chicago: Markham.

———— and Vincent Ostrom. 1973. *Understanding Urban Government: Metropolitan Reform Reconsidered*. Washington, D.C.: American Enterprise Institute.

Boulding, Kenneth E. 1963. "Toward a Pure Theory of Threat Systems." *American Economic Review*, Vol. 53 (May), 424–434.

Buchanan, James M. and Gordon Tullock. 1962. *The Calculus of Consent, Logical Foundations of Constitutional Government*. Ann Arbor: University of Michigan Press.

Burns, James MacGregor. 1963. *The Deadlock of Democracy*. Englewood Cliffs, New Jersey: Prentice-Hall.

Calhoun, John C. 1953. *A Disquisition on Government*. C. Gordon Post, ed. Indianapolis: Bobbs-Merrill.

Chomsky, Noam. 1980. *Rules and Representations*. New York: Columbia University Press.

Commons, John R. 1959. *Legal Foundations of Capitalism*. Madison: University of Wisconsin Press.

Cooke, Jacob E., ed. 1961. *The Federalist*. Middletown, Connecticut: Wesleyan University Press.

Dahl, Robert A. 1963. *A Preface to Democratic Theory*. Phoenix Books edition. Chicago: University of Chicago Press.

Dewey, John. N.d. *The Public and Its Problems*. Denver: Alan Swallow.

Diamond, Martin. N.d. "The Federalist's View of Federalism." *In* George C. S. Benson, ed. *Essays on Federalism*. Claremont, California: Claremont Men's College, Institute for Studies in Federalism.

Djilas, Milovan. 1957. *The New Class*. New York: Praeger.

Elazar, Daniel J. 1966. *American Federalism: A View from the States*. New York: Thomas Y. Crowell.

Friedmann, Wolfgang. 1964. *Law in a Changing Society*. Middlesex, England: Penguin Books.

Gasser, Adolph. 1939. *Geschichte der Volksfreiheit und der Demokratie*. Aarau, Switzerland: Verlag H. R. Sauerlaender.

Goodnow, Frank J. 1900. *Politics and Administration*. New York: Macmillan.

Gregg, Phillip M. 1974. "Units and Levels of Analysis: A Problem of Policy Analysis in Federal Systems." *Publius,* Vol. 4 (Fall), 59–86.

Hamilton, Alexander, John Jay, and James Madison. N.d. *The Federalist*. Edward Mead Earle, ed. New York: Modern Library.

———. N.d. *The Federalist Papers*. Clinton Rossiter, ed. New York: Mentor Books, New American Library of World Literature.

Hobbes, Thomas. 1949. *De Cive or the Citizen*. Sterling P. Lamprecht, ed. New York: Appleton-Century-Crofts.

———. 1960. *Leviathan or the Matter, Forme and Power of a Commonwealth Ecclesiastical and Civil*. Michael Oakeshott, ed. Oxford: Basil Blackwell.

Hofstadter, Richard. 1954. *The American Political Tradition and the Men Who Made It*. Vintage Books edition. New York: Random House.

Hohfeld, Wesley N. 1964. *Fundamental Legal Conceptions*. W. W. Cook, ed. New Haven, Connecticut: Yale University Press.

Hume, David. 1948. *Hume's Moral and Political Philosophy*. Henry D. Aiken, ed. New York: Hafner.

Johnson, Nevil. 1977. *In Search of the Constitution: Reflections on State and Society in Britain*. Oxford: Pergamon Press.

Kaufmann, Franz-Xaver, Giandomenico Majone, and Vincent Ostrom, eds. 1986. *Guidance, Control, and Evaluation in the Public Sector*. Berlin and New York: Walter de Gruyter.

King, Martin Luther. 1967. "A Letter from Birmingham Jail." *In* Thomas R. Dye and Brett W. Hawkins, eds. *Politics in the Metropolis*. Columbus, Ohio: Charles E. Merrill Books.

Kiser, Larry L. and Elinor Ostrom. 1982. "The Three Worlds of Action: A Metatheoretical Synthesis of Institutional Approaches." *In* Elinor Ostrom, ed. *Strategies of Political Inquiry*. Beverly Hills: Sage Publications, 179–222.

Langer, Susanne K. 1948. *Philosophy in a New Key*. New York: Mentor Books, New Library of World Literature.

Lasswell, Harold D. 1958. *Politics: Who Gets What, When, How*. New York: Meridian Books.

——— and Abraham Kaplan. 1950. *Power and Society: A Framework for Political Inquiry*. New Haven, Connecticut: Yale University Press.

Lenin, V. I. 1932. *State and Revolution*. New York: International Publishers.

———. N.d. *What Is to Be Done?* In *Selected Works*, Vol. II, 25–192. New York: International Publishers.

Locke, John. 1952. *The Second Treatise of Government*. Thomas P. Peardon, ed. New York: Liberal Arts Press.

Lowi, Theodore J. 1979. *The End of Liberalism*. Second edition. New York: W. W. Norton.

Lutz, Donald S. 1980. *Popular Consent and Popular Control: Whig Political Theory in the Early State Constitutions*. Baton Rouge: Louisiana State University Press.

Michels, Robert. 1966. *Political Parties: A Sociological Study of the Oligarchical Tendencies of Modern Democracy*. S. M. Lipset, ed. New York: The Free Press.

Montesquieu, Charles Louis de Secondat. 1966. *The Spirit of the Laws*. New York: Hafner.

Olson, Mancur, Jr. 1965. *The Logic of Collective Action, Public Goods and the Theory of Groups*. Cambridge, Massachusetts: Harvard University Press.

Ostrogorski, Moisei. 1964. *Democracy and the Organization of Political Parties*. Volume II: The United States. Garden City, New York: Anchor Books.

Ostrom, Elinor. 1972. "Metropolitan Reform: Propositions Derived from Two Traditions." *Social Science Quarterly*, Vol. 53 (December), 474–493.

————, Roger B. Parks, and Gordon P. Whitaker. 1975. "Defining and Measuring Structural Variations in Interorganizational Arrangements." *Publius*, Vol. 4 (Fall), 87–108.

Ostrom, Vincent. 1967. "Water and Politics California Style." *Arts and Architecture* (July/August), 14–16, 32.

————. 1969. "Operational Federalism: Organization for the Provision of Public Services in the American Federal System." *Public Choice*, Vol. 6 (Spring), 1–17.

————. 1973. "Can Federalism Make a Difference?" *Publius*, Vol. 3 (Fall), 197–238.

————. 1974. *The Intellectual Crisis in American Public Administration*. University, Alabama: University of Alabama Press.

———— and Elinor Ostrom. 1965. "A Behavioral Approach to the Study of Intergovernmental Relations." *Annals of the American Academy of Political and Social Science*, Vol. 359 (May), 137–146.

————. 1977. "Public Goods and Public Choices." *In* E. S. Savas, ed. *Alternatives for Delivering Public Services: Toward Improved Performance*. Boulder: Westview Press.

————, Charles M. Tiebout, and Robert Warren. 1961. "The Organization of Government in Metropolitan Areas: A Theoretical Inquiry." *American Political Science Review*, Vol. 55 (December), 831–842.

Padover, Saul K., ed. 1965. *The Forging of American Federalism: Selected Writings of James Madison*. Harper Torchbooks edition. New York: Harper and Row.

Peppin, John C. 1941. "Municipal Home Rule in California." *California Law Review*, Vol. 30 (November), 1–45.

Polanyi, Michael. 1951. *The Logic of Liberty, Reflection and Rejoinders.* Chicago: University of Chicago Press.

———. 1962. *Personal Knowledge.* Chicago: University of Chicago Press.

Reuss, Henry S. 1970. *Revenue Sharing: Crutch or Catalyst for State and Local Government?* New York: Praeger.

Rheinstein, Max, ed. 1967. *Max Weber on Law in Economy and Society.* Clarion Bond edition. New York: Simon and Schuster.

Riker, William H. 1964. *Federalism: Origin, Operation, Significance.* Boston: Little, Brown.

———. 1982. *Liberalism Against Populism.* San Francisco: W. H. Freeman.

Roirdon, William L. 1963. *Plunkitt of Tammany Hall.* New York: E. P. Dutton.

Rousseau, Jean-Jacques. 1978. *On the Social Contract.* Roger D. Masters, ed. New York: St. Martin's Press.

Schelling, Thomas C. 1963. *The Strategy of Conflict.* Cambridge, Massachusetts: Harvard University Press.

Searle, John R. 1969. *Speech Acts: An Essay in the Philosophy of Language.* New York: Cambridge University Press.

Smith, Adam. N.d. *The Theory of Moral Sentiments.* Indianapolis: Liberty Press.

Solberg, Winton U., ed. 1958. *The Federal Convention and the Formation of the American States.* Indianapolis: Bobbs-Merrill.

Storing, Herbert J. 1981. *The Complete Anti-Federalist.* Chicago: University of Chicago Press.

Sundquist, James L. 1969. *Making Federalism Work.* Washington, D.C.: Brookings Institution.

Tocqueville, Alexis de. 1945. *Democracy in America.* Phillips Bradley, ed. New York: Alfred A. Knopf.

———. 1955. *The Old Regime and the French Revolution.* Garden City, New York: Doubleday.

———. 1959. *The Recollections of Alexis de Tocqueville.* J. P. Mayer, ed. New York: Meridian Books.

Weber, Max. 1967. *On Law in Economy and Society.* Max Rheinstein, ed. New York: Simon and Schuster.

Wilson, Woodrow. 1887. "The Study of Administration." *Political Science Quarterly,* Vol. 2 (June), 197–220.

———. 1956. *Congressional Government: A Study in American Politics.* Meridian Books edition. New York: Meridian Books.

Yarbrough, Jean. 1985. "Rethinking 'The Federalist View of Federalism.'" *Publius,* Vol. 15 (Winter), 31–53.